Hands-On Gradient Boosting with XGBoost and scikit-learn

Perform accessible machine learning and extreme gradient boosting with Python

Corey Wade

BIRMINGHAM—MUMBAI

Hands-On Gradient Boosting with XGBoost and scikit-learn

Commissioning Editor: Veena Pagare

Acquisition Editor: Ali Abidi

Senior Editor: David Sugarman

Content Development Editor: Tazeen Shaikh

Technical Editor: Sonam Pandey

Copy Editor: Safis Editing

Project Coordinator: Aishwarya Mohan

Proofreader: Safis Editing

Indexer: Priyanka Dhadke

Production Designer: Nilesh Mohite

First published: October 2020

Production reference: 1151020

Published by Packt Publishing Ltd.
Livery Place
35 Livery Street
Birmingham
B3 2PB, UK.

ISBN 978-1-83921-835-4

www.packt.com

To my sister, Anne. Thanks for recommending the bootcamp.

– Corey

Packt.com

Subscribe to our online digital library for full access to over 7,000 books and videos, as well as industry leading tools to help you plan your personal development and advance your career. For more information, please visit our website.

Why subscribe?

- Spend less time learning and more time coding with practical eBooks and Videos from over 4,000 industry professionals

- Improve your learning with Skill Plans built especially for you

- Get a free eBook or video every month

- Fully searchable for easy access to vital information

- Copy and paste, print, and bookmark content

Did you know that Packt offers eBook versions of every book published, with PDF and ePub files available? You can upgrade to the eBook version at packt.com and as a print book customer, you are entitled to a discount on the eBook copy. Get in touch with us at customercare@packtpub.com for more details.

At www.packt.com, you can also read a collection of free technical articles, sign up for a range of free newsletters, and receive exclusive discounts and offers on Packt books and eBooks.

Contributors

About the author

Corey Wade, M.S. Mathematics, M.F.A. Writing and Consciousness, is the founder and director of Berkeley Coding Academy, where he teaches machine learning and AI to teens from all over the world. Additionally, Corey chairs the Math Department at the Independent Study Program of Berkeley High School, where he teaches programming and advanced math. His additional experience includes teaching natural language processing with Hello World, developing data science curricula with Pathstream, and publishing original statistics (3NG) and machine learning articles with Towards Data Science, Springboard, and Medium. Corey is co-author of the *Python Workshop*, also published by Packt.

I want to thank the Packt team and my family, in particular Jetta and Josephine, for giving me the space and time to complete this book when life moved in unexpected directions, as it so often does.

Foreword

Over the last decade, Data Science has become a household term - data is the new oil, and machine learning is the new electricity. Virtually, every industry has grown leaps and bounds as the information age has transitioned into the data age. Academic departments all over the globe have sprung into action, applying and developing the techniques and discoveries for and from the data science playbook. In light of all of this development, there is a growing need for books (and authors) like this one.

More than just a moneymaker, machine learning shows great promise as a problem solver and a crucial tool in managing global crises. 2020 has been a year full of challenges, imploring machine learning to come to the aid of humanity. In California alone, over 4 million acres have burned from wildfires this year. Not to mention the COVID-19 pandemic, which to date has resulted in over 36 million cases and 1 million deaths worldwide (WorldMeter.info).

This book provides readers with practical training in one of the most exciting developments in machine learning: gradient boosting. Gradient boosting was the elegant answer to the foibles of the already magnanimous Random Forest algorithm and has proven to be a formidable asset in the Predictive Analytics toolbox. Moreover, Wade has chosen to focus on XGBoost, an extremely flexible and successful implementation thereof. In fact, in addition to having a serious presence in both industry and academia, XGBoost has consistently ranked as a top (quite possibly THE top) performing algorithm in data competitions based on structured tabular data containing numerical and categorical features.

As Hands-On Gradient Boosting with XGBoost and scikit-learn goes to print, author Corey Wade and his family are standing at ground zero, challenged by the acrid smokey breeze in the San Francisco Bay Area while practicing social distancing to avoid the novel coronavirus, COVID-19. This may be the perfect setting, albeit morbidly so, for motivating Wade to guide the next wave of problem solvers. He has put his heart and soul, as well as his intellect and grit, into researching and presenting what is quite likely the most complete source of information regarding the XGBoost implementation of Gradient Boosting.

Readers should know that they are benefitting not only from a great analyst and data scientist but also from an experienced and genuine teacher in Corey Wade. He has the bug, as we say in education: a passion to give, to help, and to disseminate critical knowledge to thirsting intellects.

Kevin Glynn

Data Scientist & Educator

About the reviewers

Andrew Greenwald holds an MSc in computer science from Drexel University and a BSc in electrical engineering with a minor in mathematics from Villanova University. He started his career designing solid-state circuits to test electronic components. For the past 25 years, he has been developing software for IT infrastructure, financial markets, and defense applications. He is currently applying machine learning to cybersecurity, developing models to detect zero-day malware. Andrew lives in Austin, Texas, with his wife and three sons.

Michael Bironneau is a mathematician and software engineer with a Ph.D. in mathematics from Loughborough University. He has been creating commercial and scientific software since the age of 11 when he first used the TI-BASIC programming language on his TI-82 graphing calculator to automate the math homework.

He is currently the CTO of Open Energi, a technology company that uses AI to reduce energy costs and carbon emissions of over 50 types of flexible energy assets, such as electric vehicles and supermarket refrigerators.

He has authored Machine Learning with Go Quick Start Guide, Packt in 2019.

Packt is searching for authors like you

If you're interested in becoming an author for Packt, please visit `authors.packtpub.com` and apply today. We have worked with thousands of developers and tech professionals, just like you, to help them share their insight with the global tech community. You can make a general application, apply for a specific hot topic that we are recruiting an author for, or submit your own idea.

Table of Contents

3

Bagging with Random Forests

4

From Gradient Boosting to XGBoost

Section 2: XGBoost

5

XGBoost Unveiled

6

XGBoost Hyperparameters

7
Discovering Exoplanets with XGBoost

Section 3: Advanced XGBoost

8
XGBoost Alternative Base Learners

9
XGBoost Kaggle Masters

10
XGBoost Model Deployment

Other Books You May Enjoy

Index

Preface

XGBoost is an industry-proven, open-source software library that provides a gradient boosting framework for scaling billions of data points quickly and efficiently.

The book introduces machine learning and XGBoost in scikit-learn before building up to the theory behind gradient boosting. You'll cover decision trees and analyze bagging in the machine learning context, learning hyperparameters that extend to XGBoost along the way. You'll build gradient boosting models from scratch and extend gradient boosting to big data while recognizing speed limitations using timers. Details in XGBoost are explored with a focus on speed enhancements and deriving parameters mathematically. With the help of detailed case studies, you'll practice building and fine-tuning XGBoost classifiers and regressors using scikit-learn and the original Python API. You'll leverage XGBoost hyperparameters to improve scores, correct missing values, scale imbalanced datasets, and fine-tune alternative base learners. Finally, you'll apply advanced XGBoost techniques like building non-correlated ensembles, stacking models, and preparing models for industry deployment using sparse matrices, customized transformers, and pipelines.

By the end of the book, you'll be able to build high-performing machine learning models using XGBoost with minimal errors and maximum speed.

Who this book is for

This book is for data science professionals and enthusiasts, data analysts, and developers who want to build fast and accurate machine learning models that scale with big data. Proficiency in Python along with a basic understanding of linear algebra will help you to get the most out of this book.

What this book covers

Chapter 1, *Machine Learning Landscape*, presents XGBoost within the general context of machine learning by introducing linear regression and logistic regression before comparing results with XGBoost. pandas is introduced to preprocess raw data for machine learning by converting categorical columns and clearing null values in a variety of ways.

Chapter 2, *Decision Trees in Depth*, presents a detailed examination of decision tree hyperparameters that are used by XGBoost, along with a graphical and statistical analysis of variance and bias that highlights the importance of overfitting, a theme touched on throughout the book.

Chapter 3, *Bagging with Random Forests*, presents a general survey of random forests as an XGBoost competitor with a focus on bagging. Additional XGBoost hyperparameters shared with random forests such as n_esimtators and subsample are thoroughly covered.

Chapter 4, *From Gradient Boosting to XGBoost*, covers boosting fundamentals, building a booster from scratch in scikit-learn, fine-tuning new XGBoost hyperparameters such as eta, and comparing runtimes between gradient boosting and XGBoost to highlight XGBoost's impressive speed.

Chapter 5, *XGBoost Unveiled*, analyzes the mathematical derivations of XGBoost algorithms and features a historically relevant case study featuring XGBoost's role as the winning model in the Higgs Boson Kaggle Competition. Standard XGBoost parameters are discussed, base models are built, and the original Python API is covered.

Chapter 6, *XGBoost Hyperparameters*, covers all essential XGBoost hyperparameters, summarizes previous tree ensemble hyperparameters, and uses original grid search functions to fine-tune XGBoost models to optimize scores.

Chapter 7, *Discovering Exoplanets with XGBoost*, gives you the opportunity to discover exoplanets with XGBoost in a top-to-bottom case study. The pitfalls of imbalanced datasets are analyzed with the confusion matrix and classification report leading to different scoring metrics and the important XGBoost hyperparameter scale_pos_weight.

Chapter 8, *XGBoost Alternative Base Learners*, covers the full range of XGBoost boosters including gbtree, dart, and gblinear for regression and classification. Random forests are presented as base learners, and as XGBoost alternative models with the new XGBRFRegressor and XGBRFClassifier classes.

Chapter 9, XGBoost Kaggle Masters, presents tips and tricks that XGBoost Kaggle winners have used to win competitions such as advanced feature engineering, building non-correlated machine ensembles, and stacking.

Chapter 10, XGBoost Model Deployment, transforms raw data into XGBoost machine learning predictions through the use of customized transformers to handle mixed data and machine learning pipelines to make predictions on incoming data with a fine-tuned XGBoost model.

To get the most out of this book

Readers should be proficient in Python at the level of slicing lists, writing your own functions, and using dot-notation. General familiarity with linear algebra at the level of accessing rows and columns in matrices will be sufficient. A background in pandas and machine learning is helpful but not required as all code and concepts are explained along the way.

This book uses the latest versions of Python in Jupyter Notebook with the Anaconda distribution. Anaconda is highly recommended since all major data science libraries are included. It's worth updating Anaconda before getting started. The following section provides detailed instructions to set up your coding environment like ours.

Setting up your coding environment

The following table summarizes the essential software used in this book.

Software/Hardware covered in the book	OS Requirements
Anaconda: Jupyter Notebooks / sklearn 0.23	Windows, macOS X, and Linux (Any)
Anaconda: Python 3.7	Windows, macOS X, and Linux (Any)
xgboost 1.2	Windows, macOS X, and Linux (Any)

Here are instructions for uploading this software to your system.

Anaconda

The data science libraries that you will need in this book along with Jupyter Notebooks, scikit-learn (sklearn), and Python may be installed together using Anaconda, which is recommended.

Here are the steps to install Anaconda on your computer as of 2020:

1. Go to `https://www.anaconda.com/products/individual`.

2. Click **Download** on the following screen, which does not yet start the download, but presents you with a variety of options (see step 3):

Individual Edition

Your data science toolkit

With over 20 million users worldwide, the open-source Individual Edition (Distribution) is the easiest way to perform Python/R data science and machine learning on a single machine. Developed for solo practitioners, it is the toolkit that equips you to work with thousands of open-source packages and libraries.

Figure 0.1 – Preparing to download Anaconda

3. Select your installer. The **64-Bit Graphical Installer** is recommended for Windows and Mac. Make sure that you select from the top two rows under Python 3.7 since Python 3.7 is used throughout this book:

Anaconda Installers

Windows ⊞	MacOS	Linux △
Python 3.7	Python 3.7	Python 3.7
64-Bit Graphical Installer (466 MB)	64-Bit Graphical Installer (442 MB)	64-Bit (x86) Installer (522 MB)
32-Bit Graphical Installer (423 MB)	64-Bit Command Line Installer (430 MB)	64-Bit (Power8 and Power9) Installer (276 MB)
Python 2.7	Python 2.7	Python 2.7
64-Bit Graphical Installer (413 MB)	64-Bit Graphical Installer (637 MB)	64-Bit (x86) Installer (477 MB)
32-Bit Graphical Installer (356 MB)	64-Bit Command Line Installer (409 MB)	64-Bit (Power8 and Power9) Installer (295 MB)

Figure 0.2 – Anaconda Installers

4. After your download begins, continue with the prompts on your computer to complete the installation:

> **Warning for Mac users**
> If you run into the error **You cannot install Anaconda3 in this location**, do not panic. Just click on the highlighted row **Install for me only** and the **Continue** button will present as an option.

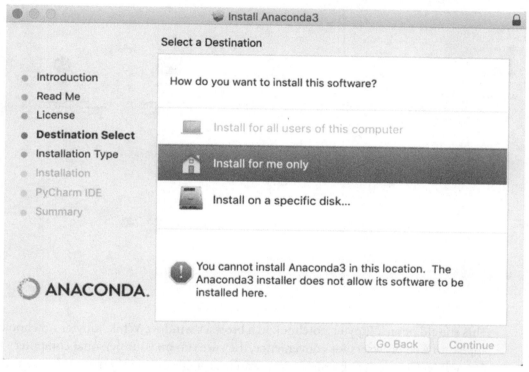

Figure 0.3 – Warning for Mac Users – Just click Install for me only then Continue

Using Jupyter notebooks

Now that you have Anaconda installed, you may open a Jupyter notebook to use Python 3.7. Here are the steps to open a Jupyter notebook:

1. Click on **Anaconda-Navigator** on your computer.

2. Click **Launch** under **Jupyter Notebook** as shown in the following screenshot:

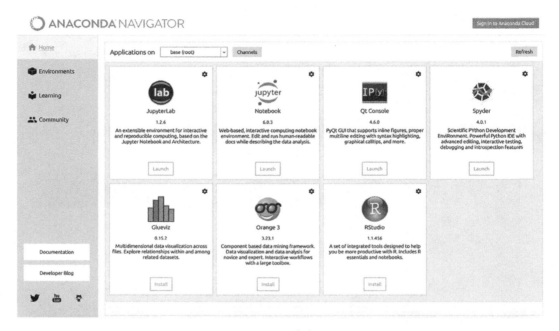

Figure 0.4 – Anaconda home screen

This should open a Jupyter notebook in a browser window. While Jupyter notebooks appear in web browsers for convenience, they are run on your personal computer, not online. Google Colab notebooks are an acceptable online alternative, but in this book, Jupyter notebooks are used exclusively.

3. Select **Python 3** from the **New** tab present on the right side of your Jupyter notebook as shown in the following screenshot:

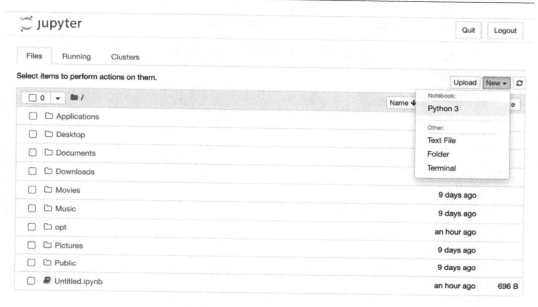

Figure 0.5 – Jupyter notebook home screen

This should bring you to the following screen:

Figure 0.6 – Inside a Jupyter notebook

Congratulations! You are now ready to run Python code! Just type anything in the cell, such as `print('hello xgboost!')`, and press *Shift + Enter* to run the code.

> **Troubleshooting Jupyter notebooks**
>
> If you have trouble running or installing Jupyter notebooks, please visit Jupyter's official troubleshooting guide: `https://jupyter-notebook.readthedocs.io/en/stable/troubleshooting.html`.

XGBoost

At the time of writing, XGBoost is not yet included in Anaconda so it must be installed separately.

Here are the steps for installing XGBoost on your computer:

1. Go to `https://anaconda.org/conda-forge/xgboost`. Here is what you should see:

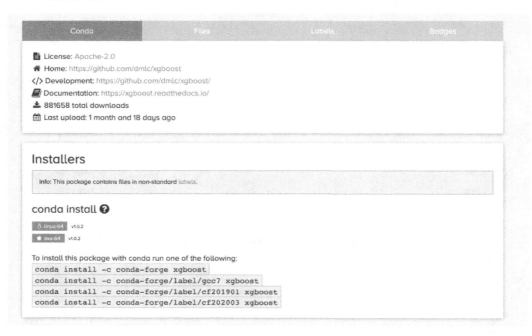

Figure 0.7 – Anaconda recommendations to install XGBoost

2. Copy the first line of code in the preceding screenshot, as shown here:

```
conda install -c conda-forge xgboost
```

Figure 0.8 – Package installation

3. Open the Terminal on your computer.

    If you do not know where your Terminal is located, search `Terminal` for Mac and `Windows Terminal` for Windows.

4. Paste the following code into your Terminal, press *Enter*, and follow any prompts:

```
conda install -c conda-forge xgboost
```

5. Verify that the installation has worked by opening a new Jupyter notebook as outlined in the previous section. Then enter `import xgboost` and press *Shift + Enter*. You should see the following:

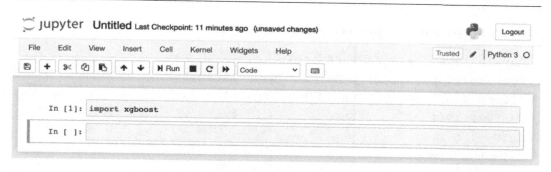

Figure 0.9 – Successful import of XGBoost in a Jupyter notebook

If you got no errors, congratulations! You now have all the necessary technical requirements to run code in this book.

> **Tip**
>
> If you received errors trying to set up your coding environment, please go back through the previous steps, or consider reviewing the Anaconda error documentation presented here: https://docs.anaconda.com/anaconda/user-guide/troubleshooting/. Previous users of Anaconda should update Anaconda by entering conda update conda in the Terminal. If you have trouble uploading XGBoost, see the official documentation at https://xgboost.readthedocs.io/en/latest/build.html.

Versions

Here is code that you may run in a Jupyter notebook to see what versions of the following software you are using:

```python
import platform; print(platform.platform())
import sys; print("Python", sys.version)
import numpy; print("NumPy", numpy.__version__)
import scipy; print("SciPy", scipy.__version__)
import sklearn; print("Scikit-Learn", sklearn.__version__)
import xgboost; print("XGBoost", xgboost.__version__)
```

Here are the versions used to generate code in this book:

```
Darwin-19.6.0-x86_64-i386-64bit
Python 3.7.7 (default, Mar 26 2020, 10:32:53)
[Clang 4.0.1 (tags/RELEASE_401/final)]
NumPy 1.19.1
SciPy 1.5.2
Scikit-Learn 0.23.2
XGBoost 1.2.0
```

It's okay if you have different versions than ours. Software is updated all the time, and you may obtain better results by using newer versions when released. If you are using older versions, however, it's recommended that you update using Anaconda by running `conda update conda` in the terminal. You may also run `conda update xgboost` if you installed an older version of XGBoost previously and forged it with Anaconda as outlined in the previous section.

Accessing code files

If you are using the digital version of this book, we advise you to type the code yourself or access the code via the GitHub repository (link available in the next section). Doing so will help you avoid any potential errors related to the copying and pasting of code.

The code bundle for the book is also hosted on GitHub at `https://github.com/PacktPublishing/Hands-On-Gradient-Boosting-with-XGBoost-and-Scikit-learn`. In case there's an update to the code, it will be updated on the existing GitHub repository.

We also have other code bundles from our rich catalog of books and videos available at `https://github.com/PacktPublishing/`. Check them out!

Download the color images

We also provide a PDF file that has color images of the screenshots/diagrams used in this book. You can download it here:

`https://static.packt-cdn.com/downloads/9781839218354_ColorImages.pdf`.

Conventions used

There are a number of text conventions used throughout this book.

`Code in text`: Indicates code words in text, database table names, folder names, filenames, file extensions, pathnames, dummy URLs, user input, and Twitter handles. Here is an example: "The `AdaBoostRegressor` and `AdaBoostClassifier` algorithms may be downloaded from the `sklearn.ensemble` library and fit to any training set."

A block of code is set as follows:

```
X_bikes = df_bikes.iloc[:,:-1]
y_bikes = df_bikes.iloc[:,-1]
from sklearn.model_selection import train_test_split
X_train, X_test, y_train, y_test = train_test_split(X_bikes, y_bikes, random_state=2)
```

When we wish to draw your attention to a particular part of a code block, the relevant lines or items are set in bold:

```
Stopping. Best iteration:
[1] validation_0-error:0.118421

Accuracy: 88.16%
```

> **Tips or important notes**
> Appear like this.

Get in touch

Feedback from our readers is always welcome.

General feedback: If you have questions about any aspect of this book, mention the book title in the subject of your message and email us at `customercare@packtpub.com`.

Errata: Although we have taken every care to ensure the accuracy of our content, mistakes do happen. If you have found a mistake in this book, we would be grateful if you would report this to us. Please visit `www.packtpub.com/support/errata`, selecting your book, clicking on the Errata Submission Form link, and entering the details.

Piracy: If you come across any illegal copies of our works in any form on the Internet, we would be grateful if you would provide us with the location address or website name. Please contact us at copyright@packt.com with a link to the material.

If you are interested in becoming an author: If there is a topic that you have expertise in and you are interested in either writing or contributing to a book, please visit authors.packtpub.com.

Reviews

Please leave a review. Once you have read and used this book, why not leave a review on the site that you purchased it from? Potential readers can then see and use your unbiased opinion to make purchase decisions, we at Packt can understand what you think about our products, and our authors can see your feedback on their book. Thank you!

For more information about Packt, please visit packt.com.

Section 1: Bagging and Boosting

An XGBoost model using scikit-learn defaults opens the book after preprocessing data with pandas and building standard regression and classification models. The practical theory behind XGBoost is explored by advancing through decision trees (XGBoost base learners), random forests (bagging), and gradient boosting to compare scores and fine-tune ensemble and tree-based hyperparameters.

This section comprises the following chapters:

- *Chapter 1, Machine Learning Landscape*
- *Chapter 2, Decision Trees in Depth*
- *Chapter 3, Bagging with Random Forests*
- *Chapter 4, From Gradient Boosting to XGBoost*

1
Machine Learning Landscape

Welcome to *Hands-On Gradient Boosting with XGBoost and Scikit-Learn*, a book that will teach you the foundations, tips, and tricks of XGBoost, the best machine learning algorithm for making predictions from tabular data.

The focus of this book is **XGBoost**, also known as **Extreme Gradient Boosting**. The structure, function, and raw power of XGBoost will be fleshed out in increasing detail in each chapter. The chapters unfold to tell an incredible story: the story of XGBoost. By the end of this book, you will be an expert in leveraging XGBoost to make predictions from real data.

In the first chapter, XGBoost is presented in a sneak preview. It makes a guest appearance in the larger context of **machine learning** regression and classification to set the stage for what's to come.

This chapter focuses on preparing data for machine learning, a process also known as **data wrangling**. In addition to building machine learning models, you will learn about using efficient **Python** code to load data, describe data, handle null values, transform data into numerical columns, split data into training and test sets, build machine learning models, and implement **cross-validation**, as well as comparing **linear regression** and **logistic regression** models with XGBoost.

The concepts and libraries presented in this chapter are used throughout the book.

This chapter consists of the following topics:

- Previewing XGBoost
- Wrangling data
- Predicting regression
- Predicting classification

Previewing XGBoost

Machine learning gained recognition with the first neural network in the 1940s, followed by the first machine learning checker champion in the 1950s. After some quiet decades, the field of machine learning took off when **Deep Blue** famously beat world chess champion Gary Kasparov in the 1990s. With a surge in computational power, the 1990s and early 2000s produced a plethora of academic papers revealing new machine learning algorithms such as **random forests** and **AdaBoost**.

The general idea behind boosting is to transform weak learners into strong learners by iteratively improving upon errors. The key idea behind **gradient boosting** is to use gradient descent to minimize the errors of the residuals. This evolutionary strand, from standard machine learning algorithms to gradient boosting, is the focus of the first four chapters of this book.

XGBoost is short for Extreme Gradient Boosting. The *Extreme* part refers to pushing the limits of computation to achieve gains in accuracy and speed. XGBoost's surging popularity is largely due to its unparalleled success in **Kaggle competitions**. In Kaggle competitions, competitors build machine learning models in attempts to make the best predictions and win lucrative cash prizes. In comparison to other models, XGBoost has been crushing the competition.

Understanding the details of XGBoost requires understanding the landscape of machine learning within the context of gradient boosting. In order to paint a full picture, we start at the beginning, with the basics of machine learning.

What is machine learning?

Machine learning is the ability of computers to learn from data. In 2020, machine learning predicts human behavior, recommends products, identifies faces, outperforms poker professionals, discovers exoplanets, identifies diseases, operates self-driving cars, personalizes the internet, and communicates directly with humans. Machine learning is leading the artificial intelligence revolution and affecting the bottom line of nearly every major corporation.

In practice, machine learning means implementing computer algorithms whose weights are adjusted when new data comes in. Machine learning algorithms learn from datasets to make predictions about species classification, the stock market, company profits, human decisions, subatomic particles, optimal traffic routes, and more.

Machine learning is the best tool at our disposal for transforming big data into accurate, actionable predictions. Machine learning, however, does not occur in a vacuum. Machine learning requires rows and columns of data.

Data wrangling

Data wrangling is a comprehensive term that encompasses the various stages of data preprocessing before machine learning can begin. Data loading, data cleaning, data analysis, and data manipulation are all included within the sphere of data wrangling.

This first chapter presents data wrangling in detail. The examples are meant to cover standard data wrangling challenges that can be swiftly handled by **pandas**, Python's special library for handling data analytics. Although no experience with **pandas** is required, basic knowledge of **pandas** will be beneficial. All code is explained so that readers new to **pandas** may follow along.

Dataset 1 – Bike rentals

The bike rentals dataset is our first dataset. The data source is the UCI Machine Learning Repository (https://archive.ics.uci.edu/ml/index.php), a world-famous data warehouse that is free to the public. Our bike rentals dataset has been adjusted from the original dataset (https://archive.ics.uci.edu/ml/datasets/bike+sharing+dataset) by sprinkling in null values so that you can gain practice in correcting them.

Accessing the data

The first step in data wrangling is to access the data. This may be achieved with the following steps:

1. Download the data. All files for this book have been stored on GitHub. You may download all files to your local computer by pressing the **Clone** button. Here is a visual:

Figure 1.1 – Accessing data

After downloading the data, move it to a convenient location, such as a `Data` folder on your desktop.

2. Open a Jupyter Notebook. You will find the link to download Jupyter Notebooks in the preface. Click on **Anaconda**, and then click on **Jupyter Notebooks**. Alternatively, type `jupyter notebook` in the terminal. After the web browser opens, you should see a list of folders and files. Go to the same folder as the bike rentals dataset and select **New: Notebook: Python 3**. Here is a visual guide:

Figure 1.2 – Visual guide to accessing the Jupyter Notebook

> **Tip**
> If you are having difficulties opening a Jupyter Notebook, see Jupyter's official trouble-shooting guide: `https://jupyter-notebook.readthedocs.io/en/stable/troubleshooting.html`.

3. Enter the following code in the first cell of your Jupyter Notebook:

```
import pandas as pd
```

Press *Shift + Enter* to run the cell. Now you may access the `pandas` library when you write `pd`.

4. Load the data using `pd.read_csv`. Loading data requires a `read` method. The `read` method stores the data as a DataFrame, a `pandas` object for viewing, analyzing, and manipulating data. When loading the data, place the filename in quotation marks, and then run the cell:

```
df_bikes = pd.read_csv('bike_rentals.csv')
```

If your data file is in a different location than your Jupyter Notebook, you must provide a file directory, such as `Downloads/bike_rental.csv`.

Now the data has been properly stored in a DataFrame called `df_bikes`.

> **Tip**
>
> **Tab completion**: When coding in Jupyter Notebooks, after typing a few characters, press the *Tab* button. For CSV files, you should see the filename appear. Highlight the name with your cursor and press *Enter*. If the filename is the only available option, you may press *Enter*. Tab completion will make your coding experience faster and more reliable.

5. Display the data using `.head()`. The final step is to view the data to ensure that it has loaded correctly. `.head()` is a DataFrame method that displays the first five rows of the DataFrame. You may place any positive integer in parentheses to view any number of rows. Enter the following code and press *Shift + Enter*:

```
df_bikes.head()
```

Here is a screenshot of the first few lines along with the expected output:

```
# Import pandas
import pandas as pd
```

```
# Upload 'bike_rentals.csv' to dataFrame
df_bikes = pd.read_csv('bike_rentals.csv')
```

```
# Display first 5 rows
df_bikes.head()
```

	instant	dteday	season	yr	mnth	holiday	weekday	workingday	weathersit	temp	atemp	hum	windspeed	casual	registered	cnt
0	1	2011-01-01	1.0	0.0	1.0	0.0	6.0	0.0	2	0.344167	0.363625	0.805833	0.160446	331	654	985
1	2	2011-01-02	1.0	0.0	1.0	0.0	0.0	0.0	2	0.363478	0.353739	0.696087	0.248539	131	670	801
2	3	2011-01-03	1.0	0.0	1.0	0.0	1.0	1.0	1	0.196364	0.189405	0.437273	0.248309	120	1229	1349
3	4	2011-01-04	1.0	0.0	1.0	0.0	2.0	1.0	1	0.200000	0.212122	0.590435	0.160296	108	1454	1562
4	5	2011-01-05	1.0	0.0	1.0	0.0	3.0	1.0	1	0.226957	0.229270	0.436957	0.186900	82	1518	1600

Figure 1.3 – The bike_rental.csv output

Now that we have access to the data, let's take a look at three methods to understand the data.

Understanding the data

Now that the data has been loaded, it's time to make sense of the data. Understanding the data is essential to making informed decisions down the road. Here are three great methods for making sense of the data.

.head()

You have already seen .head(), a widely used method to interpret column names and numbers. As the preceding output reveals, dteday is a date, while instant is an ordered index.

.describe()

Numerical statistics may be viewed by using .describe() as follows:

```
df_bikes.describe()
```

Here is the expected output:

	instant	season	yr	mnth	holiday	weekday	workingday	weathersit	temp	atemp	hum	windspeed
count	731.000000	731.000000	730.000000	730.000000	731.000000	731.000000	731.000000	731.000000	730.000000	730.000000	728.000000	726.000000
mean	366.000000	2.496580	0.500000	6.512329	0.028728	2.997264	0.682627	1.395349	0.495587	0.474512	0.627987	0.190476
std	211.165812	1.110807	0.500343	3.448303	0.167155	2.004787	0.465773	0.544894	0.183094	0.163017	0.142331	0.077725
min	1.000000	1.000000	0.000000	1.000000	0.000000	0.000000	0.000000	1.000000	0.059130	0.079070	0.000000	0.022392
25%	183.500000	2.000000	0.000000	4.000000	0.000000	1.000000	0.000000	1.000000	0.336875	0.337794	0.521562	0.134494
50%	366.000000	3.000000	0.500000	7.000000	0.000000	3.000000	1.000000	1.000000	0.499167	0.487364	0.627083	0.180971
75%	548.500000	3.000000	1.000000	9.750000	0.000000	5.000000	1.000000	2.000000	0.655625	0.608916	0.730104	0.233218
max	731.000000	4.000000	1.000000	12.000000	1.000000	6.000000	1.000000	3.000000	0.861667	0.840896	0.972500	0.507463

Figure 1.4 – The .describe() output

You may need to scroll to the right to see all of the columns.

Comparing the mean and median (50%) gives an indication of skewness. As you can see, mean and median are close to one another, so the data is roughly symmetrical. The max and min values of each column, along with the quartiles and standard deviation (std), are also presented.

.info()

Another great method is `.info()`, which displays general information about the columns and rows:

```
df_bikes.info()
```

Here is the expected output:

```
<class 'pandas.core.frame.DataFrame'>
RangeIndex: 731 entries, 0 to 730
Data columns (total 16 columns):
 #   Column      Non-Null Count  Dtype
---  ------      --------------  -----
 0   instant     731 non-null    int64
 1   dteday      731 non-null    object
 2   season      731 non-null    float64
 3   yr          730 non-null    float64
 4   mnth        730 non-null    float64
 5   holiday     731 non-null    float64
 6   weekday     731 non-null    float64
 7   workingday  731 non-null    float64
 8   weathersit  731 non-null    int64
 9   temp        730 non-null    float64
 10  atemp       730 non-null    float64
 11  hum         728 non-null    float64
 12  windspeed   726 non-null    float64
 13  casual      731 non-null    int64
 14  registered  731 non-null    int64
 15  cnt         731 non-null    int64
dtypes: float64(10), int64(5), object(1)
memory usage: 91.5+ KB
```

As you can see, `.info()` gives the number of rows, number of columns, column types, and non-null values. Since the number of non-null values differs between columns, null values must be present.

Correcting null values

If null values are not corrected, unexpected errors may arise down the road. In this subsection, we present a variety of methods that may be used to correct null values. Our examples are designed not only to handle null values but also to highlight the breadth and depth of pandas.

The following methods may be used to correct null values.

Finding the number of null values

The following code displays the total number of null values:

```
df_bikes.isna().sum().sum()
```

Here is the outcome:

```
12
```

Note that two .sum() methods are required. The first method sums the null values of each column, while the second method sums the column counts.

Displaying null values

You can display all rows containing null values with the following code:

```
df_bikes[df_bikes.isna().any(axis=1)]
```

This code may be broken down as follows: df_bikes[conditional] is a subset of df_bikes that meets the condition in brackets. .df_bikes.isna().any gathers any and all null values while (axis=1) specifies values in the columns. In pandas, rows are axis 0 and columns are axis 1.

Here is the expected output:

	instant	dteday	season	yr	mnth	holiday	weekday	workingday	weathersit	temp	atemp	hum	windspeed	casual	registered	cnt
56	57	2011-02-26	1.0	0.0	2.0	0.0	6.0	0.0	1	0.282500	0.282192	0.537917	NaN	424	1545	1969
81	82	2011-03-23	2.0	0.0	3.0	0.0	3.0	1.0	2	0.346957	0.337939	0.839565	NaN	203	1918	2121
128	129	2011-05-09	2.0	0.0	5.0	0.0	1.0	1.0	1	0.532500	0.525246	0.588750	NaN	664	3698	4362
129	130	2011-05-10	2.0	0.0	5.0	0.0	2.0	1.0	1	0.532500	0.522721	NaN	0.115671	694	4109	4803
213	214	2011-08-02	3.0	0.0	8.0	0.0	2.0	1.0	1	0.783333	0.707071	NaN	0.205850	801	4044	4845
298	299	2011-10-26	4.0	0.0	10.0	0.0	3.0	1.0	2	0.484167	0.472846	0.720417	NaN	404	3490	3894
388	389	2012-01-24	1.0	1.0	1.0	0.0	2.0	1.0	1	0.342500	0.349108	NaN	0.123767	439	3900	4339
528	529	2012-06-12	2.0	1.0	6.0	0.0	2.0	1.0	2	0.653333	0.597875	0.833333	NaN	477	4495	4972
701	702	2012-12-02	4.0	1.0	12.0	0.0	0.0	0.0	2	NaN	NaN	0.823333	0.124379	892	3757	4649
730	731	2012-12-31	1.0	NaN	NaN	0.0	1.0	0.0	2	0.215833	0.223487	0.577500	0.154846	439	2290	2729

Figure 1.5 – Bike Rentals dataset null values

As you can see from the output, there are null values in the `windspeed`, `humidity`, and `temperature` columns along with the last row.

> **Tip**
>
> If this is your first time working with **pandas**, it may take time to get used to the notation. Check out Packt's *Hands-On Data Analysis with Pandas* for a great introduction: `https://subscription.packtpub.com/book/data/9781789615326`.

Correcting null values

Correcting null values depends on the column and dataset. Let's go over some strategies.

Replacing with the median/mean

One common strategy is to replace null values with the median or mean. The idea here is to replace null values with the average column value.

For the `'windspeed'` column, the null values may be replaced with the `median` value as follows:

```
df_bikes['windspeed'].fillna((df_bikes['windspeed'].median()),
  inplace=True)
```

`df_bikes['windspeed'].fillna` means that the null values of the `'windspeed'` column will be filled. `df_bikes['windspeed'].median()` is the median of the `'windspeed'` column. Finally, `inplace=True` ensures that the changes are permanent.

> **Tip**
>
> The median is often a better choice than the mean. The median guarantees that half the data is greater than the given value and half the data is lower. The mean, by contrast, is vulnerable to **outliers**.

In the previous cell, `df_bikes[df_bikes.isna().any(axis=1)]` revealed rows 56 and 81 with null values for windspeed. These rows may be displayed using `.iloc`, short for **index location**:

```
df_bikes.iloc[[56, 81]]
```

Here is the expected output:

	instant	dteday	season	yr	mnth	holiday	weekday	workingday	weathersit	temp	atemp	hum	windspeed	casual	registered	cnt
56	57	2011-02-26	1.0	0.0	2.0	0.0	6.0	0.0	1	0.282500	0.282192	0.537917	0.180971	424	1545	1969
81	82	2011-03-23	2.0	0.0	3.0	0.0	3.0	1.0	2	0.346957	0.337939	0.839565	0.180971	203	1918	2121

Figure 1.6 – Rows 56 and 81

As expected, the null values have been replaced with the windspeed median.

> **Tip**
> It's common for users to make mistakes with single or double brackets when using **pandas**. .iloc uses single brackets for one index as follows: df_bikes.iloc[56]. Now, df_bikes also accepts a list inside brackets to allow multiple indices. Multiple indices require double brackets as follows: df_bikes.iloc[[56, 81]]. Please see https://pandas.pydata.org/pandas-docs/stable/reference/api/pandas.DataFrame.iloc.html for further documentation.

Groupby with the median/mean

It's possible to get more nuanced when correcting null values by using a **groupby**.

A groupby organizes rows by shared values. Since there are four shared seasons spread out among the rows, a groupby of seasons results in a total of four rows, one for each season. But each season comes from many different rows with different values. We need a way to combine, or aggregate, the values. Choices for the aggregate include .sum(), .count(), .mean(), and .median(). We use .median().

Grouping df_bikes by season with the .median() aggregate is achieved as follows:

```
df_bikes.groupby(['season']).median()
```

Here is the expected output:

	instant	yr	mnth	holiday	weekday	workingday	weathersit	temp	atemp	hum	windspeed	casual	registered	cnt
season														
1.0	366.0	0.5	2.0	0.0	3.0	1.0	1.0	0.285833	0.282821	0.543750	0.202750	218.0	1867.0	2209.0
2.0	308.5	0.5	5.0	0.0	3.0	1.0	1.0	0.562083	0.538212	0.646667	0.191546	867.0	3844.0	4941.5
3.0	401.5	0.5	8.0	0.0	3.0	1.0	1.0	0.714583	0.656575	0.635833	0.165115	1050.5	4110.5	5353.5
4.0	493.0	0.5	11.0	0.0	3.0	1.0	1.0	0.410000	0.409708	0.661042	0.167918	544.5	3815.0	4634.5

Figure 1.7 – The output of grouping df_bikes by season

As you can see, the column values are the medians.

To correct the null values in the hum column, short for **humidity**, we can take the median humidity by season.

The code for correcting null values in the hum column is df_bikes['hum'] = df_bikes['hum'].fillna().

The code that goes inside fillna is the desired values. The values obtained from groupby require the transform method as follows:

```
df_bikes.groupby('season')['hum'].transform('median')
```

Here is the combined code in one long step:

```
df_bikes['hum'] = df_bikes['hum'].fillna(df_bikes.
groupby('season')['hum'].transform('median'))
```

You may verify the transformation by checking df_bikes.iloc[[129, 213, 388]].

Obtaining the median/mean from specific rows

In some cases, it may be advantageous to replace null values with data from specific rows.

When correcting temperature, aside from consulting historical records, taking the mean temperature of the day before and the day after should give a good estimate.

To find null values of the 'temp' column, enter the following code:

```
df_bikes[df_bikes['temp'].isna()]
```

Here is the expected output:

	instant	dteday	season	yr	mnth	holiday	weekday	workingday	weathersit	temp	atemp	hum	windspeed	casual	registered	cnt
701	702	2012-12-02	4.0	1.0	12.0	0.0	0.0	0.0	2	NaN	NaN	0.823333	0.124379	892	3757	4649

Figure 1.8 – The output of the 'temp' column

As you can see, index 701 contains null values.

To find the mean temperature of the day before and the day after the 701 index, complete the following steps:

1. Sum the temperatures in rows 700 and 702 and divide by 2. Do this for the 'temp' and 'atemp' columns:

```
mean_temp = (df_bikes.iloc[700]['temp'] + df_bikes.
iloc[702]['temp'])/2
```
```
mean_atemp = (df_bikes.iloc[700]['atemp'] + df_bikes.
iloc[702]['atemp'])/2
```

2. Replace the null values:

```
df_bikes['temp'].fillna((mean_temp), inplace=True)
```
```
df_bikes['atemp'].fillna((mean_atemp), inplace=True)
```

You may verify on your own that the null values have been filled as expected.

Extrapolate dates

Our final strategy to correct null values involves dates. When real dates are provided, date values may be extrapolated.

df_bikes['dteday'] is a date column; however, the type of column revealed by df_bikes.info() is an object, commonly represented as a string. Date objects such as years and months must be extrapolated from datetime types. df_bikes['dteday'] may be converted to a 'datetime' type using the to_datetime method, as follows:

```
df_bikes['dteday'] = pd.to_datetime(df_bikes['dteday'],infer_
datetime_format=True)
```

infer_datetime_format=True allows **pandas** to decide the kind of datetime object to store, a safe option in most cases.

To extrapolate individual columns, first import the datetime library:

```
import datetime as dt
```

We can now extrapolate dates for the null values using some different approaches. A standard approach is convert the 'mnth' column to the correct months extrapolated from the 'dteday' column. This has the advantage of correcting any additional errors that may have surfaced in conversions, assuming of course that the 'dteday' column is correct.

The code is as follows:

```
ddf_bikes['mnth'] = df_bikes['dteday'].dt.month
```

It's important to verify the changes. Since the null date values were in the last row, we can use .tail(), a DataFrame method similar to .head(), that shows the last five rows:

```
df_bikes.tail()
```

Here is the expected output:

	instant	dteday	season	yr	mnth	holiday	weekday	workingday	weathersit	temp	atemp	hum	windspeed	casual	registered	cnt
726	727	2012-12-27	1.0	1.0	12	0.0	4.0	1.0	2	0.254167	0.226642	0.652917	0.350133	247	1867	2114
727	728	2012-12-28	1.0	1.0	12	0.0	5.0	1.0	2	0.253333	0.255046	0.590000	0.155471	644	2451	3095
728	729	2012-12-29	1.0	1.0	12	0.0	6.0	0.0	2	0.253333	0.242400	0.752917	0.124383	159	1182	1341
729	730	2012-12-30	1.0	1.0	12	0.0	0.0	0.0	1	0.255833	0.231700	0.483333	0.350754	364	1432	1796
730	731	2012-12-31	1.0	NaN	12	0.0	1.0	0.0	2	0.215833	0.223487	0.577500	0.154846	439	2290	2729

Figure 1.9 – The output of the extrapolated date values

As you can see, the month values are all correct, but the year value needs to be changed.

The years of the last five rows in the 'dteday' column are all 2012, but the corresponding year provided by the 'yr' column is 1.0. Why?

The data is normalized, meaning it's converted to values between 0 and 1.

Normalized data is often more efficient because machine learning weights do not have to adjust for different ranges.

You can use the .loc method to fill in the correct value. The .loc method is used to locate entries by row and column as follows:

```
df_bikes.loc[730, 'yr'] = 1.0
```

Now that you have practiced correcting null values and have gained significant experience with **pandas**, it's time to address non-numerical columns.

Deleting non-numerical columns

For machine learning, all data columns should be numerical. According to `df.info()`, the only column that is not numerical is `df_bikes['dteday']`. Furthermore, it's redundant since all date information exists in other columns.

The column may be deleted as follows:

```
df_bikes = df_bikes.drop('dteday', axis=1)
```

Now that we have all numerical columns and no null values, we are ready for machine learning.

Predicting regression

Machine learning algorithms aim to predict the values of one output column using data from one or more input columns. The predictions rely on mathematical equations determined by the general class of machine learning problems being addressed. Most supervised learning problems are classified as regression or classification. In this section, machine learning is introduced in the context of regression.

Predicting bike rentals

In the bike rentals dataset, `df_bikes['cnt']` is the number of bike rentals in a given day. Predicting this column would be of great use to a bike rental company. Our problem is to predict the correct number of bike rentals on a given day based on data such as whether this day is a holiday or working day, forecasted temperature, humidity, windspeed, and so on.

According to the dataset, `df_bikes['cnt']` is the sum of `df_bikes['casual']` and `df_bikes['registered']`. If `df_bikes['registered']` and `df_bikes['casual']` were included as input columns, predictions would always be 100% accurate since these columns would always sum to the correct result. Although perfect predictions are ideal in theory, it makes no sense to include input columns that would be unknown in reality.

All current columns may be used to predict `df_bikes['cnt']` except for `'casual'` and `'registered'`, as explained previously. Drop the `'casual'` and `'registered'` columns using the `.drop` method as follows:

```
df_bikes = df_bikes.drop(['casual', 'registered'], axis=1)
```

The dataset is now ready.

Saving data for future use

The bike rentals dataset will be used multiple times in this book. Instead of running this notebook each time to perform data wrangling, you can export the clean dataset to a CSV file for future use:

```
df_bikes.to_csv('bike_rentals_cleaned.csv', index=False)
```

The index=False parameter prevents an additional column from being created by the index.

Declaring predictor and target columns

Machine learning works by performing mathematical operations on each of the predictor columns (input columns) to determine the target column (output column).

It's standard to group the predictor columns with a capital X, and the target column as a lowercase y. Since our target column is the last column, splitting the data into predictor and target columns may be done via slicing using index notation:

```
X = df_bikes.iloc[:,:-1]
y = df_bikes.iloc[:,-1]
```

The comma separates columns from rows. The first colon, :, means that all rows are included. After the comma, :-1 means start at the first column and go all the way to the last column without including it. The second -1 takes the last column only.

Understanding regression

Predicting the number of bike rentals, in reality, could result in any **non-negative integer**. When the target column includes a range of unlimited values, the machine learning problem is classified as **regression**.

The most common regression algorithm is linear regression. Linear regression takes each predictor column as a **polynomial variable** and multiplies the values by **coefficients** (also called **weights**) to predict the target column. **Gradient descent** works under the hood to minimize the error. The predictions of linear regression could be any real number.

Before running linear regression, we must split the data into a training set and a test set. The training set fits the data to the algorithm, using the target column to minimize the error. After a model is built, it's scored against the test data.

The importance of holding out a test set to score the model cannot be overstated. In the world of big data, it's common to **overfit** the data to the training set because there are so many data points to train on. Overfitting is generally bad because the model adjusts itself too closely to outliers, unusual instances, and temporary trends. Strong machine learning models strike a nice balance between generalizing well to new data and accurately picking up on the nuances of the data at hand, a concept explored in detail in *Chapter 2, Decision Trees in Depth.*

Accessing scikit-learn

All machine learning libraries will be handled through **scikit-learn**. Scikit-learn's range, ease of use, and computational power place it among the most widespread machine learning libraries in the world.

Import `train_test_split` and `LinearRegression` from scikit-learn as follows:

```
from sklearn.model_selection import train_test_split
from sklearn.linear_model import LinearRegression
```

Next, split the data into the training set and test set:

```
X_train, X_test, y_train, y_test = train_test_split(X, y,
random_state=2)
```

Note the `random_state=2` parameter. Whenever you see `random_state=2`, this means that you are choosing the seed of a pseudo-random number generator to ensure reproducible results.

Silencing warnings

Before building your first machine learning model, silence all warnings. Scikit-learn includes warnings to notify users of future changes. In general, it's not advisable to silence warnings, but since our code has been tested, it's recommended to save space in your Jupyter Notebook.

Warnings may be silenced as follows:

```
import warnings
warnings.filterwarnings('ignore')
```

It's time to build your first model.

Modeling linear regression

A linear regression model may be built with the following steps:

1. Initialize a machine learning model:

    ```
    lin_reg = LinearRegression()
    ```

2. Fit the model on the training set. This is where the machine learning model is built. Note that X_train is the predictor column and y_train is the target column.

    ```
    lin_reg.fit(X_train, y_train)
    ```

3. Make predictions for the test set. The predictions of X_test, the predictor columns in the test set, are stored as y_pred using the .predict method on lin_reg:

    ```
    y_pred = lin_reg.predict(X_test)
    ```

4. Compare the predictions with the test set. Scoring the model requires a basis of comparison. The standard for linear regression is the **root mean squared error** (**RMSE**). The RMSE requires two pieces: mean_squared_error, the sum of the squares of differences between predicted and actual values, and the square root, to keep the units the same. mean_squared_error may be imported, and the square root may be taken with **Numerical Python**, popularly known as **NumPy**, a blazingly fast library designed to work with **pandas**.

5. Import mean_squared_error and NumPy, and then compute the mean squared error and take the square root:

    ```
    from sklearn.metrics import mean_squared_error
    import numpy as np
    mse = mean_squared_error(y_test, y_pred)
    rmse = np.sqrt(mse)
    ```

6. Print your results:

    ```
    print("RMSE: %0.2f" % (rmse))
    ```

    The outcome is as follows:

    ```
    RMSE: 898.21
    ```

Here is a screenshot of all the code to build your first machine learning model:

```
# Initialize LinearRegression model
lin_reg = LinearRegression()

# Fit lin_reg on training data
lin_reg.fit(X_train, y_train)

# Predict X_test using lin_reg
y_pred = lin_reg.predict(X_test)

# Import mean_squared_error
from sklearn.metrics import mean_squared_error

# Import numpy
import numpy as np

# Compute mean_squared_error as mse
mse = mean_squared_error(y_test, y_pred)

# Compute root mean squared error as rmse
rmse = np.sqrt(mse)

# Display root mean squared error
print("RMSE: %0.2f" % (rmse))
```

```
RMSE: 898.21
```

Figure 1.10 – Code to build your machine learning model

It's hard to know whether an error of 898 rentals is good or bad without knowing the expected range of rentals per day.

The `.describe()` method may be used on the `df_bikes['cnt']` column to obtain the range and more:

```
df_bikes['cnt'].describe()
```

Here is the output:

```
count     731.000000
mean     4504.348837
std      1937.211452
min        22.000000
25%      3152.000000
50%      4548.000000
75%      5956.000000
max      8714.000000
Name: cnt, dtype: float64
```

With a range of 22 to 8714, a mean of 4504, and a standard deviation of 1937, an RMSE of 898 isn't bad, but it's not great either.

XGBoost

Linear regression is one of many algorithms that may be used to solve regression problems. It's possible that other regression algorithms will produce better results. The general strategy is to experiment with different regressors to compare scores. Throughout this book, you will experiment with a wide range of regressors, including decision trees, random forests, gradient boosting, and the focus of this book, XGBoost.

A comprehensive introduction to XGBoost will be provided later in this book. For now, note that XGBoost includes a regressor, called XGBRegressor, that may be used on any regression dataset, including the bike rentals dataset that has just been scored. Let's now use the XGBRegressor to compare results on the bike rentals dataset with linear regression.

You should have already installed XGBoost in the preface. If you have not done so, install XGBoost now.

XGBRegressor

After XGBoost has been installed, the XGBoost regressor may be imported as follows:

```
from xgboost import XGBRegressor
```

The general steps for building XGBRegressor are the same as with LinearRegression. The only difference is to initialize XGBRegressor instead of LinearRegression:

1. Initialize a machine learning model:

   ```
   xg_reg = XGBRegressor()
   ```

2. Fit the model on the training set. If you get some warnings from XGBoost here, don't worry:

   ```
   xg_reg.fit(X_train, y_train)
   ```

3. Make predictions for the test set:

   ```
   y_pred = xg_reg.predict(X_test)
   ```

4. Compare the predictions with the test set:

   ```
   mse = mean_squared_error(y_test, y_pred)
   rmse = np.sqrt(mse)
   ```

5. Print your results:

```
print("RMSE: %0.2f" % (rmse))
```

The output is as follows:

```
RMSE: 705.11
```

XGBRegressor performs substantially better!

The reason why XGBoost often performs better than others will be explored in *Chapter 5, XGBoost Unveiled*.

Cross-validation

One test score is not reliable because splitting the data into different training and test sets would give different results. In effect, splitting the data into a training set and a test set is arbitrary, and a different random_state will give a different RMSE.

One way to address the score discrepancies between different splits is **k-fold cross-validation**. The idea is to split the data multiple times into different training sets and test sets, and then to take the mean of the scores. The number of splits, called **folds**, is denoted by **k**. It's standard to use k = 3, 4, 5, or 10 splits.

Here is a visual description of cross-validation:

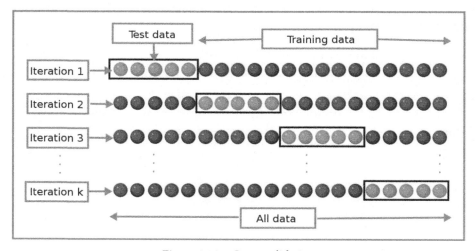

Figure 1.11 – Cross-validation

(Redrawn from https://commons.wikimedia.org/wiki/File:K-fold_cross_validation_EN.svg)

Cross-validation works by fitting a machine learning model on the first training set and scoring it against the first test set. A different training set and test set are provided for the second split, resulting in a new machine learning model with its own score. A third split results in a new model and scores it against another test set.

There is going to be overlap in the training sets, but not the test sets.

Choosing the number of folds is flexible and depends on the data. Five folds is standard because 20% of the test set is held back each time. With 10 folds, only 10% of the data is held back; however, 90% of the data is available for training and the mean is less vulnerable to outliers. For a smaller datatset, three folds may work better.

At the end, there will be k different scores evaluating the model against k different test sets. Taking the mean score of the k folds gives a more reliable score than any single fold.

`cross_val_score` is a convenient way to implement cross-validation. `cross_val_score` takes a machine learning algorithm as input, along with the predictor and target columns, with optional additional parameters that include a scoring metric and the desired number of folds.

Cross-validation with linear regression

Let's use cross-validation with `LinearRegression`.

First, import `cross_val_score` from the `cross_val_score` library:

```
from sklearn.model_selection import cross_val_score
```

Now use cross-validation to build and score a machine learning model in the following steps:

1. Initialize a machine learning model:

    ```
    model = LinearRegression()
    ```

2. Implement `cross_val_score` with the model, X, y, scoring=`'neg_mean_squared_error'`, and the number of folds, `cv=10`, as input:

    ```
    scores = cross_val_score(model, X, y, scoring='neg_mean_squared_error', cv=10)
    ```

> **Tip**
>
> Why `scoring='neg_mean_squared_error'`? Scikit-learn is designed to select the highest score when training models. This works well for accuracy, but not for errors when the lowest is best. By taking the negative of each mean squared error, the lowest ends up being the highest. This is compensated for later with `rmse = np.sqrt(-scores)`, so the final results are positive.

3. Find the RMSE by taking the square root of the negative scores:

```
rmse = np.sqrt(-scores)
```

4. Display the results:

```
print('Reg rmse:', np.round(rmse, 2))
print('RMSE mean: %0.2f' % (rmse.mean()))
```

The output is as follows:

```
Reg rmse: [ 504.01  840.55 1140.88  728.39  640.2
969.95
1133.45 1252.85 1084.64  1425.33]
RMSE mean: 972.02
```

Linear regression has a mean error of `972.06`. This is slightly better than the `980.38` obtained before. The point here is not whether the score is better or worse. The point is that it's a better estimation of how linear regression will perform on unseen data.

Using cross-validation is always recommended for a better estimate of the score.

> **About the print function**
>
> When running your own machine learning code, the global `print` function is often not necessary, but it is helpful if you want to print out multiple lines and format the output as shown here.

Cross-validation with XGBoost

Now let's use cross-validation with `XGBRegressor`. The steps are the same, except for initializing the model:

1. Initialize a machine learning model:

```
model = XGBRegressor()
```

2. Implement `cross_val_score` with the model, X, y, scoring, and the number of folds, `cv`, as input:

```
scores = cross_val_score(model, X, y, scoring='neg_mean_
squared_error', cv=10)
```

3. Find the RMSE by taking the square root of the negative scores:

```
rmse = np.sqrt(-scores)
```

4. Print the results:

```
print('Reg rmse:', np.round(rmse, 2))
print('RMSE mean: %0.2f' % (rmse.mean()))
```

The output is as follows:

```
Reg rmse: [ 717.65   692.8    520.7    737.68   835.96
1006.24   991.34   747.61   891.99 1731.13]
RMSE mean: 887.31
```

`XGBRegressor` wins again, besting linear regression by about 10%.

Predicting classification

You learned that XGBoost may have an edge in regression, but what about classification? XGBoost has a classification model, but will it perform as accurately as well tested classification models such as logistic regression? Let's find out.

What is classification?

Unlike with regression, when predicting target columns with a limited number of outputs, a machine learning algorithm is categorized as a classification algorithm. The possible outputs may include the following:

- Yes, No
- Spam, Not Spam
- 0, 1
- Red, Blue, Green, Yellow, Orange

Dataset 2 – The census

We will move a little more swiftly through the second dataset, the Census Income Data Set (`https://archive.ics.uci.edu/ml/datasets/Census+Income`), to predict personal income.

Data wrangling

Before implementing machine learning, the dataset must be preprocessed. When testing new algorithms, it's essential to have all numerical columns with no null values.

Data loading

Since this dataset is hosted directly on the UCI Machine Learning website, it can be downloaded directly from the internet using `pd.read_csv`:

```
df_census = pd.read_csv('https://archive.ics.uci.edu/ml/
machine-learning-databases/adult/adult.data')
df_census.head()
```

Here is the expected output:

	39	State-gov	77516	Bachelors	13	Never-married	Adm-clerical	Not-in-family	White	Male	2174	0	40	United-States	<=50K
0	50	Self-emp-not-inc	83311	Bachelors	13	Married-civ-spouse	Exec-managerial	Husband	White	Male	0	0	13	United-States	<=50K
1	38	Private	215646	HS-grad	9	Divorced	Handlers-cleaners	Not-in-family	White	Male	0	0	40	United-States	<=50K
2	53	Private	234721	11th	7	Married-civ-spouse	Handlers-cleaners	Husband	Black	Male	0	0	40	United-States	<=50K
3	28	Private	338409	Bachelors	13	Married-civ-spouse	Prof-specialty	Wife	Black	Female	0	0	40	Cuba	<=50K
4	37	Private	284582	Masters	14	Married-civ-spouse	Exec-managerial	Wife	White	Female	0	0	40	United-States	<=50K

Figure 1.12 – The Census Income DataFrame

The output reveals that the column headings represent the entries of the first row. When this happens, the data may be reloaded with the `header=None` parameter:

```
df_census = pd.read_csv('https://archive.ics.uci.edu/ml/
machine-learning-databases/adult/adult.data', header=None)
df_census.head()
```

Here is the expected output without the header:

	0	1	2	3	4	5	6	7	8	9	10	11	12	13	14
0	39	State-gov	77516	Bachelors	13	Never-married	Adm-clerical	Not-in-family	White	Male	2174	0	40	United-States	<=50K
1	50	Self-emp-not-inc	83311	Bachelors	13	Married-civ-spouse	Exec-managerial	Husband	White	Male	0	0	13	United-States	<=50K
2	38	Private	215646	HS-grad	9	Divorced	Handlers-cleaners	Not-in-family	White	Male	0	0	40	United-States	<=50K
3	53	Private	234721	11th	7	Married-civ-spouse	Handlers-cleaners	Husband	Black	Male	0	0	40	United-States	<=50K
4	28	Private	338409	Bachelors	13	Married-civ-spouse	Prof-specialty	Wife	Black	Female	0	0	40	Cuba	<=50K

Figure 1.13 – The header=None parameter output

As you can see, the column names are still missing. They are listed on the Census Income Data Set website (`https://archive.ics.uci.edu/ml/datasets/Census+Income`) under *Attribute Information*.

Column names may be changed as follows:

```
df_census.columns=['age', 'workclass', 'fnlwgt', 'education',
  'education-num', 'marital-status', 'occupation',
  'relationship', 'race', 'sex', 'capital-gain', 'capital-loss',
  'hours-per-week', 'native-country', 'income']
df_census.head()
```

Here is the expected output with column names:

	age	workclass	fnlwgt	education	education-num	marital-status	occupation	relationship	race	sex	capital-gain	capital-loss	hours-per-week	native-country	income
0	39	State-gov	77516	Bachelors	13	Never-married	Adm-clerical	Not-in-family	White	Male	2174	0	40	United-States	<=50K
1	50	Self-emp-not-inc	83311	Bachelors	13	Married-civ-spouse	Exec-managerial	Husband	White	Male	0	0	13	United-States	<=50K
2	38	Private	215646	HS-grad	9	Divorced	Handlers-cleaners	Not-in-family	White	Male	0	0	40	United-States	<=50K
3	53	Private	234721	11th	7	Married-civ-spouse	Handlers-cleaners	Husband	Black	Male	0	0	40	United-States	<=50K
4	28	Private	338409	Bachelors	13	Married-civ-spouse	Prof-specialty	Wife	Black	Female	0	0	40	Cuba	<=50K

Figure 1.14 – Expected column names

As you can see, the column names have been restored.

Null values

A great way to check null values is to look at the DataFrame `.info()` method:

```
df_census.info()
```

The output is as follows:

```
<class 'pandas.core.frame.DataFrame'>
RangeIndex: 32561 entries, 0 to 32560
Data columns (total 15 columns):
 #   Column          Non-Null Count   Dtype
---  ------          --------------   -----
 0   age             32561 non-null   int64
 1   workclass       32561 non-null   object
 2   fnlwgt          32561 non-null   int64
 3   education       32561 non-null   object
```

4	education-num	32561 non-null	int64
5	marital-status	32561 non-null	object
6	occupation	32561 non-null	object
7	relationship	32561 non-null	object
8	race	32561 non-null	object
9	sex	32561 non-null	object
10	capital-gain	32561 non-null	int64
11	capital-loss	32561 non-null	int64
12	hours-per-week	32561 non-null	int64
13	native-country	32561 non-null	object
14	income	32561 non-null	object

```
dtypes: int64(6), object(9)
memory usage: 3.7+ MB
```

Since all columns have the same number of non-null rows, we can infer that there are no null values.

Non-numerical columns

All columns of the dtype object must be transformed into numerical columns. A **pandas** get_dummies method takes the non-numerical unique values of every column and converts them into their own column, with 1 indicating presence and 0 indicating absence. For instance, if the column values of a DataFrame called "Book Types" were "hardback," "paperback," or "ebook," pd.get_dummies would create three new columns called "hardback," "paperback," and "ebook" replacing the "Book Types" column.

Here is a "Book Types" DataFrame:

	Book Types
0	hardback
1	paperback
2	ebook

Figure 1.15 – A "Book Types" DataFrame

Here is the same DataFrame after `pd.get_dummies`:

	hardback	paperback	ebook
0	1	0	0
1	0	1	0
2	0	0	1

Figure 1.16 – The new DataFrame

`pd.get_dummies` will create many new columns, so it's worth checking to see whether any columns may be eliminated. A quick review of the `df_census` data reveals an `'education'` column and an `education_num` column. The `education_num` column is a numerical conversion of `'education'`. Since the information is the same, the `'education'` column may be deleted:

```
df_census = df_census.drop(['education'], axis=1)
```

Now use `pd.get_dummies` to transform the non-numerical columns into numerical columns:

```
df_census = pd.get_dummies(df_census)
df_census.head()
```

Here is the expected output:

	age	fnlwgt	education-num	capital-gain	capital-loss	hours-per-week	workclass_?	workclass_Federal-gov	workclass_Local-gov	workclass_Never-worked	...	native-country_Scotland	native-country_South	native-country_Taiwan	native-country_Thailand	native-co Trinadad&1
0	39	77516	13	2174	0	40	0	0	0	0	...	0	0	0	0	
1	50	83311	13	0	0	13	0	0	0	0	...	0	0	0	0	
2	38	215646	9	0	0	40	0	0	0	0	...	0	0	0	0	
3	53	234721	7	0	0	40	0	0	0	0	...	0	0	0	0	
4	28	338409	13	0	0	40	0	0	0	0	...	0	0	0	0	

5 rows × 94 columns

Figure 1.17 – pd.get_dummies – non-numerical to numerical columns

As you can see, new columns are created using a `column_value` syntax referencing the original column. For example, `native-country` is an original column, and Taiwan is one of many values. The new `native-country_Taiwan` column has a value of 1 if the person is from Taiwan and 0 otherwise.

> **Tip**
>
> Using `pd.get_dummies` may increase memory usage, as can be verified using the `.info()` method on the DataFrame in question and checking the last line. **Sparse matrices** may be used to save memory where only values of 1 are stored and values of 0 are not stored. For more information on sparse matrices, see *Chapter 10, XGBoost Model Deployment*, or visit SciPy's official documentation at `https://docs.scipy.org/doc/scipy/reference/`.

Target and predictor columns

Since all columns are numerical with no null values, it's time to split the data into target and predictor columns.

The target column is whether or not someone makes 50K. After `pd.get_dummies`, two columns, `df_census['income_<=50K']` and `df_census['income_>50K']`, are used to determine whether someone makes 50K. Since either column will work, we delete `df_census['income_ <=50K']`:

```
df_census = df_census.drop('income_ <=50K', axis=1)
```

Now split the data into `X` (predictor columns) and `y` (target column). Note that `-1` is used for indexing since the last column is the target column:

```
X = df_census.iloc[:,:-1]
y = df_census.iloc[:,-1]
```

It's time to build machine learning classifiers!

Logistic regression

Logistic regression is the most fundamental classification algorithm. Mathematically, logistic regression works in a manner similar to linear regression. For each column, logistic regression finds an appropriate weight, or coefficient, that maximizes model accuracy. The primary difference is that instead of summing each term, as in linear regression, logistic regression uses the **sigmoid function**.

Here is the sigmoid function and the corresponding graph:

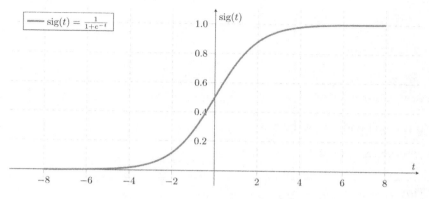

Figure 1.18 – Sigmoid function graph

The sigmoid is commonly used for classification. All values greater than 0.5 are matched to 1, and all values less than 0.5 are matched to 0.

Implementing logistic regression with scikit-learn is nearly the same as implementing linear regression. The main differences are that the predictor column should fit into categories, and the error should be in terms of accuracy. As a bonus, the error is in terms of accuracy by default, so explicit scoring parameters are not required.

You may import logistic regression as follows:

```
from sklearn.linear_model import LogisticRegression
```

The cross-validation function

Let's use cross-validation on logistic regression to predict whether someone makes over 50K.

Instead of copying and pasting, let's build a cross-validation classification function that takes a machine learning algorithm as input and has the accuracy score as output using `cross_val_score`:

```
def cross_val(classifier, num_splits=10):
    model = classifier
    scores = cross_val_score(model, X, y, cv=num_splits)
    print('Accuracy:', np.round(scores, 2))
    print('Accuracy mean: %0.2f' % (scores.mean()))
```

Now call the function with logistic regression:

```
cross_val(LogisticRegression())
```

The output is as follows:

```
Accuracy: [0.8   0.8   0.79 0.8   0.79 0.81 0.79 0.79 0.8   0.8 ]
Accuracy mean: 0.80
```

80% accuracy isn't bad out of the box.

Let's see whether XGBoost can do better.

> **Tip**
> Any time you find yourself copying and pasting code, look for a better way!
> One aim of computer science is to avoid repetition. Writing your own data
> analysis and machine learning functions will make your life easier and your
> work more efficient in the long run.

The XGBoost classifier

XGBoost has a regressor and a classifier. To use the classifier, import the following algorithm:

```
from xgboost import XGBClassifier
```

Now run the classifier in the cross_val function with one important addition. Since there are 94 columns, and XGBoost is an ensemble method, meaning that it combines many models for each run, each of which includes 10 splits, we are going to limit n_estimators, the number of models, to 5. Normally, XGBoost is very fast. In fact, it has a reputation for being the fastest boosting ensemble method out there, a reputation that we will check in this book! For our initial purposes, however, 5 estimators, though not as robust as the default of 100, is sufficient. Details on choosing n_estimators will be a focal point of *Chapter 4, From Gradient Boosting to XGBoost*:

```
cross_val(XGBClassifier(n_estimators=5))
```

The output is as follows:

```
Accuracy: [0.85 0.86 0.87 0.85 0.86 0.86 0.86 0.87 0.86 0.86]
Accuracy mean: 0.86
```

As you can see, XGBoost scores higher than logistic regression out of the box.

Summary

Your journey through XGBoost has officially begun! You started this chapter by learning the fundamentals of data wrangling and **pandas**, essential skills for all machine learning practitioners, with a focus on correcting null values. Next, you learned how to build machine learning models in scikit-learn by comparing linear regression with XGBoost. Then, you prepared a dataset for classification and compared logistic regression with XGBoost. In both cases, XGBoost was the clear winner.

Congratulations on building your first XGBoost models! Your initiation into data wrangling and machine learning using the **pandas**, NumPy, and scikit-learn libraries is complete.

In *Chapter 2, Decision Trees in Depth*, you will improve your machine learning skills by building decision trees, the base learners of XGBoost machine learning models, and fine-tuning hyperparameters to improve results.

2
Decision Trees in Depth

In this chapter, you will gain proficiency with **decision trees**, the primary machine learning algorithm from which XGBoost models are built. You will also gain first-hand experience in the science and art of **hyperparameter fine-tuning**. Since decision trees are the foundation of XGBoost models, the skills that you learn in this chapter are essential to building robust XGBoost models going forward.

In this chapter, you will build and evaluate **decision tree classifiers** and **decision tree regressors**, visualize and analyze decision trees in terms of variance and bias, and fine-tune decision tree hyperparameters. In addition, you will apply decision trees to a case study that predicts heart disease in patients.

This chapter covers the following main topics:

- Introducing decision trees with XGBoost
- Exploring decision trees
- Contrasting variance and bias
- Tuning decision tree hyperparameters
- Predicting heart disease – a case study

Introducing decision trees with XGBoost

XGBoost is an **ensemble method**, meaning that it is composed of different machine learning models that combine to work together. The individual models that make up the ensemble in XGBoost are called **base learners**.

Decision trees, the most commonly used XGBoost base learners, are unique in the machine learning landscape. Instead of multiplying column values by numeric weights, as in linear regression and logistic regression (*Chapter 1*, *Machine Learning Landscape*), decision trees split the data by asking questions about the columns. In fact, building decision trees is like playing a game of 20 Questions.

For instance, a decision tree may have a temperature column, and that column could branch into two groups, one with temperatures above 70 degrees, and one with temperatures below 70 degrees. The next split could be based on the seasons, following one branch if it's summer and another branch otherwise. Now the data has been split into four separate groups. This process of splitting data into new groups via branching continues until the algorithm reaches a desired level of accuracy.

A decision tree can create thousands of branches until it uniquely maps each sample to the correct target in the training set. This means that the training set can have 100% accuracy. Such a model, however, will not generalize well to new data.

Decision trees are prone to overfitting the data. In other words, decision trees can map too closely to the training data, a problem explored later in this chapter in terms of variance and bias. Hyperparameter fine-tuning is one solution to prevent overfitting. Another solution is to aggregate the predictions of many trees, a strategy that **Random Forests** and XGBoost employ.

While Random Forests and XGBoost will be the focus of subsequent chapters, we now take a deep look inside decision trees.

Exploring decision trees

Decision Trees work by splitting the data into *branches*. The branches are followed down to *leaves* where predictions are made. Understanding how branches and leaves are created is much easier with a practical example. Before going into further detail, let's build our first decision tree model.

First decision tree model

We start by building a decision tree to predict whether someone makes over 50K US dollars using the Census dataset from *Chapter 1, Machine Learning Landscape*:

1. First, open a new Jupyter Notebook and start with the following imports:

```
import pandas as pd
import numpy as np
import warnings
warnings.filterwarnings('ignore')
```

2. Next, open the file `'census_cleaned.csv'` that has been uploaded for you at `https://github.com/PacktPublishing/Hands-On-Gradient-Boosting-with-XGBoost-and-Scikit-learn/tree/master/Chapter02`. If you downloaded all files for this book from the Packt GitHub page, as recommended in the *preface*, you can navigate to *Chapter 2, Decision Trees in Depth*, after launching Anaconda in the same way that you navigate to other chapters. Otherwise, go our GitHub page and clone the files now:

```
df_census = pd.read_csv('census_cleaned.csv')
```

3. After uploading the data into a DataFrame, declare your predictor and target columns, X and y, as follows:

```
X = df_census.iloc[:,:-1]
y = df_census.iloc[:,-1]
```

4. Next, import `train_test_split` to split the data into training and tests set with `random_state=2` to ensure consistent results:

```
from sklearn.model_selection import train_test_split
X_train, X_test, y_train, y_test = train_test_split(X, y,
random_state=2)
```

    As with other machine learning classifiers, when using decision trees, we initialize the model, fit it on the training set, and test it using `accuracy_score`.

The `accuracy_score` determines the number of correct predictions divided by the total number of predictions. If 19 of 20 predictions are correct, the `accuracy_score` is 95%.

First, import the `DecisionTreeClassifier` and `accuracy_score`:

```
from sklearn.tree import DecisionTreeClassifier
from sklearn.metrics import accuracy_score
```

Next, we build a decision tree classifier with the standard steps:

1. Initialize a machine learning model with `random_state=2` to ensure consistent results:

    ```
    clf = DecisionTreeClassifier(random_state=2)
    ```

2. Fit the model on the training set:

    ```
    clf.fit(X_train, y_train)
    ```

3. Make predictions for the test set:

    ```
    y_pred = clf.predict(X_test)
    ```

4. Compare predictions with the test set:

    ```
    accuracy_score(y_pred, y_test)
    ```

    The `accuracy_score` is as follows:

    ```
    0.8131679154894976
    ```

An accuracy of 81% is comparable to the accuracy of Logistic Regression from the same dataset in *Chapter 1, Machine Learning Landscape*.

Now that you have seen how to build a decision tree, let's take a look inside.

Inside a decision tree

Decision Trees come with nice visuals that reveal their inner workings.

Here is a decision tree from the Census dataset with only two splits:

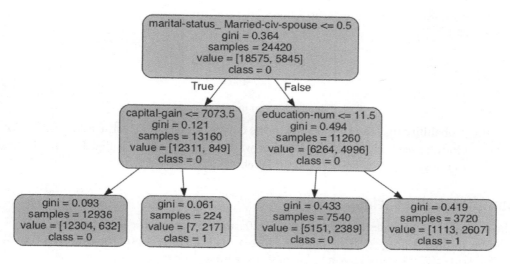

Figure 2.1 – Census dataset decision tree

The top of the tree is the root, the **True/False** arrows are branches, and the data points are nodes. At the end of the tree, the nodes are classified as leaves. Let's study the preceding diagram in depth.

Root

The root of the tree is at the top. The first line reads **marital-status_Married-civ-spouse <=5**. **marital-status** is a binary column, so all values are **0** (negative) or **1** (positive). The first split is based on whether someone is married or not. The left side of the tree is the **True** branch, meaning the user is unmarried, and the right side is the **False** branch, meaning the user is married.

Gini criterion

The second line of the root reads **gini=0.364**. This is the error method the decision tree uses to decide how splits should be made. The goal is to find a split that leads to the lowest error. A Gini index of 0 means 0 errors. A gini index of 1 means all errors. A gini index of 0.5, which shows an equal distribution of elements, means the predictions are no better than random guessing. The closer to 0, the lower the error. At the root, a gini of 0.364 means the training set is imbalanced with 36.4 percent of class 1.

The equation for the gini index is as follows:

$$gini = 1 - \sum_{i=1}^{c} (pi)^2$$

Figure 2.2 – gini index equation

P_i is the probability that the split results in the correct value, and c is the total number of classes: 2 in the preceding example. Another way of looking at this is that P_i is the fraction of items in the set with the correct output label.

Samples, values, class

The root of the tree states that there are 24,420 samples. This is the total number of samples in the training set. The following line reads [**18575 , 5845**]. The ordering is 0 then 1, so 18,575 samples have a value of 0 (they make less than 50K) and 5,845 have a value of 1 (they make more than 50K).

True/false nodes

Following the first branch, you see **True** on the left side, and **False** on the right. The pattern of True – left and False – right continues throughout the tree.

In the left node in the second row, the split **capital_gain <= 7073.5** is applied to subsequent nodes. The remaining information comes from the split above the previous branch. Of the 13,160 unmarried people, 12,311 have an income of less than 50K, while 849 have an income of more than 50K. The gini index, **0.121**, is a very good score.

Stumps

It's possible to have a tree with only one split. Such a tree is called a **stump**. Although stumps are not powerful predictors in themselves, stumps can become powerful when used as boosters, as covered in *Chapter 4, From Gradient Boosting to XGBoost*.

Leaves

The nodes at the end of the tree are leaves. The leaves contain all final predictions.

The far-left leaf has a gini index of **0.093**, correctly predicting 12,304 of 12,938 cases, which is 95%. We are 95% confident that unmarried users with capital gains of less than 7,073.50 do not make more than 50K.

Other leaves may be interpreted similarly.

Now let's see where these predictions go wrong.

Contrasting variance and bias

Imagine that you have the data points displayed in the following graph. Your task is to fit a line or curve that will allow you to make predictions for new points.

Here is a graph of random points:

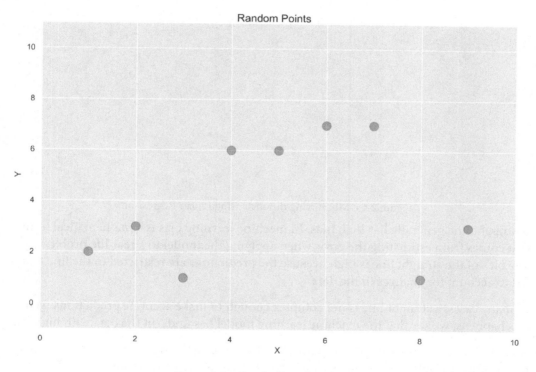

Figure 2.3 – Graph of random points

One idea is to use Linear Regression, which minimizes the square of the distance between each point and the line, as shown in the following graph:

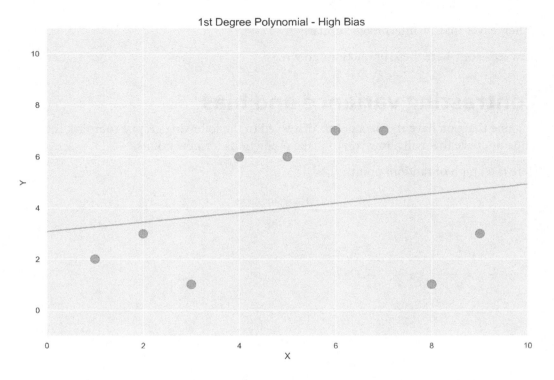

Figure 2.4 – Minimizing distance using Linear Regression

A straight line generally has high **bias**. In machine learning bias is a mathematical term that comes from estimating the error when applying the model to a real-life problem. The bias of the straight line is high because the predictions are restricted to the line and fail to account for changes in the data.

In many cases, a straight line is not complex enough to make accurate predictions. When this happens, we say that the machine learning model has underfit the data with high bias.

A second option is to fit the points with an eight-degree polynomial. Since there are only nine points, an eight-degree polynomial will fit the data perfectly, as you can see in the following graph:

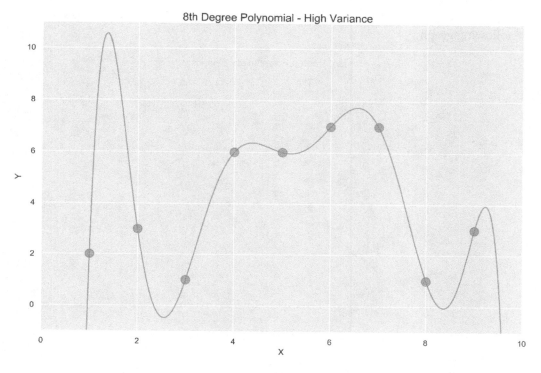

Figure 2.5 – Eight-degree poynomial

This model has high **variance**. In machine learning, variance is a mathematical term indicating how much a model will change given a different set of training data. Formally, variance is the measure of the squared deviation between a random variable and its mean. Given nine different data points in the training set, the eighth-degree polynomial will be completely different, resulting in high variance.

Models with high variance often overfit the data. These models do not generalize well to new data points because they have fit the training data too closely.

In the world of big data, overfitting is a big problem. More data results in larger training sets, and machine learning models like decision trees fit the training data too well.

As a final option, consider a third-degree polynomial that fits the data points as shown in the following graph:

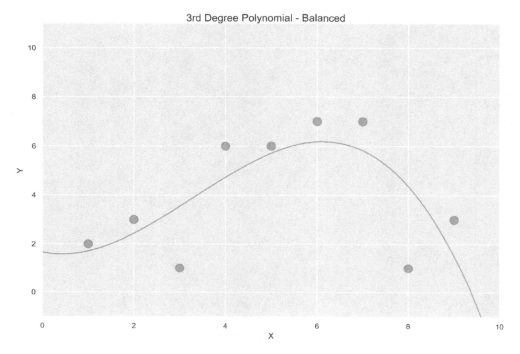

Figure 2.6 – Third-degree polynomial

This third-degree polynomial provides a nice balance between variance and bias, following the curve generally, yet adapting to the variation. Low variance means that a different training set will not result in a curve that differs by a significant amount. Low bias indicates that the error when applying this model to a real-world situation will not be too high. In machine learning, the combination of low variance and low bias is ideal.

One of the best machine learning strategies to strike a nice balance between variance and bias is to fine-tune hyperparameters.

Tuning decision tree hyperparameters

Hyperparameters are not the same as parameters.

In machine learning, parameters are adjusted when the model is being tuned. The weights in linear and Logistic Regression, for example, are parameters adjusted during the build phase to minimize errors. Hyperparameters, by contrast, are chosen in advance of the build phase. If no hyperparameters are selected, default values are used.

Decision Tree regressor

The best way to learn about hyperparameters is through experimentation. Although there are theories behind the range of hyperparameters chosen, results trump theory. Different datasets see improvements with different hyperparameter values.

Before selecting hyperparameters, let's start by finding a baseline score using a `DecisionTreeRegressor` and `cross_val_score` with the following steps:

1. Download the `'bike_rentals_cleaned'` dataset and split it into `X_bikes` (predictor columns) and `y_bikes` (training columns):

    ```
    df_bikes = pd.read_csv('bike_rentals_cleaned.csv')
    X_bikes = df_bikes.iloc[:,:-1]
    y_bikes = df_bikes.iloc[:,-1]
    ```

2. Import the `DecisionTreeRegressor` and `cross_val_score`:

    ```
    from sklearn.tree import DecisionTreeRegressor
    from sklearn.model_selection import cross_val_score
    ```

3. Initialize `DecisionTreeRegressor` and fit the model in `cross_val_score`:

    ```
    reg = DecisionTreeRegressor(random_state=2)
    scores = cross_val_score(reg, X_bikes, y_bikes,
    scoring='neg_mean_squared_error', cv=5)
    ```

4. Compute the **root mean squared error** (**RMSE**) and print the results:

    ```
    rmse = np.sqrt(-scores)
    print('RMSE mean: %0.2f' % (rmse.mean()))
    ```

    The result is as follows:

    ```
    RMSE mean: 1233.36
    ```

The RMSE is `1233.36`. This is worse than the `972.06` obtained from Linear Regression in *Chapter 1, Machine Learning Landscape*, and from the `887.31` obtained by XGBoost.

Is the model overfitting the data because the variance is too high?

This question may be answered by seeing how well the decision tree makes predictions on the training set alone. The following code checks the error of the training set, before it makes predictions on the test set:

```
reg = DecisionTreeRegressor()
reg.fit(X_train, y_train)
y_pred = reg.predict(X_train)
from sklearn.metrics import mean_squared_error
reg_mse = mean_squared_error(y_train, y_pred)
reg_rmse = np.sqrt(reg_mse)
reg_rmse
```

The result is as follows:

```
0.0
```

A RMSE of 0.0 means that the model has perfectly fit every data point! This perfect score combined with a cross-validation error of 1233.36 is proof that the decision tree is overfitting the data with high variance. The training set fit perfectly, but the test set missed badly.

Hyperparameters may rectify the situation.

Hyperparameters in general

Hyperparameter details for all scikit-learn models may be viewed on scikit-learn's official documentation pages.

Here is an excerpt from the DecisionTreeRegressor website (`https://scikit-learn.org/stable/modules/generated/sklearn.tree.DecisionTreeRegressor.html`).

> **Note**
> *sklearn* is short for *scikit-learn*.

sklearn.tree.DecisionTreeRegressor

class sklearn.tree.**DecisionTreeRegressor**(*criterion='mse', splitter='best', max_depth=None, min_samples_split=2, min_samples_leaf=1, min_weight_fraction_leaf=0.0, max_features=None, random_state=None, max_leaf_nodes=None, min_impurity_decrease=0.0, min_impurity_split=None, presort='deprecated', ccp_alpha=0.0*)   [source]

A decision tree regressor.

Read more in the User Guide.

Parameters:	**criterion : *{"mse", "friedman_mse", "mae"}, default="mse"***
	The function to measure the quality of a split. Supported criteria are "mse" for the mean squared error, which is equal to variance reduction as feature selection criterion and minimizes the L2 loss using the mean of each terminal node, "friedman_mse", which uses mean squared error with Friedman's improvement score for potential splits, and "mae" for the mean absolute error, which minimizes the L1 loss using the median of each terminal node.
	New in version 0.18: Mean Absolute Error (MAE) criterion.
	splitter : *{"best", "random"}, default="best"*
	The strategy used to choose the split at each node. Supported strategies are "best" to choose the best split and "random" to choose the best random split.
	max_depth : *int, default=None*
	The maximum depth of the tree. If None, then nodes are expanded until all leaves are pure or until all leaves contain less than min_samples_split samples.
	min_samples_split : *int or float, default=2*
	The minimum number of samples required to split an internal node:
	• If int, then consider `min_samples_split` as the minimum number.
	• If float, then `min_samples_split` is a fraction and `ceil(min_samples_split * n_samples)` are the

Figure 2.7. Excerpt of DecisionTreeRegressor official documentation page

The official documentation explains the meaning behind the hyperparameters. Note that **Parameters** here is short for *hyperparameters*. When working on your own, checking the official documentation is your most reliable resource.

Let's go over the hyperparameters one at a time.

max_depth

max_depth defines the depth of the tree, determined by the number of times splits are made. By default, there is no limit to max_depth, so there may be hundreds or thousands of splits that result in overfitting. By limiting max_depth to smaller numbers, variance is reduced, and the model generalizes better to new data.

How can you choose the best number for max_depth?

You can always try max_depth=1, then max_depth=2, then max_depth=3, and so on, but this process would be exhausting. Instead, you may use a wonderful tool called GridSearchCV.

GridSearchCV

`GridSearchCV` searches a grid of hyperparameters using cross-validation to deliver the best results.

`GridSearchCV` functions as any machine learning algorithm, meaning that it's fit on a training set, and scored on a test set. The primary difference is that `GridSearchCV` checks all hyperparameters before finalizing a model.

The key with `GridSearchCV` is to establish a dictionary of hyperparameter values. There is no correct set of values to try. One strategy is to select a smallest and largest value with evenly spaced numbers in between. Since we are trying to reduce overfitting, the general idea is to try more values on the lower side for `max_depth`.

Import `GridSearchCV` and define a list of hyperparameters for `max_depth` as follows:

```
from sklearn.model_selection import GridSearchCV
params = {'max_depth':[None,2,3,4,6,8,10,20]}
```

The `params` dictionary contains one key, `'max_depth'`, written as a string, and one value, a list of numbers that we have chosen. Note that `None` is the default, meaning that there is no limit to `max_depth`.

> **Tip**
> Generally speaking, decreasing max hyperparameters and increasing min hyperparameters will reduce variation and prevent overfitting.

Next, initialize a `DecisionTreeRegressor`, and place it inside of `GridSearchCV` along with `params` and the scoring metric:

```
reg = DecisionTreeRegressor(random_state=2)
grid_reg = GridSearchCV(reg, params, scoring='neg_mean_squared_
error', cv=5, n_jobs=-1)
grid_reg.fit(X_train, y_train)
```

Now that `GridSearchCV` has been fit on the data, you can view the best hyperparameters as follows:

```
best_params = grid_reg.best_params_
print("Best params:", best_params)
```

The result is as follows:

```
Best params: {'max_depth': 6}
```

As you can see, a `max_depth` value of 6 resulted in the best cross-validation score in the training set.

The training score may be displayed using the `best_score` attribute:

```
best_score = np.sqrt(-grid_reg.best_score_)
print("Training score: {:.3f}".format(best_score))
```

The score is as follows:

```
Training score: 951.938
```

The test score may be displayed as follows:

```
best_model = grid_reg.best_estimator_
y_pred = best_model.predict(X_test)
rmse_test = mean_squared_error(y_test, y_pred)**0.5
print('Test score: {:.3f}'.format(rmse_test))
```

The score is as follows:

```
Test score: 864.670
```

Variance has been substantially reduced.

min_samples_leaf

`min_samples_leaf` provides a restriction by increasing the number of samples that a leaf may have. As with `max_depth`, `min_samples_leaf` is designed to reduce overfitting.

When there are no restrictions, `min_samples_leaf=1` is the default, meaning that leaves may consist of unique samples (prone to overfitting). Increasing `min_samples_leaf` reduces variance. If `min_samples_leaf=8`, all leaves must contain eight or more samples.

Testing a range of values for `min_samples_leaf` requires going through the same process as before. Instead of copying and pasting, we write a function that displays the best parameters, training score, and test score using `GridSearchCV` with `DecisionTreeRegressor(random_state=2)` assigned to `reg` as a default parameter:

```
def grid_search(params, reg=DecisionTreeRegressor(random_
state=2)):
```

```
grid_reg = GridSearchCV(reg, params,
scoring='neg_mean_squared_error', cv=5, n_jobs=-1):
grid_reg.fit(X_train, y_train)

best_params = grid_reg.best_params_
print("Best params:", best_params)

best_score = np.sqrt(-grid_reg.best_score_)
print("Training score: {:.3f}".format(best_score))

y_pred = grid_reg.predict(X_test)
rmse_test = mean_squared_error(y_test, y_pred)**0.5
print('Test score: {:.3f}'.format(rmse_test))
```

> **Tip**
>
> When writing your own functions, it's advantageous to include default keyword arguments. A default keyword argument is a named parameter with a default value that may be changed for later use and testing. Default keyword arguments greatly enhance the capabilities of Python.

When choosing the range of hyperparameters, it's helpful to know the size of the training set on which the model is built. Pandas comes with a nice method, `.shape`, that returns the rows and columns of the data:

```
X_train.shape
```

The rows and columns of data are as follows:

```
(548, 12)
```

Since the training set has `548` rows, this helps determine reasonable values for `min_samples_leaf`. Let's try [1, 2, 4, 6, 8, 10, 20, 30] as the input of our `grid_search`:

```
grid_search(params={'min_samples_leaf':[1, 2, 4, 6, 8, 10, 20, 30]})
```

The score is as follows:

```
Best params: {'min_samples_leaf': 8}
Training score: 896.083
Test score: 855.620
```

Since the test score is better than the training score, variance has been reduced.

What happens when we put `min_samples_leaf` and `max_depth` together? Let's see:

```
grid_search(params={'max_depth':[None,2,3,4,6,8,10,20],'min_
samples_leaf':[1,2,4,6,8,10,20,30]})
```

The score is as follows:

```
Best params: {'max_depth': 6, 'min_samples_leaf': 2}
Training score: 870.396
Test score: 913.000
```

The result may be a surprise. Even though the training score has improved, the test score has not. `min_samples_leaf` has decreased from 8 to 2, while `max_depth` has remained the same.

> **Tip**
> This is a valuable lesson in hyperparameter tuning: Hyperparameters should not be chosen in isolation.

As for reducing variance in the preceding example, limiting `min_samples_leaf` to values greater than three may help:

```
grid_search(params={'max_depth':[6,7,8,9,10],'min_samples_
leaf':[3,5,7,9]})
```

The score is as follows:

```
Best params: {'max_depth': 9, 'min_samples_leaf': 7}
Training score: 888.905
Test score: 878.538
```

As you can see, the test score has improved.

We will now explore the remaining decision tree hyperparameters without individual testing.

max_leaf_nodes

`max_leaf_nodes` is similar to `min_samples_leaf`. Instead of specifying the number of samples per leaf, it specifies the total number of leaves. So, `max_leaf_nodes=10` means that the model cannot have more than 10 leaves. It could have fewer.

max_features

max_features is an effective hyperparameter for reducing variance. Instead of considering every possible feature for a split, it chooses from a select number of features each round.

It's standard to see max_features with the following options:

- 'auto' is the default, which provides no limitations.
- 'sqrt' is the square root of the total number of features.
- 'log2' is the log of the total number of features in base 2. 32 columns resolves to 5 since $2 ^5 = 32$.

min_samples_split

Another splitting technique is min_samples_split. As the name indicates, min_samples_split provides a limit to the number of samples required before a split can be made. The default is 2, since two samples may be split into one sample each, ending as single leaves. If the limit is increased to 5, no further splits are permitted for nodes with five samples or fewer.

splitter

There are two options for splitter, 'random' and 'best'. Splitter tells the model how to select the feature to split each branch. The 'best' option, the default, selects the feature that results in the greatest gain of information. The 'random' option, by contrast, selects the split randomly.

Changing splitter to 'random' is a great way to prevent overfitting and diversify trees.

criterion

The criterion for splitting decision tree regressors and classifiers are different. The criterion provides the method the machine learning model uses to determine how splits should be made. It's the scoring method for splits. For each possible split, the criterion calculates a number for a possible split and compares it to other options. The split with the best score wins.

The options for decision tree regressors are mse (mean squared error), friedman_mse, (which includes Friedman's adjustment), and mae (mean absolute error). The default is mse.

For classifiers, `gini`, which was described earlier, and `entropy` usually give similar results.

min_impurity_decrease

Previously known as `min_impurity_split`, `min_impurity_decrease` results in a split when the impurity is greater than or equal to this value.

Impurity is a measure of how pure the predictions are for every node. A tree with 100% accuracy would have an impurity of 0.0. A tree with 80% accuracy would have an impurity of 0.20.

Impurity is an important idea in Decision Trees. Throughout the tree-building process, impurity should continually decrease. Splits that result in the greatest decrease of impurity are chosen for each node.

The default value is `0.0`. This number can be increased so that trees stop building when a certain threshold is reached.

min_weight_fraction_leaf

`min_weight_fraction_leaf` is the minimum weighted fraction of the total weights required to be a leaf. According to the documentation, *Samples have equal weight when sample_weight is not provided.*

For practical purposes, `min_weight_fraction_leaf` is another hyperparameter that reduces variance and prevents overfitting. The default is 0.0. Assuming equal weights, a restriction of 1%, 0.01, would require at least 5 of the 500 samples to be a leaf.

ccp_alpha

The `ccp_alpha` hyperparameter will not be discussed here, as it is designed for pruning after the tree has been built. For a full discussion, check out minimal cost complexity pruning: `https://scikit-learn.org/stable/modules/tree.html#minimal-cost-complexity-pruning`.

Putting it all together

When fine-tuning hyperparameters, several factors come into play:

- The amount of time allotted
- The number of hyperparameters
- The number of decimal places of accuracy desired

The time spent, number of hyperparameters fine-tuned, and accuracy desired depend on you, the dataset, and the project at hand. Since hyperparameters are interrelated, it's not required to modify them all. Fine-tuning a smaller range may lead to better results.

Now that you understand the fundamentals of decision trees and decision tree hyperparameters, it's time to apply what you have learned.

> **Tip**
> There are too many decision tree hyperparameters to consistently use them all. In my experience, `max_depth`, `max_features`, `min_samples_leaf`, `max_leaf_nodes`, `min_impurity_decrease`, and `min_samples_split` are often sufficient.

Predicting heart disease – a case study

You have been asked by a hospital to use machine learning to predict heart disease. Your job is to develop a model and highlight two to three important features that doctors and nurses can focus on to improve patient health.

You decide to use a decision tree classifier with fine-tuned hyperparameters. After the model has been built, you will interpret results using `feature_importances_`, an attribute that determines the most important features in predicting heart disease.

Heart Disease dataset

The Heart Disease dataset has been uploaded to GitHub as `heart_disease.csv`. This is a slight modification to the original Heart Disease dataset (`https://archive.ics.uci.edu/ml/datasets/Heart+Disease`) provided by the UCI Machine Learning Repository (`https://archive.ics.uci.edu/ml/index.php`) with null values cleaned up for your convenience.

Upload the file and display the first five rows as follows:

```
df_heart = pd.read_csv('heart_disease.csv')
df_heart.head()
```

The preceding code produces the following table:

	age	sex	cp	trestbps	chol	fbs	restecg	thalach	exang	oldpeak	slope	ca	thal	target
0	63	1	3	145	233	1	0	150	0	2.3	0	0	1	1
1	37	1	2	130	250	0	1	187	0	3.5	0	0	2	1
2	41	0	1	130	204	0	0	172	0	1.4	2	0	2	1
3	56	1	1	120	236	0	1	178	0	0.8	2	0	2	1
4	57	0	0	120	354	0	1	163	1	0.6	2	0	2	1

Figure 2.8 – heart_disease.csv output

The target column, conveniently labeled 'target' is binary, with 1 indicating that the patient has heart disease and 0 indicating that they do not.

Here are the meanings of the predictor columns, taken from the data source linked previously:

- age: Age in years
- sex: Sex (1 = male; 0 = female)
- cp: Chest pain type (1 = typical angina, 2 = atypical angina, 3 = non-anginal pain, 4 = asymptomatic)
- trestbps: Resting blood pressure (in mm Hg on admission to the hospital)
- chol: Serum cholesterol in mg/dl 6 fbs: (fasting blood sugar > 120 mg/dl) (1 = true; 0 = false)
- fbs: Fasting blood sugar > 120 mg/dl (1 = true; 0 = false)
- restecg: Resting electrocardiographic results (0 = normal, 1 = having ST-T wave abnormality (T wave inversions and/or ST elevation or depression of > 0.05 mV), 2 = showing probable or definite left ventricular hypertrophy by Estes' criteria)
- thalach: Maximum heart rate achieved
- exang: Exercise induced angina (1 = yes; 0 = no)
- oldpeak: ST depression induced by exercise relative to rest
- slope: The slope of the peak exercise ST segment (1 = upsloping, 2 = flat, 3 = downsloping)
- ca: Number of major vessels (0-3) colored by fluoroscopy
- thal: 3 = normal; 6 = fixed defect; 7 = reversible defect

Split the data into training and test sets in preparation for machine learning:

```
X = df_heart.iloc[:,:-1]
y = df_heart.iloc[:,-1]
from sklearn.model_selection import train_test_split
X_train, X_test, y_train, y_test = train_test_split(X, y,
random_state=2)
```

You are now ready to make predictions.

Decision Tree classifier

Before implementing hyperparameters, it's helpful to have a baseline model for comparison.

Use `cross_val_score` with a `DecisionTreeClassifier` as follows:

```
model = DecisionTreeClassifier(random_state=2)
scores = cross_val_score(model, X, y, cv=5)
print('Accuracy:', np.round(scores, 2))
print('Accuracy mean: %0.2f' % (scores.mean()))
Accuracy: [0.74 0.85 0.77 0.73 0.7 ]
```

The result is as follows:

```
Accuracy mean: 0.76
```

The initial accuracy is 76%. Let's see what gains can be made with hyperparameter fine-tuning.

RandomizedSearch CLF function

When fine-tuning many hyperparameters, `GridSearchCV` can take too much time. The scikit-learn library provides `RandomizedSearchCV` as a wonderful alternative. `RandomizedSearchCV` works in the same way as `GridSearchCV`, but instead of trying all hyperparameters, it tries a random number of combinations. It's not meant to be exhaustive. It's meant to find the best combinations in limited time.

Here's a function that uses `RandomizedSearchCV` to return the best model along with the scores. The inputs are `params` (a dictionary of hyperparameters to test), `runs` (number of hyperparameter combinations to check), and `DecisionTreeClassifier`:

```
def randomized_search_clf(params, runs=20,
clf=DecisionTreeClassifier(random_state=2)):
```

```
rand_clf = RandomizedSearchCV(clf, params, n_iter=runs,
cv=5, n_jobs=-1, random_state=2)
rand_clf.fit(X_train, y_train)
best_model = rand_clf.best_estimator_
best_score = rand_clf.best_score_
print("Training score: {:.3f}".format(best_score))
y_pred = best_model.predict(X_test)
accuracy = accuracy_score(y_test, y_pred)
print('Test score: {:.3f}'.format(accuracy))
return best_model
```

Now, let's pick a range of hyperparameters.

Choosing hyperparameters

There is no single correct approach for choosing hyperparameters. Experimentation is the name of the game. Here is an initial list, placed inside the `randomized_search_clf` function. These numbers have been chosen with the aim of reducing variance and trying an expansive range:

```
randomized_search_clf(params={'criterion':['entropy',
'gini'],'splitter':['random', 'best'], 'min_weight_fraction_
leaf':[0.0, 0.0025, 0.005, 0.0075, 0.01],'min_samples_
split':[2, 3, 4, 5, 6, 8, 10],
'min_samples_leaf':[1, 0.01, 0.02, 0.03, 0.04],
'min_impurity_decrease':[0.0, 0.0005, 0.005, 0.05, 0.10, 0.15,
0.2],'max_leaf_nodes':[10, 15, 20, 25, 30, 35, 40, 45, 50,
None],'max_features':['auto', 0.95, 0.90, 0.85, 0.80, 0.75,
0.70],'max_depth':[None, 2,4,6,8],
'min_weight_fraction_leaf':[0.0, 0.0025, 0.005, 0.0075, 0.01,
0.05]})
```

```
Training score: 0.798
```

```
Test score: 0.855
```

```
DecisionTreeClassifier(class_weight=None, criterion='entropy',
max_depth=8, max_features=0.8, max_leaf_nodes=45, min_
impurity_decrease=0.0, min_impurity_split=None, min_samples_
leaf=0.04, min_samples_split=10,min_weight_fraction_leaf=0.05,
presort=False, random_state=2, splitter='best')
```

This is a definite improvement, and the model generalizes well on the test set. Let's see if we can do better by narrowing the range.

Narrowing the range

Narrowing the range is one strategy to improve hyperparameters.

As an example, using a baseline of max_depth=8 chosen from the best model, we may narrow the range to from 7 to 9.

Another strategy is to stop checking hyperparameters whose defaults are working fine. entropy, for instance, is not recommended over 'gini' as the differences are very slight. min_impurity_split and min_impurity_decrease may also be left at their defaults.

Here is a new hyperparameter range with an increase of 100 runs:

```
randomized_search_clf(params={'max_depth':[None, 6, 7],
'max_features':['auto', 0.78], 'max_leaf_nodes':[45, None],
'min_samples_leaf':[1, 0.035, 0.04, 0.045, 0.05],
'min_samples_split':[2, 9, 10],
'min_weight_fraction_leaf': [0.0, 0.05, 0.06, 0.07],
}, runs=100)
```

```
Training score: 0.802
Test score: 0.868
DecisionTreeClassifier(class_weight=None, criterion='gini',
max_depth=7,max_features=0.78, max_leaf_nodes=45, min_
impurity_decrease=0.0, min_impurity_split=None, min_samples_
leaf=0.045, min_samples_split=9, min_weight_fraction_leaf=0.06,
presort=False, random_state=2, splitter='best')
```

This model is more accurate in the training and test score.

For a proper baseline of comparison, however, it's essential to put the new model into cross_val_clf. This may be achieved by copying and pasting the preceding model:

```
model = DecisionTreeClassifier(class_weight=None,
criterion='gini', max_depth=7, max_features=0.78, max_
leaf_nodes=45, min_impurity_decrease=0.0, min_impurity_
split=None, min_samples_leaf=0.045, min_samples_split=9,
min_weight_fraction_leaf=0.06, presort=False, random_state=2,
splitter='best')
```

```
scores = cross_val_score(model, X, y, cv=5)
print('Accuracy:', np.round(scores, 2))
print('Accuracy mean: %0.2f' % (scores.mean()))
Accuracy: [0.82 0.9  0.8  0.8  0.78]
```

The result is as follows:

```
Accuracy mean: 0.82
```

This is six percentage points higher than the default model. When it comes to predicting heart disease, more accuracy can save lives.

feature_importances_

The final piece of the puzzle is to communicate the most important features of the machine learning model. Decision trees come with a nice attribute, `feature_importances_`, that does exactly this.

First, we need to finalize the best model. Our function returned the best model, but it has not been saved.

When testing, it's important not to mix and match training and test sets. After a final model has been selected, however, fitting the model on the entire dataset can be beneficial. Why? Because the goal is to test the model on data that has never been seen and fitting the model on the entire dataset may lead to additional gains in accuracy.

Let's define the model using the best hyperparameters and fit it on the entire dataset:

```
best_clf = DecisionTreeClassifier(class_weight=None,
criterion='gini', max_depth=9,
max_features=0.8, max_leaf_nodes=47,
min_impurity_decrease=0.0, min_impurity_split=None,
min_samples_leaf=1, min_samples_split=8,
min_weight_fraction_leaf=0.05, presort=False,
random_state=2, splitter='best')
best_clf.fit(X, y)
```

In order to determine the most important features, we can run the `feature_importances_` attribute on `best_clf`:

```
best_clf.feature_importances_
array([0.04826754, 0.04081653, 0.48409586, 0.00568635,
0.        , 0., 0., 0.00859483, 0., 0.02690379, 0., 0.18069065,
0.20494446])
```

It's not easy to interpret these results. The following code zips the columns along with the most important features into a dictionary before displaying them in reverse order for a clean output that is easy to interpret:

```
feature_dict = dict(zip(X.columns, best_clf.feature_
importances_))
```

```
# Import operator
import operator
```

```
Sort dict by values (as list of tuples)
sorted(feature_dict.items(), key=operator.itemgetter(1),
reverse=True)[0:3]
```

```
[('cp', 0.4840958610240171),
 ('thal', 0.20494445570568706),
 ('ca', 0.18069065321397942)]
```

The three most important features are as follows:

- 'cp': Chest pain type (1 = typical angina, 2 = atypical angina, 3 = non-anginal pain, 4 = asymptomatic)

- 'thalach': Maximum heart rate achieved

- 'ca': Number of major vessels (0-3) colored by fluoroscopy

These numbers may be interpreted as their explanation of variance, so 'cp' accounts for 48% of the variance, which is more than 'thal' and 'ca' combined.

You can tell the doctors and nurses that your model predicts if the patient has a heart disease with 82% accuracy using chest pain, maximum heart rate, and fluoroscopy as the three most important characteristics.

Summary

In this chapter, you have taken a big leap toward mastering XGBoost by examining decision trees, the primary XGBoost base learners. You built decision tree regressors and classifiers by fine-tuning hyperparameters with `GridSearchCV` and `RandomizedSearchCV`. You visualized decision trees and analyzed their errors and accuracy in terms of variance and bias. Furthermore, you learned about an indispensable tool, `feature_importances_`, which is used to communicate the most important features of your model that is also an attribute of XGBoost.

In the next chapter, you will learn how to build Random Forests, our first ensemble method and a rival of XGBoost. The applications of Random Forests are important for comprehending the difference between bagging and boosting, generating machine learning models comparable to XGBoost, and learning about the limitations of Random Forests that facilitated the development of XGBoost in the first place.

3
Bagging with Random Forests

In this chapter, you will gain proficiency in building **random forests**, a leading competitor to XGBoost. Like XGBoost, random forests are ensembles of decision trees. The difference is that random forests combine trees via **bagging**, while XGBoost combines trees via **boosting**. Random forests are a viable alternative to XGBoost with advantages and limitations that are highlighted in this chapter. Learning about random forests is important because they provide valuable insights into the structure of tree-based ensembles (XGBoost), and they allow a deeper understanding of boosting in comparison and contrast with their own method of bagging.

In this chapter, you will build and evaluate **random forest classifiers** and **random forest regressors**, gain mastery of random forest hyperparameters, learn about bagging in the machine learning landscape, and explore a case study that highlights some random forest limitations that spurred the development of gradient boosting (XGBoost).

This chapter covers the following main topics:

- Bagging ensembles
- Exploring random forests
- Tuning random forest hyperparameters
- Pushing random forest boundaries – case study

Technical requirements

The code for this chapter is available at `https://github.com/PacktPublishing/Hands-On-Gradient-Boosting-with-XGBoost-and-Scikit-learn/tree/master/Chapter03`

Bagging ensembles

In this section, you will learn why ensemble methods are usually superior to individual machine learning models. Furthermore, you will learn about the technique of bagging. Both are essential features of random forests.

Ensemble methods

In machine learning, an ensemble method is a machine learning model that aggregates the predictions of individual models. Since ensemble methods combine the results of multiple models, they are less prone to error, and therefore tend to perform better.

Imagine your goal is to determine whether a house will sell within the first month of being on the market. You run several machine learning algorithms and find that **logistic regression** gives 80% accuracy, **decision trees** 75% accuracy, and **k-nearest neighbors** 77% accuracy.

One option is to use logistic regression, the most accurate model, as your final model. A more compelling option is to combine the predictions of each individual model.

For classifiers, the standard option is to take the majority vote. If at least two of three models predict that a house will sell within the first month, the prediction is *YES*. Otherwise, it's *NO*.

Overall accuracy is usually higher with ensemble methods. For a prediction to be wrong, it's not enough for one model to get it wrong; the majority of classifiers must get it wrong.

Ensemble methods are generally classified into two types. The first type combines different machine learning models, such as scikit-learn's `VotingClassifier`, as chosen by the user. The second type of ensemble method combines many versions of the same model, as is the case with XGBoost and random forests.

Random forests are among the most popular and widespread of all ensemble methods. The individual models of random forests are decision trees, the focus of the previous chapter, *Chapter 2, Decision Trees in Depth*. A random forest may consist of hundreds or thousands of decision trees whose predictions are combined for the final result.

Although random forests use majority rules for classifiers, and the average of all models for regressors, they also use a special method called bagging, short for bootstrap aggregation, to select individual trees.

Bootstrap aggregation

Bootstrapping means sampling with replacement.

Imagine you have a bag of 20 shaded marbles. You are going to select 10 marbles, one at a time. Each time you select a marble, you put it back in the bag. This means that it's possible, though extremely unlikely, that you could pick the same marble 10 times.

It's more likely that you will pick some marbles more than once, and some not at all.

Here is a visual of the marbles:

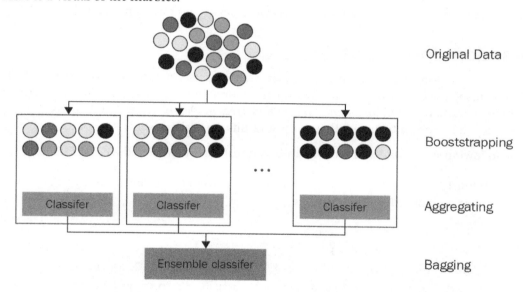

Figure 3.1 – Visual demonstration of bagging (Redrawn from: Siakorn, Wikimedia Commons, `https://commons.wikimedia.org/wiki/File:Ensemble_Bagging.svg`)

As you can see from the preceding diagram, bootstrap samples are achieved by sampling with replacement. If the marbles were not replaced, it would be impossible to obtain a sample with more black (*blue* in the original diagram) marbles than the original bag, as in the far-right box.

When it comes to random forests, bootstrapping works under the hood. The bootstrapping occurs when each decision tree is made. If the decision trees all consisted of the same samples, the trees would give similar predictions making the aggregate result similar to the individual tree. Instead, with random forests, the trees are built using bootstrapping, usually with the same number of samples as in the original dataset. Mathematical estimations are that two-thirds of the samples for each tree are unique, and one-third include duplicates.

After the bootstrapping phase of the model-build, each decision tree makes its own individual predictions. The result is a forest of trees whose predictions are aggregated into one final prediction using majority rules for classifiers and the average for regressors.

In summary, a random forest aggregates the predictions of bootstrapped decision trees. This general ensemble method is known in machine learning as bagging.

Exploring random forests

To get a better sense of how random forests work, let's build one using scikit-learn.

Random forest classifiers

Let's use a random forest classifier to predict whether a user makes more or less than USD 50,000 using the census dataset we cleaned and scored in *Chapter 1, Machine Learning Landscape*, and revisited in *Chapter 2, Decision Trees in Depth*. We are going to use `cross_val_score` to ensure that our test results generalize well:

The following steps build and score a random forest classifier using the census dataset:

1. Import `pandas`, `numpy`, `RandomForestClassifier`, and `cross_val_score` before silencing warnings:

    ```
    import pandas as pd
    import numpy as np
    from sklearn.ensemble import RandomForestClassifier
    from sklearn.model_selection import cross_val_score
    import warnings
    warnings.filterwarnings('ignore')
    ```

2. Load the dataset `census_cleaned.csv` and split it into X (a predictor column) and y (a target column):

    ```
    df_census = pd.read_csv('census_cleaned.csv')
    X_census = df_census.iloc[:,:-1]
    y_census = df_census.iloc[:,-1]
    ```

    With our imports and data ready to go, it's time to build a model.

3. Next, we initialize the random forest classifier. In practice, ensemble algorithms work just like any other machine learning algorithm. A model is initialized, fit to the training data, and scored against the test data.

We initialize a random forest by setting the following hyperparameters in advance:

a) `random_state=2` to ensure that your results are consistent with ours.

b) `n_jobs=-1` to speed up computations by taking advantage of parallel processing.

c) `n_estimators=10`, a previous scikit-learn default sufficient to speed up computations and avoid ambiguity; new defaults have set `n_estimators=100`. `n_esmitators` will be explored in further detail in the next section:

```
rf = RandomForestClassifier(n_estimators=10, random_
state=2, n_jobs=-1)
```

4. Now we'll use `cross_val_score`. `Cross_val_score` requires a model, predictor columns, and a target column as inputs. Recall that `cross_val_score` splits, fits, and scores the data:

```
scores = cross_val_score(rf, X_census, y_census, cv=5)
```

5. Display the results:

```
print('Accuracy:', np.round(scores, 3))
print('Accuracy mean: %0.3f' % (scores.mean()))
Accuracy: [0.851 0.844 0.851 0.852 0.851]
Accuracy mean: 0.850
```

The default random forest classifier provides a better score for the census dataset than the decision tree in *Chapter 2, Decision Trees in Depth* (81%), but not quite as good as XGBoost in *Chapter 1, Machine Learning Landscape* (86%). Why does it perform better than individual decision trees?

The improved performance is likely on account of the bagging method described in the previous section. With 10 trees in this forest (since `n_estimators=10`), each prediction is based on 10 decision trees instead of 1. The trees are bootstrapped, which increases diversity, and aggregated, which reduces variance.

By default, random forest classifiers select from the square root of the total number of features when looking for a split. So, if there are 100 features (columns), each decision tree will only consider 10 features when choosing a split. Thus two trees with duplicate samples may give very different predictions due to the different splits. This is another way that random forests reduce variance.

In addition to classification, random forests also work with regression.

Random forest regressors

In a random forest regressor, the samples are bootstrapped, as with the random forest Classifier, but the max number of features is the total number of features instead of the square root. This change is due to experimental results (see `https://orbi.uliege.be/bitstream/2268/9357/1/geurts-mlj-advance.pdf`).

Furthermore, the final prediction is made by taking the average of the predictions of all the trees, instead of a majority rules vote.

To see a random forest regressor in action, complete the following steps:

1. Upload the bike rental dataset from *Chapter 2, Decision Trees in Depth*, and pull up the first five rows for a refresher:

    ```
    df_bikes = pd.read_csv('bike_rentals_cleaned.csv')
    df_bikes.head()
    ```

    The preceding code should result in the following output:

	instant	season	yr	mnth	holiday	weekday	workingday	weathersit	temp	atemp	hum	windspeed	cnt
0	1	1.0	0.0	1.0	0.0	6.0	0.0	2	0.344167	0.363625	0.805833	0.160446	985
1	2	1.0	0.0	1.0	0.0	0.0	0.0	2	0.363478	0.353739	0.696087	0.248539	801
2	3	1.0	0.0	1.0	0.0	1.0	1.0	1	0.196364	0.189405	0.437273	0.248309	1349
3	4	1.0	0.0	1.0	0.0	2.0	1.0	1	0.200000	0.212122	0.590435	0.160296	1562
4	5	1.0	0.0	1.0	0.0	3.0	1.0	1	0.226957	0.229270	0.436957	0.186900	1600

Figure 3.2 – Bike rentals dataset – cleaned

2. Split the data into X and y, the predictive and target columns:

    ```
    X_bikes = df_bikes.iloc[:,:-1]
    y_bikes = df_bikes.iloc[:,-1]
    ```

3. Import the regressor, then initialize it using the same default hyperparameters, n_estimators=10, random_state=2, and n_jobs=-1:

    ```
    from sklearn.ensemble import RandomForestRegressor
    rf = RandomForestRegressor(n_estimators=10, random_state=2, n_jobs=-1)
    ```

4. Now we need to use `cross_val_score`. Place the regressor, `rf`, along with predictor and target columns inside `cross_val_score`. Note that the negative mean squared error (`'neg_mean_squared_error'`) should be defined as the scoring parameter. Select 10 folds (`cv=10`):

```
scores = cross_val_score(rf, X_bikes, y_bikes,
    scoring='neg_mean_squared_error', cv=10)
```

5. Find and display the **root mean squared error (RMSE)**:

```
rmse = np.sqrt(-scores)
print('RMSE:', np.round(rmse, 3))
print('RMSE mean: %0.3f' % (rmse.mean()))
```

The output is as follows:

```
RMSE: [ 801.486  579.987  551.347  846.698  895.05
 1097.522  893.738  809.284  833.488 2145.046]
RMSE mean: 945.365
```

The random forest performs respectably, though not as well as other models that we have seen. We will further examine the bike rentals dataset in the case study later in this chapter to see why.

Next, let's examine random forest hyperparameters in detail.

Random forest hyperparameters

The range of random forest hyperparameters is large, unless one already has a working knowledge of decision tree hyperparameters, as covered in *Chapter 2, Decision Trees in Depth*.

In this section, we will go over additional random forest hyperparameters before grouping the hyperparameters that you have already seen. Many of these hyperparameters will be used by XGBoost.

oob_score

Our first hyperparameter, and perhaps the most intriguing, is `oob_score`.

Random forests select decision trees via bagging, meaning that samples are selected with replacement. After all of the samples have been chosen, some samples should remain that have not been chosen.

It's possible to hold back these samples as the test set. After the model is fit on one tree, the model can immediately be scored against this test set. When the hyperparameter is set to `oob_score=True`, this is exactly what happens.

In other words, `oob_score` provides a shortcut to get a test score. `oob_score` may be printed out immediately after the model has been fit.

Let's use `oob_score` on the census dataset to see how it works in practice. Since we are using `oob_score` to test the model, it's not necessary to split the data into a training set and test set.

The random forest may be initialized as usual with `oob_score=True`:

```
rf = RandomForestClassifier(oob_score=True, n_estimators=10,
random_state=2, n_jobs=-1)
```

Next, `rf` may be fit on the data:

```
rf.fit(X_census, y_census)
```

Since `oob_score=True`, the score is available after the model has been fit. It may be accessed using the model attribute `.oob_score_` as follows (note the underscore after `score`):

```
rf.oob_score_
```

The score is as follows:

```
0.8343109855348423
```

As described previously, `oob_score` is created by scoring samples on individual trees excluded during the training phase. When the number of trees in the forest is small, as is the case with 10 estimators, there may not be enough test samples to maximize accuracy.

More trees mean more samples, and often greater accuracy.

n_estimators

Random forests are powerful when there are many trees in the forest. How many is enough? Recently, scikit-learn defaults changed from 10 to 100. While 100 trees may be enough to cut down on variance and obtain good scores, for larger datasets, 500 or more trees may be required.

Let's start with `n_estimators=50` to see how `oob_score` changes:

```
rf = RandomForestClassifier(n_estimators=50, oob_score=True,
random_state=2, n_jobs=-1)
rf.fit(X_census, y_census)
rf.oob_score_
```

The score is as follows:

```
0.8518780135745216
```

A definite improvement. What about 100 trees?

```
rf = RandomForestClassifier(n_estimators=100, oob_score=True,
random_state=2, n_jobs=-1)
rf.fit(X_census, y_census)
rf.oob_score_
```

The score is as follows:

```
0.8551334418476091
```

The gain is smaller. As `n_estimators` continues to rise, scores will eventually level off.

warm_start

The `warm_start` hyperparameter is great for determining the number of trees in the forest (`n_estimators`). When `warm_start=True`, adding more trees does not require starting over from scratch. If you change `n_estimators` from 100 to 200, it may take twice as long to build the forest with 200 trees. When `warm_start=True`, the random forest with 200 trees does not start from scratch, but rather starts where the previous model stopped.

`warm_start` may be used to plot various scores with a range of `n_estimators`.

As an example, the following code takes increments of 50 trees, starting with 50 and ending at 500, to display a range of scores. This code may take time to run as it is building 10 random forests by adding 50 new trees each round! The code is broken down in the following steps:

1. Import matplotlib and seaborn, then set the seaborn dark grid with `sns.set()`:

    ```
    import matplotlib.pyplot as plt
    import seaborn as sns
    sns.set()
    ```

2. Initialize an empty list of scores and initialize a random forest classifier with 50 estimators, making sure that warm_start=True and oob_score=True:

```
oob_scores = []
rf = RandomForestClassifier(n_estimators=50, warm_
start=True, oob_score=True, n_jobs=-1, random_state=2)
```

3. Fit rf to the dataset, then append oob_score to the oob_scores list:

```
rf.fit(X_census, y_census)
oob_scores.append(rf.oob_score_)
```

4. Prepare a list of estimators that contains the number of trees starting with 50:

```
est = 50
estimators=[est]
```

5. Write a for loop that adds 50 trees each round. For each round, add 50 to est, append est to the estimators list, change n_estimators with rf.set_params(n_estimators=est), fit the random forest on the data, then append the new oob_score_:

```
for i in range(9):
    est += 50
    estimators.append(est)
    rf.set_params(n_estimators=est)
    rf.fit(X_census, y_census)
    oob_scores.append(rf.oob_score_)
```

6. For a nice display, show a larger graph, then plot the estimators and oob_scores. Add the appropriate labels, then save and show the graph:

```
plt.figure(figsize=(15,7))
plt.plot(estimators, oob_scores)
plt.xlabel('Number of Trees')
plt.ylabel('oob_score_')
plt.title('Random Forest Warm Start', fontsize=15)
plt.savefig('Random_Forest_Warm_Start', dpi=325)
plt.show()
```

This generates the following graph:

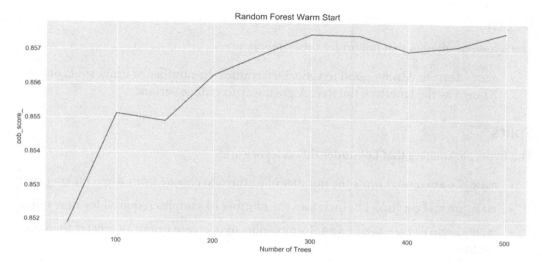

Figure 3.3 – Random forest Warm Start – oob_score per number of trees

As you can see, the number of trees tends to peak at around 300. It's more costly and time-consuming to use more trees than 300, and the gains are minimal at best.

bootstrap

Although random forests are traditionally bootstrapped, the bootstrap hyperparameter may be set to False. If bootstrap=False, oob_score cannot be included since oob_score is only possible when samples have been left out.

We will not pursue this option, although it makes sense if underfitting occurs.

Verbose

The verbose hyperparameter may be changed to a higher number to display more information when building a model. You may try it on your own for experimentation. When building large models, verbose=1 may provide helpful information along the way.

Decision Tree hyperparameters

The remaining hyperparameters all come from decision trees. It turns out that decision tree hyperparameters are not as significant within random forests since random forests cut down on variance by design.

Here are decision tree hyperparameters grouped according to category for you to review.

Depth

The hyperparameters that fall under this category are:

- `max_depth`: Always good to tune. Determines the number of times splits occur. Known as the length of the tree. A great way to reduce variance.

Splits

The hyperparameters that fall under this category are:

- `max_features`: Limits the number of features to choose from when making splits.

- `min_samples_split`: Increases the number of samples required for new splits.

- `min_impurity_decrease`: Limits splits to decrease impurity greater than the set threshold.

Leaves

The hyperparameters that fall under this category are:

- `min_samples_leaf`: Increases the minimum number of samples required for a node to be a leaf.

- `min_weight_fraction_leaf`: The fraction of the total weights required to be a leaf.

For more information on the preceding hyperparameters, check out the official random forest regressor documentation: `https://scikit-learn.org/stable/modules/generated/sklearn.ensemble.RandomForestRegressor.html`

Pushing random forest boundaries – case study

Imagine you work for a bike rental company and your goal is to predict the number of bike rentals per day depending upon the weather, the time of day, the time of year, and the growth of the company.

Earlier in this chapter, you implemented a random forest regressor with cross-validation to obtain an RMSE of 945 bikes. Your goal is to modify the random forest to obtain the lowest error score possible.

Preparing the dataset

Earlier in this chapter, you downloaded the dataset `df_bikes` and split it into `X_bikes` and `y_bikes`. Now that you are doing some serious testing, you decide to split `X_bikes` and `y_bikes` into training sets and test sets as follows:

```
from sklearn.model_selection import train_test_split
X_train, X_test, y_train, y_test = train_test_split(X_bikes,
y_bikes, random_state=2)
```

n_estimators

Start by choosing a reasonable value for `n_estimators`. Recall that `n_estimators` can be increased to improve accuracy at the cost of computational resources and time.

The following is a graph of RMSE using the `warm_start` method for a variety of `n_estimators` using the same general code provided previously under the *warm_start* heading:

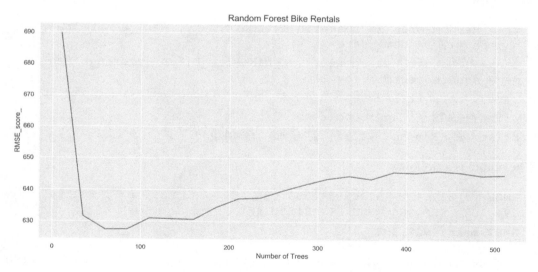

Figure 3.4 – Random forest Bike Rentals – RMSE per number of trees

This graph is very interesting. The random forest provides the best score with 50 estimators. After 100 estimators, the error gradually starts to go up, a concept that will be revisited later.

For now, it's sensible to use `n_estimators=50` as the starting point.

cross_val_score

With errors ranging from 620 to 690 bike rentals according to the preceding graph, it's time to see how the dataset performs with cross-validation using `cross_val_score`. Recall that in cross-validation the purpose is to divide the samples into *k* different folds, and to use all samples as test sets over the different folds. Since all samples are used to test the model, `oob_score` will
not work.

The following code contains the same steps that you used earlier in the chapter:

1. Initialize the model.
2. Score the model, using `cross_val_score` with the model, predictor columns, target column, scoring, and the number of folds as parameters.
3. Compute the RMSE.
4. Display the cross-validation scores and the mean.

Here is the code:

```
rf = RandomForestRegressor(n_estimators=50, warm_start=True,
n_jobs=-1, random_state=2)
scores = cross_val_score(rf, X_bikes, y_bikes, scoring='neg_
mean_squared_error', cv=10)
rmse = np.sqrt(-scores)
print('RMSE:', np.round(rmse, 3))
print('RMSE mean: %0.3f' % (rmse.mean()))
```

The output is as follows:

```
RMSE: [ 836.482   541.898   533.086   812.782   894.877   881.117
794.103   828.968   772.517 2128.148]
RMSE mean: 902.398
```

This score is better than earlier in the chapter. Notice that the error in the last fold is much higher according to the last entry in the RMSE array. This could be due to errors within the data or outliers.

Fine-tuning hyperparameters

It's time to create a grid of hyperparameters to fine-tune our model using `RandomizedSearchCV`. Here is a function that uses `RandomizedSearchCV` to display the RMSEs along with the mean score and best hyperparameters:

```python
from sklearn.model_selection import RandomizedSearchCV
def randomized_search_reg(params, runs=16,
reg=RandomForestRegressor(random_state=2, n_jobs=-1)):
    rand_reg = RandomizedSearchCV(reg, params, n_iter=runs,
scoring='neg_mean_squared_error', cv=10, n_jobs=-1, random_
state=2)
    rand_reg.fit(X_train, y_train)
    best_model = rand_reg.best_estimator_
    best_params = rand_reg.best_params_
    print("Best params:", best_params)
    best_score = np.sqrt(-rand_reg.best_score_)
    print("Training score: {:.3f}".format(best_score))
    y_pred = best_model.predict(X_test)
    from sklearn.metrics import mean_squared_error as MSE
    rmse_test = MSE(y_test, y_pred)**0.5
    print('Test set score: {:.3f}'.format(rmse_test))
```

Here is a starter's grid of hyperparameters placed inside the new `randomized_search_reg` function to obtain the first results:

```python
randomized_search_reg(params={'min_weight_fraction_leaf':[0.0,
0.0025, 0.005, 0.0075, 0.01, 0.05],'min_samples_split':[2,
0.01, 0.02, 0.03, 0.04, 0.06, 0.08, 0.1],'min_samples_
leaf':[1,2,4,6,8,10,20,30],'min_impurity_decrease':[0.0, 0.01,
0.05, 0.10, 0.15, 0.2],'max_leaf_nodes':[10, 15, 20, 25, 30,
35, 40, 45, 50, None], 'max_features':['auto', 0.8, 0.7, 0.6,
0.5, 0.4],'max_depth':[None,2,4,6,8,10,20]})
```

The output is as follows:

```
Best params: {'min_weight_fraction_leaf': 0.0, 'min_samples_
split': 0.03, 'min_samples_leaf': 6, 'min_impurity_decrease':
0.05, 'max_leaf_nodes': 25, 'max_features': 0.7, 'max_depth':
None}
Training score: 759.076
Test set score: 701.802
```

This is a major improvement. Let's see if we can do better by narrowing the range:

```
randomized_search_reg(params={'min_samples_leaf':
[1,2,4,6,8,10,20,30], 'min_impurity_decrease':[0.0, 0.01, 0.05,
0.10, 0.15, 0.2],'max_features':['auto', 0.8, 0.7, 0.6, 0.5,
0.4], 'max_depth':[None,2,4,6,8,10,20]})
```

The output is as follows:

```
Best params: {'min_samples_leaf': 1, 'min_impurity_decrease':
0.1, 'max_features': 0.6, 'max_depth': 10}
Training score: 679.052
Test set score: 626.541
```

The score has improved yet again.

Now let's increase the number of runs, and give more options for max_depth:

```
randomized_search_reg(params={'min_samples_
leaf':[1,2,4,6,8,10,20,30],'min_impurity_decrease':[0.0, 0.01,
0.05, 0.10, 0.15, 0.2],'max_features':['auto', 0.8, 0.7, 0.6,
0.5, 0.4],'max_depth':[None,4,6,8,10,12,15,20]}, runs=20)
```

The output is as follows:

```
Best params: {'min_samples_leaf': 1, 'min_impurity_decrease':
0.1, 'max_features': 0.6, 'max_depth': 12}
Training score: 675.128
Test set score: 619.014
```

The score keeps getting better. At this point, it may be worth narrowing the ranges further, based upon the previous results:

```
randomized_search_reg(params={'min_samples_leaf':[1,2,3,4,5,6],
'min_impurity_decrease':[0.0, 0.01, 0.05, 0.08, 0.10, 0.12,
0.15], 'max_features':['auto', 0.8, 0.7, 0.6, 0.5, 0.4],'max_de
pth':[None,8,10,12,14,16,18,20]})
```

The output is as follows:

```
Best params: {'min_samples_leaf': 1, 'min_impurity_decrease':
0.05, 'max_features': 0.7, 'max_depth': 18}
Training score: 679.595
Test set score: 630.954
```

The test score has gone back up. Increasing `n_estimators` at this point could be a good idea. The more trees in the forest, the more potential there may be to realize small gains.

We can also increase the number of runs to 20 to look for better hyperparameter combinations. Keep in mind that results are based on a randomized search, not a full grid search:

```
randomized_search_reg(params={'min_samples_
leaf':[1,2,4,6,8,10,20,30], 'min_impurity_decrease':[0.0,
0.01, 0.05, 0.10, 0.15, 0.2], 'max_features':['auto', 0.8,
0.7, 0.6, 0.5, 0.4],'max_depth':[None,4,6,8,10,12,15,20],'n_
estimators':[100]}, runs=20)
```

The output is as follows:

```
Best params: {'n_estimators': 100, 'min_samples_leaf': 1, 'min_
impurity_decrease': 0.1, 'max_features': 0.6, 'max_depth': 12}
Training score: 675.128
Test set score: 619.014
```

This matches the best score achieved thus far. We could keep tinkering. It's possible with enough experimentation that the test score may drop to under 600 bikes. But we also seem to be peaking around the low 600 mark.

Finally, let's place our best model in `cross_val_score` to see how the result compares with the original:

```
rf = RandomForestRegressor(n_estimators=100,  min_impurity_
decrease=0.1, max_features=0.6, max_depth=12, warm_start=True,
n_jobs=-1, random_state=2)
scores = cross_val_score(rf, X_bikes, y_bikes, scoring='neg_
mean_squared_error', cv=10)
rmse = np.sqrt(-scores)
print('RMSE:', np.round(rmse, 3))
print('RMSE mean: %0.3f' % (rmse.mean()))
```

The output is as follows:

```
RMSE: [ 818.354   514.173   547.392   814.059   769.54    730.025
831.376   794.634   756.83   1595.237]
RMSE mean: 817.162
```

The RMSE goes back up to 817. The score is much better than 903, but it's considerably worse than 619. What's going on here?

There may be an issue with the last split in cross_val_score since its score is twice as bad as the others. Let's see if shuffling the data does the trick. Scikit-learn has a shuffle module that may be imported from sklearn.utils as follows:

```
from sklearn.utils import shuffle
```

Now we can shuffle the data as follows:

```
df_shuffle_bikes = shuffle(df_bikes, random_state=2)
```

Now split the data into a new X and y and run RandomForestRegressor with cross_val_score again:

```
X_shuffle_bikes = df_shuffle_bikes.iloc[:,:-1]
y_shuffle_bikes = df_shuffle_bikes.iloc[:,-1]
rf = RandomForestRegressor(n_estimators=100, min_impurity_
decrease=0.1, max_features=0.6, max_depth=12, n_jobs=-1,
random_state=2)
scores = cross_val_score(rf, X_shuffle_bikes, y_shuffle_bikes,
scoring='neg_mean_squared_error', cv=10)
rmse = np.sqrt(-scores)
print('RMSE:', np.round(rmse, 3))
print('RMSE mean: %0.3f' % (rmse.mean()))
```

The output is as follows:

```
RMSE: [630.093 686.673 468.159 526.676 593.033 724.575 774.402
672.63  760.253  616.797]
RMSE mean: 645.329
```

In the shuffled data, there is no issue with the last split, and the score is much higher, as expected.

Random forest drawbacks

At the end of the day, the random forest is limited by its individual trees. If all trees make the same mistake, the random forest makes this mistake. There are scenarios, as is revealed in this case study before the data was shuffled, where random forests are unable to significantly improve upon errors due to challenges within the data that individual trees are unable to address.

An ensemble method capable of improving upon initial shortcomings, an ensemble method that will learn from the mistakes of trees in future rounds, could be advantageous. Boosting was designed to learn from the mistakes of trees in early rounds. Boosting, in particular gradient boosting – the focus of the next chapter – addresses this topic.

In closure, the following graph displays the results of the tuned random forest regressor and the default XGBoost regressor when increasing the number of trees in the bike rentals dataset if the data is not shuffled:

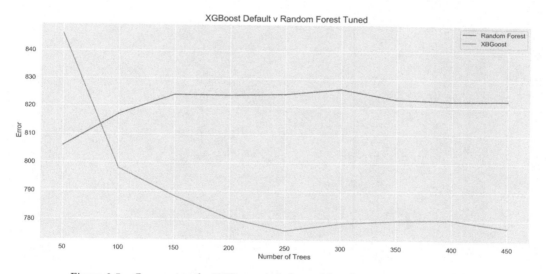

Figure 3.5 – Comparing the XGBoost default model with a tuned random forest

As you can see, XGBoost does a much better job of learning as the number of trees increases. And the XGBoost model has not even been tuned!

Summary

In this chapter, you learned about the importance of ensemble methods. In particular, you learned about bagging, the combination of bootstrapping, sampling with replacement, and aggregation, combining many models into one. You built random forest classifiers and regressors. You adjusted n_estimators with the warm_start hyperparameter and used oob_score_ to find errors. Then you modified random forest hyperparameters to fine-tune models. Finally, you examined a case study where shuffling the data gave excellent results but adding more trees to the random forest did not result in any gains with the unshuffled data, as contrasted with XGBoost.

In the next chapter, you will learn the fundamentals of boosting, an ensemble method that learns from its mistakes to improve upon accuracy as more trees are added. You will implement gradient boosting to make predictions, thereby setting the stage for Extreme gradient boosting, better known as XGBoost.

4
From Gradient Boosting to XGBoost

XGBoost is a unique form of gradient boosting with several distinct advantages, which will be explained in *Chapter 5*, *XGBoost Unveiled*. In order to understand the advantages of XGBoost over traditional gradient boosting, you must first learn how traditional gradient boosting works. The general structure and hyperparameters of traditional gradient boosting are incorporated by XGBoost. In this chapter, you will discover the power behind gradient boosting, which is at the core of XGBoost.

In this chapter, you will build gradient boosting models from scratch before comparing gradient boosting models and errors with previous results. In particular, you will focus on the **learning rate** hyperparameter to build powerful gradient boosting models that include XGBoost. Finally, you will preview a case study on exoplanets highlighting the need for faster algorithms, a critical need in the world of big data that is satisfied by XGBoost.

In this chapter, we will be covering the following main topics:

- From bagging to boosting
- How gradient boosting works
- Modifying gradient boosting hyperparameters
- Approaching big data – gradient boosting versus XGBoost

Technical requirements

The code for this chapter is available at `https://github.com/PacktPublishing/Hands-On-Gradient-Boosting-with-XGBoost-and-Scikit-learn/tree/master/Chapter04`.

From bagging to boosting

In *Chapter 3*, *Bagging with Random Forests*, you learned why ensemble machine learning algorithms such as random forests make better predictions by combining many machine learning models into one. Random forests are classified as bagging algorithms because they take the aggregates of bootstrapped samples (decision trees).

Boosting, by contrast, learns from the mistakes of individual trees. The general idea is to adjust new trees based on the errors of previous trees.

In boosting, correcting errors for each new tree is a distinct approach from bagging. In a bagging model, new trees pay no attention to previous trees. Also, new trees are built from scratch using bootstrapping, and the final model aggregates all individual trees. In boosting, however, each new tree is built from the previous tree. The trees do not operate in isolation; instead, they are built on top of one another.

Introducing AdaBoost

AdaBoost is one of the earliest and most popular boosting models. In AdaBoost, each new tree adjusts its weights based on the errors of the previous trees. More attention is paid to predictions that went wrong by adjusting weights that affect those samples at a higher percentage. By learning from its mistakes, AdaBoost can transform weak learners into strong learners. A weak learner is a machine learning algorithm that barely performs better than chance. By contrast, a stronger learner has learned a considerable amount from data and performs quite well.

The general idea behind boosting algorithms is to transform weak learners into strong learners. A weak learner is hardly better than random guessing. But there is a purpose behind the weak start. Building on this general idea, boosting works by focusing on iterative error correction, *not* by establishing a strong baseline model. If the base model is too strong, the learning process is necessarily limited, thereby undermining the general strategy behind boosting models.

Weak learners are transformed into strong learners through hundreds of iterations. In this sense, a small edge goes a long way. In fact, boosting has been one of the best general machine learning strategies in terms of producing optimal results for the past couple of decades.

A detailed study of AdaBoost is beyond the scope of this book. Like many scikit-learn models, it's straightforward to implement AdaBoost in practice. The `AdaBoostRegressor` and `AdaBoostClassifier` algorithms may be downloaded from the `sklearn.ensemble` library and fit to any training set. The most important AdaBoost hyperparameter is `n_estimators`, the number of trees (iterations) required to create a strong learner.

> **Note**
>
> For further information on AdaBoost, check out the official documentation at `https://scikit-learn.org/stable/modules/generated/sklearn.ensemble.AdaBoostClassifier.html` for classifiers and `https://scikit-learn.org/stable/modules/generated/sklearn.ensemble.AdaBoostRegressor.html` for regressors.

We will now move on to gradient boosting, a strong alternative to AdaBoost with a slight edge in performance.

Distinguishing gradient boosting

Gradient boosting uses a different approach than AdaBoost. While gradient boosting also adjusts based on incorrect predictions, it takes this idea one step further: gradient boosting fits each new tree entirely based on the errors of the previous tree's predictions. That is, for each new tree, gradient boosting looks at the mistakes and then builds a new tree completely around these mistakes. The new tree doesn't care about the predictions that are already correct.

Building a machine learning algorithm that solely focuses on the errors requires a comprehensive method that sums errors to make accurate final predictions. This method leverages residuals, the difference between the model's predictions and actual values. Here is the general idea:

Gradient boosting computes the residuals of each tree's predictions and sums all the residuals to score the model.

It's essential to understand **computing** and **summing residuals** as this idea is at the core of XGBoost, an advanced version of gradient boosting. When you build your own version of gradient boosting, the process of computing and summing residuals will become clear. In the next section, you will build your own version of a gradient boosting model. First, let's learn in detail how gradient boosting works.

How gradient boosting works

In this section, we will look under the hood of gradient boosting and build a gradient boosting model from scratch by training new trees on the errors of the previous trees. The key mathematical idea here is the residual. Next, we will obtain the same results using scikit-learn's gradient boosting algorithm.

Residuals

The residuals are the difference between the errors and the predictions of a given model. In statistics, residuals are commonly analyzed to determine how good a given linear regression model fits the data.

Consider the following examples:

1. Bike rentals

    a) *Prediction*: 759

    b) *Result*: 799

    c) *Residual*: 799 - 759 = 40

2. Income

    a) *Prediction*: 100,000

    b) *Result*: 88,000

    c) *Residual*: 88,000 –100,000 = -12,000

As you can see, residuals tell you how far the model's predictions are from reality, and they may be positive or negative.

Here is a visual example displaying the residuals of a **linear regression** line:

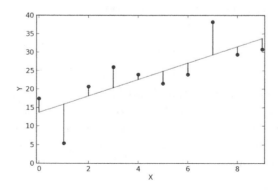

Figure 4.1 – Residuals of a linear regression line

The goal of linear regression is to minimize the square of the residuals. As the graph reveals, a visual of the residuals indicates how well the line fits the data. In statistics, linear regression analysis is often performed by graphing the residuals to gain deeper insight into the data.

In order to build a gradient boosting algorithm from scratch, we will compute the residuals of each tree and fit a new model to the residuals. Let's do this now.

Learning how to build gradient boosting models from scratch

Building a gradient boosting model from scratch will provide you with a deeper understanding of how gradient boosting works in code. Before building a model, we need to access data and prepare it for machine learning.

Processing the bike rentals dataset

We continue with the bike rentals dataset to compare new models with the previous models:

1. We will start by importing pandas and numpy. We will also add a line to silence any warnings:

    ```
    import pandas as pd
    import numpy as np
    import warnings
    warnings.filterwarnings('ignore')
    ```

2. Now, load the bike_rentals_cleaned dataset and view the first five rows:

    ```
    df_bikes = pd.read_csv('bike_rentals_cleaned.csv')
    df_bikes.head()
    ```

    Your output should look like this:

	instant	season	yr	mnth	holiday	weekday	workingday	weathersit	temp	atemp	hum	windspeed	cnt
0	1	1.0	0.0	1.0	0.0	6.0	0.0	2	0.344167	0.363625	0.805833	0.160446	985
1	2	1.0	0.0	1.0	0.0	0.0	0.0	2	0.363478	0.353739	0.696087	0.248539	801
2	3	1.0	0.0	1.0	0.0	1.0	1.0	1	0.196364	0.189405	0.437273	0.248309	1349
3	4	1.0	0.0	1.0	0.0	2.0	1.0	1	0.200000	0.212122	0.590435	0.160296	1562
4	5	1.0	0.0	1.0	0.0	3.0	1.0	1	0.226957	0.229270	0.436957	0.186900	1600

Figure 4.2 – First five rows of Bike Rental Dataset

3. Now, split the data into X and y. Then, split X and y into training and test sets:

```
X_bikes = df_bikes.iloc[:,:-1]
y_bikes = df_bikes.iloc[:,-1]
from sklearn.model_selection import train_test_split
X_train, X_test, y_train, y_test = train_test_split(X_
bikes, y_bikes, random_state=2)
```

It's time to build a gradient boosting model from scratch!

Building a gradient boosting model from scratch

Here are the steps for building a gradient boosting machine learning model from scratch:

1. Fit the data to the decision tree: You may use a decision tree stump, which has a max_depth value of 1, or a decision tree with a max_depth value of 2 or 3. The initial decision tree, called a **base learner**, should not be fine-tuned for accuracy. We want a model that focuses on learning from errors, not a model that relies heavily on the base learner.

    Initialize a decision tree with max_depth=2 and fit it on the training set as tree_1, since it's the first tree in our ensemble:

    ```
    from sklearn.tree import DecisionTreeRegressor
    tree_1 = DecisionTreeRegressor(max_depth=2, random_
    state=2)
    tree_1.fit(X_train, y_train)
    ```

2. Make predictions with the training set: Instead of making predictions with the test set, predictions in gradient boosting are initially made with the training set. Why? To compute the residuals, we need to compare the predictions while still in the training phase. The test phase of the model build comes at the end, after all the trees have been constructed. The predictions of the training set for the first round are obtained by adding the predict method to tree_1 with X_train as the input:

    ```
    y_train_pred = tree_1.predict(X_train)
    ```

3. Compute the residuals: The residuals are the differences between the predictions and the target column. The predictions of X_train, defined here as y_train_pred, are subtracted from y_train, the target column, to compute the residuals:

    ```
    y2_train = y_train - y_train_pred
    ```

> **Note**
>
> The residuals are defined as `y2_train` because they are the new target column for the next tree.

4. Fit the new tree on the residuals: Fitting a new tree on the residuals is different than fitting a model on the training set. The primary difference is in the predictions. In the bike rentals dataset, when fitting a new tree on the residuals, we should progressively get smaller numbers.

   Initialize a new tree and fit it on `X_train` and the residuals, `y2_train`:

   ```
   tree_2 = DecisionTreeRegressor(max_depth=2, random_
   state=2)
   tree_2.fit(X_train, y2_train)
   ```

5. Repeat steps 2-4: As the process continues, the residuals should gradually approach 0 from the positive and negative direction. The iterations continue for the number of estimators, `n_estimators`.

   Let's repeat the process for a third tree as follows:

   ```
   y2_train_pred = tree_2.predict(X_train)
   y3_train = y2_train - y2_train_pred
   tree_3 = DecisionTreeRegressor(max_depth=2, random_
   state=2)
   tree_3.fit(X_train, y3_train)
   ```

   This process may continue for dozens, hundreds, or thousands of trees. Under normal circumstances, you would certainly keep going. It will take more than a few trees to transform a weak learner into a strong learner. Since our goal is to understand how gradient boosting works behind the scenes, however, we will move on now that the general idea has been covered.

6. Sum the results: Summing the results requires making predictions for each tree with the test set as follows:

   ```
   y1_pred = tree_1.predict(X_test)
   y2_pred = tree_2.predict(X_test)
   y3_pred = tree_3.predict(X_test)
   ```

   Since the predictions are positive and negative differences, summing the predictions should result in predictions that are closer to the target column as follows:

   ```
   y_pred = y1_pred + y2_pred + y3_pred
   ```

7. Lastly, let's compute the **mean squared error (MSE)** to obtain the results as follows:

```
from sklearn.metrics import mean_squared_error as MSE
MSE(y_test, y_pred)**0.5
```

Here is the expected output:

```
911.0479538776444
```

Not bad for a weak learner that isn't yet strong! Now let's try to obtain the same result using scikit-learn.

Building a gradient boosting model in scikit-learn

Let's see whether we can obtain the same result as in the previous section using scikit-learn's `GradientBoostingRegressor`. This may be done through a few hyperparameter adjustments. The advantage of using `GradientBoostingRegressor` is that it's much faster to build and easier to implement:

1. First, import the regressor from the `sklearn.ensemble` library:

```
from sklearn.ensemble import GradientBoostingRegressor
```

2. When initializing `GradientBoostingRegressor`, there are several important hyperparameters. To obtain the same results, it's essential to match `max_depth=2` and `random_state=2`. Furthermore, since there are only three trees, we must have `n_estimators=3`. Finally, we must set the `learning_rate=1.0` hyperparameter. We will have much to say about `learning_rate` shortly:

```
gbr = GradientBoostingRegressor(max_depth=2, n_
estimators=3, random_state=2, learning_rate=1.0)
```

3. Now that the model has been initialized, it can be fit on the training data and scored against the test data:

```
gbr.fit(X_train, y_train)
y_pred = gbr.predict(X_test)
MSE(y_test, y_pred)**0.5
```

The result is as follows:

```
911.0479538776439
```

The result is the same to 11 decimal places!

Recall that the point of gradient boosting is to build a model with enough trees to transform a weak learner into a strong learner. This is easily done by changing n_estimators, the number of iterations, to a much larger number.

4. Let's build and score a gradient boosting regressor with 30 estimators:

```
gbr = GradientBoostingRegressor(max_depth=2, n_
estimators=30, random_state=2, learning_rate=1.0)
gbr.fit(X_train, y_train)
y_pred = gbr.predict(X_test)
MSE(y_test, y_pred)**0.5
```

The result is as follows:

```
857.1072323426944
```

The score is an improvement. Now let's look at 300 estimators:

```
gbr = GradientBoostingRegressor(max_depth=2, n_
estimators=300, random_state=2, learning_rate=1.0)
gbr.fit(X_train, y_train)
y_pred = gbr.predict(X_test)
MSE(y_test, y_pred)**0.5
```

The result is this:

```
936.3617413678853
```

This is a surprise! The score has gotten worse! Have we been misled? Is gradient boosting not all that it's cracked up to be?

Whenever you get a surprise result, it's worth double-checking the code. Now, we changed learning_rate without saying much about it. So, what happens if we remove learning_rate=1.0 and use the scikit-learn defaults?

Let's find out:

```
gbr = GradientBoostingRegressor(max_depth=2, n_estimators=300,
random_state=2)
gbr.fit(X_train, y_train)
y_pred = gbr.predict(X_test)
MSE(y_test, y_pred)**0.5
```

The result is this:

```
653.7456840231495
```

Incredible! By using the scikit-learn default for the `learning_rate` hyperparameter, the score has changed from `936` to `654`.

In the next section, we will learn more about the different gradient boosting hyperparameters with a focus on the `learning_rate` hyperparameter.

Modifying gradient boosting hyperparameters

In this section, we will focus on the `learning_rate`, the most important gradient boosting hyperparameter, with the possible exception of `n_estimators`, the number of iterations or trees in the model. We will also survey some tree hyperparameters, and `subsample`, which results in **stochastic gradient boosting**. In addition, we will use `RandomizedSearchCV` and compare results with XGBoost.

learning_rate

In the last section, changing the `learning_rate` value of `GradientBoostingRegressor` from `1.0` to scikit-learn's default, which is `0.1`, resulted in enormous gains.

`learning_rate`, also known as the *shrinkage*, shrinks the contribution of individual trees so that no tree has too much influence when building the model. If an entire ensemble is built from the errors of one base learner, without careful adjustment of hyperparameters, early trees in the model can have too much influence on subsequent development. `learning_rate` limits the influence of individual trees. Generally speaking, as `n_estimators`, the number of trees, goes up, `learning_rate` should go down.

Determining an optimal `learning_rate` value requires varying `n_estimators`. First, let's hold `n_estimators` constant and see what `learning_rate` does on its own. `learning_rate` ranges from 0 to 1. A `learning_rate` value of 1 means that no adjustments are made. The default value of `0.1` means that the tree's influence is weighted at 10%.

Here is a reasonable range to start with:

`learning_rate_values = [0.001, 0.01, 0.05, 0.1, 0.15, 0.2, 0.3, 0.5, 1.0]`

Next, we will loop through the values by building and scoring a new `GradientBoostingRegressor` to see how the scores compare:

```
for value in learning_rate_values:
    gbr = GradientBoostingRegressor(max_depth=2,    n_
```

```
estimators=300, random_state=2, learning_rate=value)
    gbr.fit(X_train, y_train)
    y_pred = gbr.predict(X_test)
    rmse = MSE(y_test, y_pred)**0.5
    print('Learning Rate:', value, ', Score:', rmse)
```

The learning rate values and scores are as follows:

```
Learning Rate: 0.001 , Score: 1633.0261400367258
Learning Rate: 0.01 , Score: 831.5430182728547
Learning Rate: 0.05 , Score: 685.0192988749717
Learning Rate: 0.1 , Score: 653.7456840231495
Learning Rate: 0.15 , Score: 687.666134269379
Learning Rate: 0.2 , Score: 664.312804425697
Learning Rate: 0.3 , Score: 689.4190385930236
Learning Rate: 0.5 , Score: 693.8856905068778
Learning Rate: 1.0 , Score: 936.3617413678853
```

As you can see from the output, the default `learning_rate` value of `0.1` gives the best score for 300 trees.

Now let's vary `n_estimators`. Using the preceding code, we can generate `learning_rate` plots with `n_estimators` of 30, 300, and 3,000 trees, as shown in the following figure:

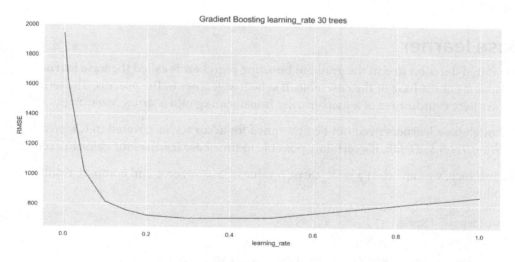

Figure 4.3 – learning_rate plot for 30 trees

As you can see, with 30 trees, the `learning_rate` value peaks at around `0.3`.

Now, let's take a look at the `learning_rate` plot for 3,000 trees:

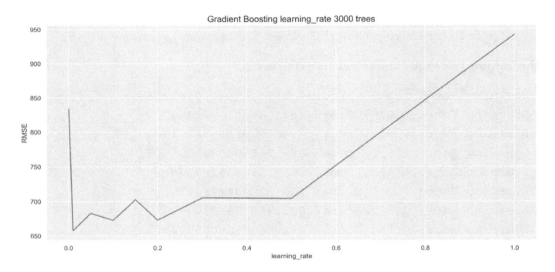

Fig 4.4 -- learning_rate plot for 3,000 trees

With 3,000 trees, the `learning_rate` value peaks at the second value, which is given as `0.05`.

These graphs highlight the importance of tuning `learning_rate` and `n_estimators` together.

Base learner

The initial decision tree in the gradient boosting regressor is called the **base learner** because it's at the base of the ensemble. It's the first learner in the process. The term *learner* here is indicative of a *weak learner* transforming into a *strong learner*.

Although base learners need not be fine-tuned for accuracy, as covered in *Chapter 2, Decision Trees in Depth*, it's certainly possible to tune base learners for gains in accuracy.

For instance, we can select a `max_depth` value of 1, 2, 3, or 4 and compare results as follows:

```
depths = [None, 1, 2, 3, 4]
for depth in depths:
    gbr = GradientBoostingRegressor(max_depth=depth, n_
estimators=300, random_state=2)
```

```
gbr.fit(X_train, y_train)
y_pred = gbr.predict(X_test)
rmse = MSE(y_test, y_pred)**0.5
print('Max Depth:', depth, ', Score:', rmse)
```

The result is as follows:

```
Max Depth: None , Score: 867.9366621617327
Max Depth: 1 , Score: 707.8261886858736
Max Depth: 2 , Score: 653.7456840231495
Max Depth: 3 , Score: 646.4045923317708
Max Depth: 4 , Score: 663.048387855927
```

A max_depth value of 3 gives the best results.

Other base learner hyperparameters, as covered in *Chapter 2, Decision Trees in Depth*, may be tuned in a similar manner.

subsample

subsample is a subset of samples. Since samples are the rows, a subset of rows means that all rows may not be included when building each tree. By changing subsample from 1.0 to a smaller decimal, trees only select that percentage of samples during the build phase. For example, subsample=0.8 would select 80% of samples for each tree.

Continuing with max_depth=3, we try a range of subsample percentages to improve results:

```
samples = [1, 0.9, 0.8, 0.7, 0.6, 0.5]
for sample in samples:
    gbr = GradientBoostingRegressor(max_depth=3, n_
estimators=300, subsample=sample, random_state=2)
    gbr.fit(X_train, y_train)
    y_pred = gbr.predict(X_test)
    rmse = MSE(y_test, y_pred)**0.5
    print('Subsample:', sample, ', Score:', rmse)
```

The result is as follows:

```
Subsample: 1 , Score: 646.4045923317708
Subsample: 0.9 , Score: 620.1819001443569
Subsample: 0.8 , Score: 617.2355650565677
Subsample: 0.7 , Score: 612.9879156983139
Subsample: 0.6 , Score: 622.6385116402317
Subsample: 0.5 , Score: 626.9974073227554
```

A subsample value of 0.7 with 300 trees and max_depth of 3 produces the best score yet.

When subsample is not equal to 1.0, the model is classified as **stochastic gradient descent**, where *stochastic* indicates that some randomness is inherent in the model.

RandomizedSearchCV

We have a good working model, but we have not yet performed a grid search, as covered in *Chapter 2, Decision Trees in Depth*. Our preliminary analysis indicates that a grid search centered around max_depth=3, subsample=0.7, n_estimators=300, and learning_rate = 0.1 is a good place to start. We have already shown that as n_estimators goes up, learning_rate should go down:

1. Here is a possible starting point:

    ```
    params={'subsample':[0.65, 0.7, 0.75],
            'n_estimators':[300, 500, 1000],
            'learning_rate':[0.05, 0.075, 0.1]}
    ```

    Since n_estimators is going up from the starting value of 300, learning_rate is going down from the starting value of 0.1. Let's keep max_depth=3 to limit the variance.

    With 27 possible combinations of hyperparameters, we use RandomizedSearchCV to try 10 of these combinations in the hopes of finding a good model.

    > **Note**
    > While 27 combinations are feasible with GridSearchCV, at some point you will end up with too many possibilities and RandomizedSearchCV will become essential. We use RandomizedSearchCV here for practice and to speed up computations.

2. Let's import `RandomizedSearchCV` and initialize a gradient boosting model:

```
from sklearn.model_selection import RandomizedSearchCV
gbr = GradientBoostingRegressor(max_depth=3, random_
state=2)
```

3. Next, initialize `RandomizedSearchCV` with `gbr` and `params` as inputs in addition to the number of iterations, the scoring, and the number of folds. Recall that `n_jobs=-1` may speed up computations and `random_state=2` ensures the consistency of results:

```
rand_reg = RandomizedSearchCV(gbr, params, n_iter=10,
scoring='neg_mean_squared_error', cv=5, n_jobs=-1,
random_state=2)
```

4. Now fit the model on the training set and obtain the best parameters and scores:

```
rand_reg.fit(X_train, y_train)
best_model = rand_reg.best_estimator_
best_params = rand_reg.best_params_
print("Best params:", best_params)
best_score = np.sqrt(-rand_reg.best_score_)
print("Training score: {:.3f}".format(best_score))
y_pred = best_model.predict(X_test)
rmse_test = MSE(y_test, y_pred)**0.5
print('Test set score: {:.3f}'.format(rmse_test))
```

The result is as follows:

```
Best params: {'learning_rate': 0.05, 'n_estimators': 300,
'subsample': 0.65}
Training score: 636.200
Test set score: 625.985
```

From here, it's worth experimenting by changing parameters individually or in pairs. Even though the best model currently has `n_estimators=300`, it's certainly possible that raising this hyperparameter will obtain better results with careful adjustment of the `learning_rate` value. `subsample` may be experimented with as well.

5. After a few rounds of experimentation, we obtained the following model:

```
gbr = GradientBoostingRegressor(max_depth=3, n_
estimators=1600, subsample=0.75, learning_rate=0.02,
random_state=2)
```
```
gbr.fit(X_train, y_train)
```
```
y_pred = gbr.predict(X_test)
```
```
MSE(y_test, y_pred)**0.5
```

The result is the following:

```
596.9544588974487
```

With a larger value for n_estimators at 1600, a smaller learning_rate value at 0.02, a comparable subsample value of 0.75, and the same max_depth value of 3, we obtained the best **Root Mean Square Error** (**RMSE**) yet at 597.

It may be possible to do better. We encourage you to try!

Now, let's see how XGBoost differs from gradient boosting using the same hyperparameters covered thus far.

XGBoost

XGBoost is an advanced version of gradient boosting with the same general structure, meaning that it transforms weak learners into strong learners by summing the residuals of trees.

The only difference in hyperparameters from the last section is that XGBoost refers to learning_rate as eta.

Let's build an XGBoost regressor with the same hyperparameters to compare the results.

Import XGBRegressor from xgboost, and then initialize and score the model as follows:

```
from xgboost import XGBRegressor
```
```
xg_reg = XGBRegressor(max_depth=3, n_estimators=1600, eta=0.02,
subsample=0.75, random_state=2)
```
```
xg_reg.fit(X_train, y_train)
```
```
y_pred = xg_reg.predict(X_test)
```
```
MSE(y_test, y_pred)**0.5
```

The result is this:

```
584.339544309016
```

The score is better. The reason as to why the score is better will be revealed in the next chapter, *Chapter 5, XGBoost Unveiled*.

Accuracy and speed are the two most important concepts when building machine learning models, and we have shown multiple times that XGBoost is very accurate. XGBoost is preferred over gradient boosting in general because it consistently delivers better results, and because it's faster, as demonstrated by the following case study.

Approaching big data – gradient boosting versus XGBoost

In the real world, datasets can be enormous, with trillions of data points. Limiting work to one computer can be disadvantageous due to the limited resources of one machine. When working with big data, the cloud is often used to take advantage of parallel computers.

Datasets are big when they push the limits of computation. So far in this book, by limiting datasets to tens of thousands of rows with a hundred or fewer columns, there should have been no significant time delays, unless you ran into errors (happens to everyone).

In this section, we examine **exoplanets** over time. The dataset has 5,087 rows and 3,189 columns that record light flux at different times of a star's life cycle. Multiplying columns and rows together results in 1.5 million data points. Using a baseline of 100 trees, we need 150 million data points to build a model.

In this section, my 2013 MacBook Air had wait times of about 5 minutes. New computers should be faster. I have chosen the exoplanet dataset so that wait times play a significant role without tying up your computer for a very long time.

Introducing the exoplanet dataset

The exoplanet dataset is taken from Kaggle and dates from around 2017: `https://www.kaggle.com/keplersmachines/kepler-labelled-time-series-data`. The dataset contains information about the light of stars. Each row is an individual star and the columns reveal different light patterns over time. In addition to light patterns, an exoplanet column is labeled 2 if the star hosts an exoplanet; otherwise, it is labeled 1.

The dataset records the light flux from thousands of stars. **Light flux**, often referred to as **luminous flux**, is the perceived brightness of a star.

Note

The perceived brightness is different than actual brightness. For instance, an incredibly bright star very far away may have a small luminous flux (looks dim), while a moderately bright star that is very close, like the sun, may have a large luminous flux (looks bright).

When the light flux of an individual star changes periodically, it is possible that the star is being orbited by an exoplanet. The assumption is that when an exoplanet orbits in front of a star, it blocks a small fraction of the light, reducing the perceived brightness by a very slight amount.

Tip

Finding exoplanets is rare. The predictive column, on whether a star hosts an exoplanet or not, has very few positive cases, resulting in an imbalanced dataset. Imbalanced datasets require extra precautions. We will cover imbalanced datasets in *Chapter 7, Discovering Exoplanets with XGBoost*, where we go into further detail with this dataset.

Next, let's access the exoplanet dataset and prepare it for machine learning.

Preprocessing the exoplanet dataset

The exoplanet dataset has been uploaded to our GitHub page at `https://github.com/PacktPublishing/Hands-On-Gradient-Boosting-with-XGBoost-and-Scikit-learn/tree/master/Chapter04`.

Here are the steps to load and preprocess the exoplanet dataset for machine learning:

1. Download `exoplanets.csv` in the same folder as your Jupyter Notebook. Then, open the file and take a look:

    ```
    df = pd.read_csv('exoplanets.csv')
    df.head()
    ```

The DataFrame will look as shown in the following figure:

	LABEL	FLUX.1	FLUX.2	FLUX.3	FLUX.4	FLUX.5	FLUX.6	FLUX.7	FLUX.8	FLUX.9
0	2	93.85	83.81	20.10	-26.98	-39.56	-124.71	-135.18	-96.27	-79.89
1	2	-38.88	-33.83	-58.54	-40.09	-79.31	-72.81	-86.55	-85.33	-83.97
2	2	532.64	535.92	513.73	496.92	456.45	466.00	464.50	486.39	436.56
3	2	326.52	347.39	302.35	298.13	317.74	312.70	322.33	311.31	312.42
4	2	-1107.21	-1112.59	-1118.95	-1095.10	-1057.55	-1034.48	-998.34	-1022.71	-989.57

5 rows × 3198 columns

Fig 4.5 – Exoplanet DataFrame

Not all columns are shown due to space limitations. The flux columns are floats, while the `Label` column is 2 for an exoplanet star and 1 for a non-exoplanet star.

2. Let's' confirm that all columns are numerical with `df.info()`:

```
df.info()
```

The result is as follows:

```
<class 'pandas.core.frame.DataFrame'>
RangeIndex: 5087 entries, 0 to 5086
Columns: 3198 entries, LABEL to FLUX.3197
dtypes: float64(3197), int64(1)
memory usage: 124.1 MB
```

As you can see from the output, `3197` columns are floats and 1 column is an `int`, so all columns are numerical.

3. Now, let's confirm the number of null values with the following code:

```
df.isnull().sum().sum()
```

The output is as follows:

```
0
```

The output reveals that there are no null values.

4. Since all columns are numerical with no null values, we may split the data into training and test sets. Note that the 0th column is the target column, `y`, and all other columns are the predictor columns, `X`:

```
X = df.iloc[:,1:]
y = df.iloc[:,0]
```

```
X_train, X_test, y_train, y_test = train_test_split(X, y,
random_state=2)
```

It's time to build a gradient boosting classifier to predict whether stars host exoplanets.

Building gradient boosting classifiers

Gradient boosting classifiers work in the same manner as gradient boosting regressors. The difference is primarily in the scoring.

Let's start by importing `GradientBoostingClassifer` and `XGBClassifier` in addition to `accuracy_score` so that we may compare both models:

```
from sklearn.ensemble import GradientBoostingClassifier
from xgboost import XGBClassifier
from sklearn.metrics import accuracy_score
```

Next, we need a way to compare models using a timer.

Timing models

Python comes with a `time` library that can be used to mark time. The general idea is to mark the time before and after a computation. The difference between these times tells us how long the computation took.

The `time` library is imported as follows:

```
import time
```

Within the `time` library, the `.time()` method marks time in seconds.

As an example, see how long it takes to run `df.info()` by assigning start and end times before and after the computation using `time.time()`:

```
start = time.time()
df.info()
end = time.time()
elapsed = end - start
print('\nRun Time: ' + str(elapsed) + ' seconds.')
```

The output is as follows:

```
<class 'pandas.core.frame.DataFrame'>
RangeIndex: 5087 entries, 0 to 5086
Columns: 3198 entries, LABEL to FLUX.3197
dtypes: float64(3197), int64(1)
memory usage: 124.1 MB
```

The runtime is as follows:

```
Run Time: 0.0525362491607666 seconds.
```

Your results will differ from ours, but hopefully it's in the same ballpark.

Let's now compare `GradientBoostingClassifier` and `XGBoostClassifier` with the exoplanet dataset for its speed using the preceding code to mark time.

> **Tip**
>
> Jupyter Notebooks come with magic functions, denoted by the `%` sign before a command. `%timeit` is one such magic function. Instead of computing how long it takes to run the code once, `%timeit` computes how long it takes to run code over multiple runs. See `ipython.readthedocs.io/en/stable/interactive/magics.html` for more information on magic functions.

Comparing speed

It's time to race `GradientBoostingClassifier` and `XGBoostClassifier` with the exoplanet dataset. We have set `max_depth=2` and `n_estimators=100` to limit the size of the model. Let's start with `GradientBoostingClassifier`:

1. First, we will mark the start time. After building and scoring the model, we will mark the end time. The following code may take around 5 minutes to run depending on the speed of your computer:

```
start = time.time()
gbr = GradientBoostingClassifier(n_estimators=100, max_
depth=2, random_state=2)
gbr.fit(X_train, y_train)
y_pred = gbr.predict(X_test)
score = accuracy_score(y_pred, y_test)
print('Score: ' + str(score))
```

```
end = time.time()
elapsed = end - start
print('\nRun Time: ' + str(elapsed) + ' seconds')
```

The result is this:

```
Score: 0.9874213836477987
Run Time: 317.6318619251251 seconds
```

`GradientBoostingRegressor` took over 5 minutes to run on my 2013 MacBook Air. Not bad for 150 million data points on an older computer.

> **Note**
> While a score of 98.7% percent is usually outstanding for accuracy, this is not the case with imbalanced datasets, as you will see in *Chapter 7, Discovering Exoplanets with XGBoost.*

2. Next, we will build an `XGBClassifier` model with the same hyperparameters and mark the time in the same manner:

```
start = time.time()
xg_reg = XGBClassifier(n_estimators=100, max_depth=2,
random_state=2)
xg_reg.fit(X_train, y_train)
y_pred = xg_reg.predict(X_test)
score = accuracy_score(y_pred, y_test)
print('Score: ' + str(score))
end = time.time()
elapsed = end - start
print('Run Time: ' + str(elapsed) + ' seconds')
```

The result is as follows:

```
Score: 0.9913522012578616
Run Time: 118.90568995475769 seconds
```

On my 2013 MacBook Air, XGBoost took under 2 minutes, making it more than twice as fast. It's also more accurate by half a percentage point.

When it comes to big data, an algorithm twice as fast can save weeks or months of computational time and resources. This advantage is huge in the world of big data.

In the world of boosting, XGBoost is the model of choice due to its unparalleled speed and impressive accuracy.

As for the exoplanet dataset, it will be revisited in *Chapter 7, Discovering Exoplanets with XGBoost*, in an important case study that reveals the challenges of working with imbalanced datasets along with a variety of potential solutions to those challenges.

> **Note**
>
> I recently purchased a 2020 MacBook Pro and updated all software. The difference in time using the same code is staggering:
>
> Gradient Boosting Run Time: 197.38 seconds
>
> XGBoost Run Time: 8.66 seconds
>
> More than a 10-fold difference!

Summary

In this chapter, you learned the difference between bagging and boosting. You learned how gradient boosting works by building a gradient boosting regressor from scratch. You implemented a variety of gradient boosting hyperparameters, including `learning_rate`, `n_estimators`, `max_depth`, and `subsample`, which results in stochastic gradient boosting. Finally, you used big data to predict whether stars have exoplanets by comparing the times of `GradientBoostingClassifier` and `XGBoostClassifier`, with `XGBoostClassifier` emerging as twice to over ten times as fast and more accurate.

The advantage of learning these skills is that you now understand when to apply XGBoost rather than similar machine learning algorithms such as gradient boosting. You can now build stronger XGBoost and gradient boosting models by properly taking advantage of core hyperparameters, including `n_estimators` and `learning_rate`. Furthermore, you have developed the capacity to time all computations instead of relying on intuition.

Congratulations! You have completed all of the preliminary XGBoost chapters. Until now, the purpose has been to introduce you to machine learning and data analytics within the larger XGBoost narrative. The aim has been to show how the need for XGBoost emerged from ensemble methods, boosting, gradient boosting, and big data.

The next chapter starts a new leg on our journey with an advanced introduction to XGBoost, where you will learn the mathematical details behind the XGBoost algorithm in addition to hardware modifications that XGBoost makes to improve speed. You'll also be building XGBoost models using the original Python API in a historically relevant case study on the discovery of the Higgs boson. The chapters that follow highlight exciting details, advantages, nuances, and tricks and tips to build swift, efficient, powerful, and industry-ready XGBoost models that you can use for years to come.

Section 2: XGBoost

XGBoost is reintroduced and examined in depth by looking at the general framework, including base models, speed enhancements, mathematical derivations, and the original Python API. XGBoost hyperparameters are analyzed, summarized, and fine-tuned in detail. Scientifically relevant case studies provide ample practice in building and fine-tuning powerful XGBoost models to correct weight imbalances and insufficient scores.

This section comprises the following chapters:

- *Chapter 5, XGBoost Unveiled*
- *Chapter 6, XGBoost Hyperparameters*
- *Chapter 7, Discovering Exoplanets with XGBoost*

5
XGBoost Unveiled

In this chapter, you will finally see **Extreme Gradient Boosting**, or **XGBoost**, as it is. XGBoost is presented in the context of the machine learning narrative that we have built up, from decision trees to gradient boosting. The first half of the chapter focuses on the theory behind the distinct advancements that XGBoost brings to tree ensemble algorithms. The second half focuses on building XGBoost models within the **Higgs Boson Kaggle Competition**, which unveiled XGBoost to the world.

Specifically, you will identify speed enhancements that make XGBoost faster, discover how XGBoost handles missing values, and learn the mathematical derivation behind XGBoost's **regularized parameter selection**. You will establish model templates for building XGBoost classifiers and regressors. Finally, you will look at the **Large Hadron Collider**, where the Higgs boson was discovered, where you will weigh data and make predictions using the original XGBoost Python API.

This chapter covers the following main topics:

- Designing XGBoost
- Analyzing XGBoost parameters
- Building XGBoost models
- Finding the Higgs boson – case study

Designing XGBoost

XGBoost is a significant upgrade from gradient boosting. In this section, you will identify the key features of XGBoost that distinguish it from gradient boosting and other tree ensemble algorithms.

Historical narrative

With the acceleration of big data, the quest to find awesome machine learning algorithms to produce accurate, optimal predictions began. Decision trees produced machine learning models that were too accurate and failed to generalize well to new data. Ensemble methods proved more effective by combining many decision trees via **bagging** and **boosting**. A leading algorithm that emerged from the tree ensemble trajectory was gradient boosting.

The consistency, power, and outstanding results of gradient boosting convinced Tianqi Chen from the University of Washington to enhance its capabilities. He called the new algorithm XGBoost, short for **Extreme Gradient Boosting**. Chen's new form of gradient boosting included built-in regularization and impressive gains in speed.

After finding initial success in Kaggle competitions, in 2016, Tianqi Chen and Carlos Guestrin authored *XGBoost: A Scalable Tree Boosting System* to present their algorithm to the larger machine learning community. You can check out the original paper at `https://arxiv.org/pdf/1603.02754.pdf`. The key points are summarized in the following section.

Design features

As indicated in *Chapter 4*, *From Gradient Boosting to XGBoost*, the need for faster algorithms is evident when dealing with big data. The *Extreme* in *Extreme Gradient Boosting* means pushing computational limits to the extreme. Pushing computational limits requires knowledge not just of model-building but also of disk-reading, compression, cache, and cores.

Although the focus of this book remains on building XGBoost models, we will take a glance under the hood of the XGBoost algorithm to distinguish key advancements, such as handling missing values, speed gains, and accuracy gains that make XGBoost faster, more accurate, and more desirable. Let's look at these key advancements next.

Handling missing values

You spent significant time in *Chapter 1*, *Machine Learning Landscape*, practicing different ways to correct **null values**. This is an essential skill for all machine learning practitioners.

XGBoost, however, is capable of handling missing values for you. There is a `missing` hyperparameter that can be set to any value. When given a missing data point, XGBoost scores different split options and chooses the one with the best results.

Gaining speed

XGBoost was specifically designed for speed. Speed gains allow machine learning models to build more quickly which is especially important when dealing with millions, billions, or trillions of rows of data. This is not uncommon in the world of big data, where each day, industry and science accumulate more data than ever before. The following new design features give XGBoost a big edge in speed over comparable ensemble algorithms:

- **Approximate split-finding algorithm**
- **Sparsity aware split-finding**
- **Parallel computing**
- **Cache-aware access**
- **Block compression and sharding**

Let's learn about these features in a bit more detail.

Approximate split-finding algorithm

Decision trees need optimal splits to produce optimal results. A *greedy algorithm* selects the best split at each step and does not backtrack to look at previous branches. Note that decision tree splitting is usually performed in a greedy manner.

XGBoost presents an exact greedy algorithm in addition to a new approximate split-finding algorithm. The split-finding algorithm uses **quantiles**, percentages that split data, to propose candidate splits. In a global proposal, the same quantiles are used throughout the entire training, and in a local proposal, new quantiles are provided for each round of splitting.

A previously known algorithm, **quantile sketch**, works well with equally weighted datasets. XGBoost presents a novel weighted quantile sketch based on merging and pruning with a theoretical guarantee. Although the mathematical details of this algorithm are beyond the scope of this book, you are encouraged to check out the appendix of the original XGBoost paper at `https://arxiv.org/pdf/1603.02754.pdf`.

Sparsity-aware split finding

Sparse data occurs when the majority of entries are 0 or null. This may occur when datasets consist primarily of null values or when they have been **one-hot encoded**. In *Chapter 1, Machine Learning Landscape*, you used pd.get_dummies to transform **categorical columns** into **numerical columns**. This resulted in a larger dataset with many values of 0. This method of converting categorical columns into numerical columns, where 1 indicates presence and 0 indicates absence, is generally referred to as one-hot encoding. You will gain practice with one-hot-encoding in *Chapter 10, XGBoost Model Deployment*.

Sparse matrices are designed to only store data points with non-zero and non-null values. This saves valuable space. A sparsity-aware split indicates that when looking for splits, XGBoost is faster because its matrices are sparse.

According to the original paper, *XGBoost: A Scalable Tree Boosting System*, the sparsity-aware split-finding algorithm performed 50 times faster than the standard approach on the **All-State-10K** dataset.

Parallel computing

Boosting is not ideal for **parallel computing** since each tree depends on the results of the previous tree. There are opportunities, however, where parallelization may take place.

Parallel computing occurs when multiple computational units are working together on the same problem at the same time. XGBoost sorts and compresses the data into blocks. These blocks may be distributed to multiple machines, or to external memory (out of core).

Sorting the data is faster with blocks. The split-finding algorithm takes advantage of blocks and the search for quantiles is faster due to blocks. In each of these cases, XGBoost provides parallel computing to expedite the model-building process.

Cache-aware access

The data on your computer is separated into **cache** and **main memory**. The cache, what you use most often, is reserved for high-speed memory. The data that you use less often is held back for lower-speed memory. Different cache levels have different orders of magnitude of latency, as outlined here: https://gist.github.com/jboner/2841832.

When it comes to gradient statistics, XGBoost uses **cache-aware prefetching**. XGBoost allocates an internal buffer, fetches the gradient statistics, and performs accumulation with mini batches. According to *XGBoost: A Scalable Tree Boosting System*, prefetching lengthens read/write dependency and reduces runtimes by approximately 50% for datasets with a large number of rows.

Block compression and sharding

XGBoost delivers additional speed gains through **block compression** and **block sharding**.

Block compression helps with computationally expensive disk reading by compressing columns. Block sharding decreases read times by sharding the data into multiple disks that alternate when reading the data.

Accuracy gains

XGBoost adds built-in regularization to achieve accuracy gains beyond gradient boosting. **Regularization** is the process of adding information to reduce variance and prevent overfitting.

Although data may be regularized through hyperparameter fine-tuning, regularized algorithms may also be attempted. For example, `Ridge` and `Lasso` are regularized machine learning alternatives to `LinearRegression`.

XGBoost includes regularization as part of the learning objective, as contrasted with gradient boosting and random forests. The regularized parameters penalize complexity and smooth out the final weights to prevent overfitting. XGBoost is a regularized version of gradient boosting.

In the next section, you will meet the math behind the learning objective of XGBoost, which combines regularization with the loss function. While you don't need to know the math to use XGBoost effectively, mathematical knowledge may provide a deeper understanding. You can skip the next section if desired.

Analyzing XGBoost parameters

In this section, we will analyze the parameters that XGBoost uses to create state-of-the-art machine learning models with a mathematical derivation.

We will maintain the distinction between parameters and hyperparameters as presented in *Chapter 2, Decision Trees in Depth*. Hyperparameters are chosen before the model is trained, whereas parameters are chosen while the model is being trained. In other words, the parameters are what the model learns from the data.

The derivation that follows is taken from the XGBoost official documentation, *Introduction to Boosted Trees*, at `https://xgboost.readthedocs.io/en/latest/tutorials/model.html`.

Learning objective

The learning objective of a machine learning model determines how well the model fits the data. In the case of XGBoost, the learning objective consists of two parts: the **loss function** and the **regularization term**.

Mathematically, XGBoost's learning objective may be defined as follows:

$$obj(\theta) = l(\theta) + \Omega(\theta)$$

Here, $l(\theta)$ is the loss function, which is the **Mean Squared Error** (**MSE**) for regression, or the log loss for classification, and $\Omega(\theta)$ is the regularization function, a penalty term to prevent over-fitting. Including a regularization term as part of the objective function distinguishes XGBoost from most tree ensembles.

Let's look at the objective function in more detail, by considering the MSE for regression.

Loss function

The loss function, defined as the MSE for regression, can be written in summation notation, as follows:

$$l(\theta) = \sum_{i=1}^{n} (y_i - \hat{y}_i)^2$$

Here, y_i is the target value for the ith row and $\hat{y}_i$ is the value predicted by the machine learning model for the ith row. The summation symbol, Σ, indicates that all rows are summed starting with $i = 1$ and ending with $i = n$, the number of rows.

The prediction, $\hat{y}_i$, for a given tree requires a function that starts at the tree root and ends at a leaf. Mathematically, this can be expressed as follows:

$$\hat{y}_i = f(x_i), f \in F$$

Here, x_i is a vector whose entries are the columns of the ith row and $f \in F$ means that the function f is a member of F, the set of all possible CART functions. **CART** is an acronym for **Classification And Regression Trees**. CART provides a real value for all leaves, even for classification algorithms.

In gradient boosting, the function that determines the prediction for the ith row includes the sum of all previous functions, as outlined in *Chapter 4, From Gradient Boosting to XGBoost*. Therefore, it's possible to write the following:

$$\hat{y}_i = \sum_{t=1}^{T} f_t(x_i), f_t \in F$$

Here, T is the number of boosted trees. In other words, to obtain the prediction for the ith tree, sum the predictions of the previous trees in addition to the prediction for the new tree. The notation $f_t \in F$ insists that the functions belong to F, the set of all possible CART functions.

The learning objective for the tth boosted tree can now be rewritten as follows:

$$obj^{(t)} = \sum_{i=1}^{n} l(y_i, \widehat{y}_i^t) + \sum_{i=1}^{t} \Omega(f_t)$$

Here, $l(y_i, \widehat{y}_i^t)$ is the general loss function of the tth boosted tree and $\Omega(f_t)$ is the regularization term.

Since boosted trees sum the predictions of previous trees, in addition to the prediction of the new tree, it must be the case that $\widehat{y}_i^t = \widehat{y}_i^{t-1} + f_t(x_i)$. This is the idea behind additive training.

By substituting this into the preceding learning objective, we obtain the following:

$$obj^{(t)} = \sum_{i=1}^{n} l\left(y_i, \widehat{y}_i^{t-1} + f_t(x_i)\right) + \Omega(f_t)$$

This can be rewritten as follows for the least square regression case:

$$obj^{(t)} = \sum_{i=1}^{n} \left(y_i - \left(\widehat{y}_i^{t-1} + f_t(x_i)\right)\right)^2 + \Omega(f_t)$$

Multiplying the polynomial out, we obtain the following:

$$obj^{(t)} = \sum_{i=1}^{n} 2(y_i - \widehat{y}_i^{t-1})f_t(x_i) + f_t(x_i)^2 + \Omega(f_t) + C$$

Here, C is a constant term that does not depend on t. In terms of polynomials, this is a quadratic equation with the variable $f_t(x_i)$. Recall that the goal is to find an optimal value of $f_t(x_i)$, the optimal function mapping the roots (samples) to the leaves (predictions).

Any sufficiently smooth function, such as second-degree polynomial (quadratic), can be approximated by a **Taylor polynomial**. XGBoost uses Newton's method with a second-degree Taylor polynomial to obtain the following:

$$obj^{(t)} = \sum_{i=1}^{n} g_i f_t(x_i) + \frac{1}{2} h_i f_t(x_i)^2 + \Omega(f_t)$$

Here, g_i and h_i can be written as the following partial derivatives:

$$g_i = \partial_{\hat{y}_i^{t-1}} l(y_i, \hat{y}_i^{t-1})$$

$$h_i = \partial_{\hat{y}_i^{t-1}}^2 l(y_i, \hat{y}_i^{t-1})$$

For a general discussion of how XGBoost uses the **Taylor expansion**, check out https://stats.stackexchange.com/questions/202858/xgboost-loss-function-approximation-with-taylor-expansion.

XGBoost implements this learning objective function by taking a solver that uses only g_i and h_i as input. Since the loss function is general, the same inputs can be used for regression and classification.

This leaves the regularization function, $\Omega(f_t)$.

Regularization function

Let w be the vector space of leaves. Then, f, the function mapping the tree root to the leaves, can be recast in terms of w, as follows:

$$f_t(x) = w_{q(x)}, w \in R^T, q: R^d \rightarrow \{1, 2, ..., T\}$$

Here, q is the function assigning data points to leaves and T is the number of leaves.

After practice and experimentation, XGBoost settled on the following as the regularization function where γ and λ are penalty constants to reduce overfitting:

$$\Omega(f) = \gamma T + \frac{1}{2}\lambda \sum_{j=1}^{T} w_j^2$$

Objective function

Combining the loss function with the regularization function, the learning objective function becomes the following:

$$obj^{(t)} = \sum_{i=1}^{n} g_i w_{q(x_i)} + \frac{1}{2} h_i w_{q(x_i)}^2 + \gamma T + \frac{1}{2}\lambda \sum_{j=1}^{T} w_j^2$$

We can define the set of indices of data points assigned to the jth leaf as follows:

$$I_j = \{i \mid q(x_i) = j\}$$

The objective function can then be written as follows:

$$obj^{(t)} = \sum_{i \in I_j} g_i w_j + \frac{1}{2} \sum_{i \in I_j} h_i w_j^2 + \gamma T + \frac{1}{2} \lambda \sum_{j=1}^{T} w_j^2$$

Finally, setting the $G_j = \sum_{i \in I_j} g_i$ and $H_j = \sum_{i \in I_j} h_i$, after rearranging the indices and combining like

terms, we obtain the final form of the objective function, which is the following:

$$obj^{(t)} = \sum_{j=1}^{T} [G_j w_j + \frac{1}{2} (H_j + \lambda) w_j^2 + \gamma T]$$

Minimizing the objective function by taking the derivative with respect to w_j and setting the left side equal to zero, we obtain the following:

$$w_j = -\frac{G_j}{H_j + \lambda}$$

This can be substituted back into the objection function to give the following:

$$obj^{(t)} = -\frac{1}{2} \sum_{j=1}^{T} \frac{G_j^2}{H_j + \lambda} + \gamma T$$

This is the result XGBoost uses to determine how well the model fits the data.

Congratulations on making it through a long and challenging derivation!

Building XGBoost models

In the first two sections, you learned how XGBoost works under the hood with parameter derivations, regularization, speed enhancements, and new features such as the `missing` parameter to compensate for null values.

In this book, we primarily build XGBoost models with scikit-learn. The scikit-learn XGBoost wrapper was released in 2019. Before full immersion with scikit-learn, building XGBoost models required a steeper learning curve. Converting NumPy arrays to `dmatrices`, for instance, was mandatory to take advantage of the XGBoost framework.

In scikit-learn, however, these conversions happen behind the scenes. Building XGBoost models in scikit-learn is very similar to building other machine learning models in scikit-learn, as you have experienced throughout this book. All standard scikit-learn methods, such as `.fit`, and `.predict`, are available, in addition to essential tools such as `train_test_split`, `cross_val_score`, `GridSearchCV`, and `RandomizedSearchCV`.

In this section, you will develop templates for building XGBoost models. Going forward, these templates can be referenced as starting points for building XGBoost classifiers and regressors.

We will build templates for two classic datasets: the **Iris dataset** for classification and the **Diabetes dataset** for regression. Both datasets are small, built into scikit-learn, and have been tested frequently throughout the machine learning community. As part of the model-building process, you will explicitly define default hyperparameters that give XGBoost great scores. These hyperparameters are explicitly defined so that you can learn what they are in preparation for adjusting them going forward.

The Iris dataset

The Iris dataset, a staple of the machine learning community, was introduced by statistician Robert Fischer in 1936. Its easy accessibility, small size, clean data, and symmetry of values have made it a popular choice for testing classification algorithms.

We will introduce the Iris dataset by downloading it directly from scikit-learn using the `datasets` library with the `load_iris()` method, as follows:

```
import pandas as pd
import numpy as np
from sklearn import datasets
iris = datasets.load_iris()
```

Scikit-learn datasets are stored as **NumPy arrays**, the array storage method of choice for machine learning algorithms. `pandas` DataFrames are used more for data analysis and data visualization. Viewing NumPy arrays as DataFrames requires the `pandas` `DataFrame` method. This scikit-learn dataset is split into predictor and target columns in advance. Bringing them together requires concatenating the NumPy arrays with the code `np.c_` before conversion. Column names are also added, as follows:

```
df = pd.DataFrame(data= np.c_[iris['data'],
 iris['target']],columns= iris['feature_names'] + ['target'])
```

You can view the first five rows of the DataFrame using `df.head()`:

```
df.head()
```

The resulting DataFrame will look like this:

	sepal length (cm)	sepal width (cm)	petal length (cm)	petal width (cm)	target
0	5.1	3.5	1.4	0.2	0.0
1	4.9	3.0	1.4	0.2	0.0
2	4.7	3.2	1.3	0.2	0.0
3	4.6	3.1	1.5	0.2	0.0
4	5.0	3.6	1.4	0.2	0.0

Figure 5.1 – The Iris dataset

The predictor columns are self-explanatory, measuring sepal and petal length and width. The target column, according to the scikit-learn documentation, `https://scikit-learn.org/stable/auto_examples/datasets/plot_iris_dataset.html`, consists of three different iris flowers, **setosa**, **versicolor**, and **virginica**. There are 150 rows.

To prepare the data for machine learning, import `train_test_split`, then split the data accordingly. You can use the original NumPy arrays, `iris['data']` and `iris['target']`, as inputs for `train_test_split`:

```
from sklearn.model_selection import train_test_split
X_train, X_test, y_train, y_test = train_test_
split(iris['data'], iris['target'], random_state=2)
```

Now that we have split the data, let's build the classification template.

XGBoost classification template

The following template is for building an XGBoost classifier, assuming the dataset has already been split into `X_train`, `X_test`, `y_train`, and `y_test` sets:

1. Import `XGBClassifier` from the `xgboost` library:

    ```
    from xgboost import XGBClassifier
    ```

2. Import a classification scoring method as needed.

    While `accuracy_score` is standard, other scoring methods, such as `auc` (**Area Under Curve**), will be discussed later:

    ```
    from sklearn.metrics import accuracy_score
    ```

3. Initialize the XGBoost classifier with hyperparameters.

    Fine-tuning hyperparameters is the focus of *Chapter 6, XGBoost Hyperparameters*. In this chapter, the most important default hyperparameters are explicitly stated ahead:

    ```
    xgb = XGBClassifier(booster='gbtree',
    objective='multi:softprob', max_depth=6, learning_
    rate=0.1, n_estimators=100, random_state=2, n_jobs=-1)
    ```

    The brief descriptions of the preceding hyperparameters are as follows:

    a) `booster='gbtree'`: The booster is the **base learner**. It's the machine learning model that is constructed during every round of boosting. You may have guessed that `'gbtree'` stands for gradient boosted tree, the XGBoost default base learner. It's uncommon but possible to work with other base learners, a strategy we employ in *Chapter 8, XGBoost Alternative Base Learners*.

    b) `objective='multi:softprob'`: Standard options for the objective can be viewed in the XGBoost official documentation, `https://xgboost.readthedocs.io/en/latest/parameter.html`, under *Learning Task Parameters*. The `multi:softprob` objective is a standard alternative to `binary:logistic` when the dataset includes multiple classes. It computes the probabilities of classification and chooses the highest one. If not explicitly stated, XGBoost will often find the right objective for you.

    c) `max_depth=6`: The `max_depth` of a tree determines the number of branches each tree has. It's one of the most important hyperparameters in making balanced predictions. XGBoost uses a default of 6, unlike random forests, which don't provide a value unless explicitly programmed.

    d) `learning_rate=0.1`: Within XGBoost, this hyperparameter is often referred to as `eta`. This hyperparameter limits the variance by reducing the weight of each tree to the given percentage. The `learning_rate` hyperparameter was explored in detail in *Chapter 4, From Gradient Boosting to XGBoost*.

    e) `n_estimators=100`: Popular among ensemble methods, `n_estimators` is the number of boosted trees in the model. Increasing this number while decreasing `learning_rate` can lead to more robust results.

4. Fit the classifier to the data.

    This is where the magic happens. The entire XGBoost system, the details explored in the previous two sections, the selection of optimal parameters, including regularization constraints, and speed enhancements, such as the approximate split-finding algorithm, and blocking and sharding all occur during this one powerful line of scikit-learn code:

    ```
    xgb.fit(X_train, y_train)
    ```

5. Predict the *y* values as `y_pred`:

    ```
    y_pred = xgb.predict(X_test)
    ```

6. Score the model by comparing `y_pred` against `y_test`:

    ```
    score = accuracy_score(y_pred, y_test)
    ```

7. Display your results:

    ```
    print('Score: ' + str(score))
    Score: 0.9736842105263158
    ```

Unfortunately, there is no official list of Iris dataset scores. There are too many to compile in one place. An initial score of 97.4 percent on the Iris dataset using default hyperparameters is very good (see https://www.kaggle.com/c/serpro-iris/leaderboard).

The XGBoost classifier template provided in the preceding paragraphs is not meant to be definitive, but rather a starting point going forward.

The Diabetes dataset

Now that you are becoming familiar with scikit-learn and XGBoost, you are developing the ability to build and score XGBoost models fairly quickly. In this section, an XGBoost regressor template is provided using `cross_val_score` with scikit-learn's Diabetes dataset.

Before building the template, import the predictor columns as X and the target columns as y, as follows:

```
X,y = datasets.load_diabetes(return_X_y=True)
```

Now that we have imported the predictor and target columns, let's start building the template.

The XGBoost regressor template (cross-validation)

Here are the essential steps to build an XGBoost regression model in scikit-learn using cross-validation, assuming that the predictor columns, X, and the target column, y, have been defined:

1. Import XGBRegressor and cross_val_score:

    ```
    from sklearn.model_selection import cross_val_score
    from xgboost import XGBRegressor
    ```

2. Initialize XGBRegressor.

    Here, we initialize XGBRegressor with objective='reg:squarederror', the MSE. The most important hyperparameter defaults are explicitly given:

    ```
    xgb = XGBRegressor(booster='gbtree',
    objective='reg:squarederror', max_depth=6, learning_
    rate=0.1, n_estimators=100, random_state=2, n_jobs=-1)
    ```

3. Fit and score the regressor with cross_val_score.

    With cross_val_score, fitting and scoring are done in one step using the model, the predictor columns, the target column, and the scoring as inputs:

    ```
    scores = cross_val_score(xgb, X, y, scoring='neg_mean_
    squared_error', cv=5)
    ```

4. Display the results.

    Scores for regression are commonly displayed as the **Root Mean Squared Error (RMSE)** to keep the units the same:

    ```
    rmse = np.sqrt(-scores)
    print('RMSE:', np.round(rmse, 3))
    print('RMSE mean: %0.3f' % (rmse.mean()))
    ```

    The result is as follows:

    ```
    RMSE: [63.033 59.689 64.538 63.699 64.661]
    RMSE mean: 63.124
    ```

Without a baseline of comparison, we have no idea what that score means. Converting the target column, y, into a pandas DataFrame with the .describe() method will give the quartiles and the general statistics of the predictor column, as follows:

```
pd.DataFrame(y).describe()
```

Here is the expected output:

	0
count	442.000000
mean	152.133484
std	77.093005
min	25.000000
25%	87.000000
50%	140.500000
75%	211.500000
max	346.000000

Figure 5.2 – Describing the statistics of y, the Diabetes target column

A score of 63.124 is less than 1 standard deviation, a respectable result.

You now have XGBoost classifier and regressor templates that can be used for building models going forward.

Now that you are accustomed to building XGBoost models in scikit-learn, it's time for a deep dive into high energy physics.

Finding the Higgs boson – case study

In this section, we will review the Higgs Boson Kaggle Competition, which brought XGBoost into the machine learning spotlight. In order to set the stage, the historical background is given before moving on to model development. The models that we build include a default model provided by XGBoost at the time of the competition and a reference to the winning solution provided by Gabor Melis. Kaggle accounts are not required for this text, so we will not take the time to show you how to make submissions. We have provided guidelines if you are interested.

Physics background

In popular culture, the Higgs boson is known as the *God particle*. Theorized by Peter Higgs in 1964, the Higgs boson was introduced to explain why particles have mass.

The search to find the Higgs boson culminated in its discovery in 2012 in the **Large Hadron Collider** at CERN (Geneva, Switzerland). Nobel Prizes were awarded and the Standard Model of physics, the model that accounts for every force known to physics except for gravity, stood taller than ever before.

The Higgs boson was discovered by smashing protons into each other at extremely high speeds and observing the results. Observations came from the **ATLAS** detector, which records data resulting from *hundreds of millions of proton-proton collisions per second*, according to the competition's technical documentation, *Learning to discover: the Higgs boson machine learning challenge,* `https://higgsml.lal.in2p3.fr/files/2014/04/documentation_v1.8.pdf`.

After discovering the Higgs boson, the next step was to precisely measure the characteristics of its decay. The ATLAS experiment found the Higgs boson decaying into two **tau** particles from data wrapped in background noise. To better understand the data, ATLAS called upon the machine learning community.

Kaggle competitions

The Kaggle competition is a machine learning competition designed to solve a particular problem. Machine learning competitions became famous in 2006 when Netflix offered 1 million dollars to anyone who could improve upon their movie recommendations by 10%. In 2009, the 1 million dollar prize was awarded to *BellKor's Pragmatic Chaos* team (`https://www.wired.com/2009/09/bellkors-pragmatic-chaos-wins-1-million-netflix-prize/`).

Many businesses, computer scientists, mathematicians, and students became aware of the increasing value that machine learning held in society. Machine learning competitions became hot, with mutual benefits going to company hosts and machine learning practitioners. Starting in 2010, many early adopters went to Kaggle to try their hand at machine learning competitions.

In 2014, Kaggle announced the *Higgs Boson Machine Learning Challenge* with ATLAS (`https://www.kaggle.com/c/higgs-boson`). With a $13,000 prize pool, 1,875 teams entered the competition.

In Kaggle competitions, training data is provided, along with a required scoring method. Teams build machine learning models on the training data before submitting their results. The target column of the test data is not provided. Multiple submissions are permitted, however, and scores are returned so that competitors can improve upon their models before the final date.

Kaggle competitions are fertile ground for testing machine learning algorithms. Unlike in industry, Kaggle competitions draw thousands of competitors, making the machine learning models that win prizes very well tested.

XGBoost and the Higgs challenge

XGBoost was released to the general public on March 27, 2014, 6 months before the Higgs challenge. In the competition, XGBoost soared, helping competitors climb the Kaggle leaderboard while saving valuable time.

Let's access the data to see what the competitors were working with.

Data

Instead of using the data provided by Kaggle, we use the original data provided by the CERN open data portal where it originated: `http://opendata.cern.ch/record/328`. The difference between the CERN data and the Kaggle data is that the CERN dataset is significantly larger. We will select the first 250,000 rows and make some modifications to match the Kaggle data.

You can download the CERN Higgs boson dataset directly from `https://github.com/PacktPublishing/Hands-On-Gradient-Boosting-with-XGBoost-and-Scikit-learn/tree/master/Chapter05`.

Read the `atlas-higgs-challenge-2014-v2.csv.gz` file into a `pandas` DataFrame. Please note that we are selecting the first 250,000 rows only, and the `compression=gzip` parameter is used since the dataset is zipped as a `csv.gz` file. After accessing the data, view the first five rows, as follows:

```
df = pd.read_csv('atlas-higgs-challenge-2014-v2.csv.gz',
nrows=250000, compression='gzip')
df.head()
```

The far-right columns of the output should be as shown in the following screenshot:

PRI_jet_leading_phi	PRI_jet_subleading_pt	PRI_jet_subleading_eta	PRI_jet_subleading_phi	PRI_jet_all_pt	Weight	Label	KaggleSet	KaggleWeight
0.444	46.062	1.24	-2.475	113.497	0.000814	s	t	0.002653
1.158	-999.000	-999.00	-999.000	46.226	0.681042	b	t	2.233584
-2.028	-999.000	-999.00	-999.000	44.251	0.715742	b	t	2.347389
-999.000	-999.000	-999.00	-999.000	-0.000	1.660654	b	t	5.446378
-999.000	-999.000	-999.00	-999.000	0.000	1.904263	b	t	6.245333

Figure 5.3 – CERN Higgs boson data – Kaggle columns included

Notice the `Kaggleset` and `KaggleWeight` columns. Since the Kaggle dataset was smaller, Kaggle used a different number for their weight column which is denoted in the preceding diagram as `KaggleWeight`. The `t` value under `Kaggleset` indicates that it's part of the training set for the Kaggle dataset. In other words, these two columns, `Kaggleset` and `KaggleWeight`, are columns in the CERN dataset designed to include information that will be used for the Kaggle dataset. In this chapter, we will restrict our subset of the CERN data to the Kaggle training set.

To match the Kaggle training data, let's delete the `Kaggleset` and `Weight` columns, convert `KaggleWeight` into `'Weight'`, and move the `'Label'` column to the last column, as follows:

```
del df[<Weight>]
del df[<KaggleSet>]
df = df.rename(columns={«KaggleWeight»: «Weight»})
```

One way to move the `Label` column is to store it as a variable, delete the column, and add a new column by assigning it to the new variable. Whenever assigning a new column to a DataFrame, the new column appears at the end:

```
label_col = df['Label']
del df['Label']
df['Label'] = label_col
```

Now that all changes have been made, the CERN data matches the Kaggle data. Go ahead and view the first five rows:

```
df.head()
```

Here is the left side of the expected output:

	EventId	DER_mass_MMC	DER_mass_transverse_met_lep	DER_mass_vis	DER_pt_h	DER_deltaeta_jet_jet	DER_mass_jet_jet	DER_prodeta_jet_jet	DER_deltar_
0	100000	138.470	51.655	97.827	27.980	0.91	124.711	2.666	
1	100001	160.937	68.768	103.235	48.146	-999.00	-999.000	-999.000	
2	100002	-999.000	162.172	125.953	35.635	-999.00	-999.000	-999.000	
3	100003	143.905	81.417	80.943	0.414	-999.00	-999.000	-999.000	
4	100004	175.864	16.915	134.805	16.405	-999.00	-999.000	-999.000	

5 rows × 33 columns

Figure 5.4 – CERN Higgs boson data – physics columns

Many columns are not shown, and an unusual value of -999.00 occurs in multiple places.

The columns beyond EventId include variables prefixed with PRI, which stands for *primitives*, which are values directly measured by the detector during collisions. By contrast, columns labeled DER are numerical derivations from these measurements.

All column names and types are revealed by df.info():

```
df.info()
```

Here is a sample of the output, with the middle columns truncated to save space:

```
<class 'pandas.core.frame.DataFrame'>
RangeIndex: 250000 entries, 0 to 249999
Data columns (total 33 columns):
 #   Column                      Non-Null Count    Dtype
---  ------                      --------------    -----
 0   EventId                     250000 non-null   int64
 1   DER_mass_MMC                250000 non-null   float64
 2   DER_mass_transverse_met_lep 250000 non-null   float64
 3   DER_mass_vis                250000 non-null   float64
 4   DER_pt_h                    250000 non-null   float64
...
 28  PRI_jet_subleading_eta      250000 non-null   float64
 29  PRI_jet_subleading_phi      250000 non-null   float64
 30  PRI_jet_all_pt              250000 non-null   float64
 31  Weight                      250000 non-null   float64
 32  Label                       250000 non-null   object
dtypes: float64(30), int64(3)
memory usage: 62.9 MB
```

All columns have non-null values, and only the final column, Label, is non-numerical. The columns can be grouped as follows:

- Column 0 : EventId – irrelevant for the machine learning model.
- Columns 1-30: Physics columns derived from LHC collisions. Details for these columns can be found in the link to the technical documentation at http://higgsml.lal.in2p3.fr/documentation. These are the machine learning predictor columns.

- Column 31 : `Weight` – this column is used to scale the data. The issue here is that Higgs boson events are very rare, so a machine learning model with 99.9 percent accuracy may not be able to find them. Weights compensate for this imbalance, but weights are not available for the test data. Strategies for dealing with weights will be discussed later in this chapter, and in *Chapter 7, Discovering Exoplanets with XGBoost*.

- Column 32: `Label` – this is the target column, labeled `s` for signal and `b` for background. The training data has been simulated from real data, so there are many more signals than otherwise would be found. The signal is the occurrence of the Higgs boson decay.

The only issue with the data is that the target column, `Label`, is not numerical. Convert the `Label` column into a numerical column by replacing the `s` values with `1` and the `b` values with `0`, as follows:

```
df['Label'].replace(('s', 'b'), (1, 0), inplace=True)
```

Now that all columns are numerical with non-null values, you can split the data into predictor and target columns. Recall that the predictor columns are indexed 1–30 and the target column is the last column, indexed `32` (or -1). Note that the `Weight` column should not be included because it's not available for the test data:

```
X = df.iloc[:,1:31]
y = df.iloc[:,-1]
```

Scoring

The Higgs Challenge is not your average Kaggle competition. In addition to the difficulty of understanding high energy physics for feature engineering (a route we will not pursue), the scoring method is not standard. The Higgs Challenge requires optimizing the **Approximate Median Significance (AMS)**.

The AMS is defined as follows:

$$\sqrt{2((s + b + b_{reg})ln(1 + \frac{s}{b + b_{reg}} - s)}$$

Here, s is the true positive rate, b is the false positive rate, and b_{reg} is a constant regularization term given as `10`.

Fortunately, XGBoost provided an AMS scoring method for the competition, so it does not need to be formally defined. A high AMS results from many true positives and few false negatives. Justification for the AMS instead of other scoring methods is given in the technical documentation at `http://higgsml.lal.in2p3.fr/documentation`.

> **Tip**
> It's possible to build your own scoring methods, but it's not usually needed. In the rare event that you need to build your own scoring method, you can check out `https://scikit-learn.org/stable/modules/model_evaluation.html` for more information.

Weights

Before building a machine learning model for the Higgs boson, it's important to understand and utilize weights.

In machine learning, weights can be used to improve the accuracy of imbalanced datasets. Consider the s (signal) and b (background) columns in the Higgs challenge. In reality, s << b, so signals are very rare among the background noise. Let's say, for example, that signals are 1,000 times rarer than background noise. You can create a weight column where b = 1 and s = 1/1000 to compensate for this imbalance.

According to the technical documentation of the competition, the weight column is a **scale factor** that, when summed, gives the expected number of signal and background events during the time of data collection in 2012. This means that weights are required for the predictions to represent reality. Otherwise, the model will predict way too many s (signal) events.

The weights should first be scaled to match the test data since the test data provides the expected number of signal and background events generated by the test set. The test data has 550,000 rows, more than twice the 250,000 rows (`len(y)`) provided by the training data. Scaling weights to match the test data can be achieved by multiplying the weight column by the percentage of increase, as follows:

```
df['test_Weight'] = df['Weight'] * 550000 / len(y)
```

Next, XGBoost provides a hyperparameter, `scale_pos_weight`, which takes the scaling factor into account. The scaling factor is the sum of the weights of the background noises divided by the sum of the weight of the signal. The scaling factor can be computed using `pandas` conditional notation, as follows:

```
s = np.sum(df[df['Label']==1]['test_Weight'])
b = np.sum(df[df['Label']==0]['test_Weight'])
```

In the preceding code, `df[df['Label']==1]` narrows the DataFrame down to rows where the `Label` column equals 1, then `np.sum` adds the values of these rows using the `test_Weight` column.

Finally, to see the actual rate, divide b by s:

```
b/s
593.9401931492318
```

In summary, the weights represent the expected number of signal and background events generated by the data. We scale the weights to match the size of the test data, then divide the sum of the background weights by the sum of the signal weights to establish the `scale_pos_weight=b/s` hyperparameter.

> **Tip**
>
> For a more detailed discussion on weights, check out the excellent introduction from KDnuggets at `https://www.kdnuggets.com/2019/11/machine-learning-what-why-how-weighting.html`.

The model

It's time to build an XGBoost model to predict the signal – that is, the simulated occurrences of the Higgs boson decay.

At the time of the competition, XGBoost was new, and the scikit-learn wrapper was not yet available. Even today (2020), the majority of information online about implementing XGBoost in Python is pre-scikit-learn. Since you are likely to encounter the pre-scikit-learn XGBoost Python API online, and this is what all competitors used in the Higgs Challenge, we present code using the original Python API in this chapter only.

Here are the steps to build an XGBoost model for the Higgs Challenge:

1. Import `xgboost` as `xgb`:

    ```
    import xgboost as xgb
    ```

2. Initialize the XGBoost model as a **DMatrix** with the missing values and weights filled in.

    All XGBoost models were initialized as a DMatrix before scikit-learn. The scikit-learn wrapper automatically converts the data into a DMatrix for you. The sparse matrices that XGBoost optimizes for speed are DMatrices.

    According to the documentation, all values set to -999.0 are unknown values. Instead of converting these values into the median, mean, mode, or other null replacement, in XGBoost, unknown values can be set to the `missing` hyperparameter. During the model build phase, XGBoost automatically chooses the value leading to the best split.

3. The `weight` hyperparameter can equal the new column, `df['test_Weight']`, as defined in the `weight` section:

    ```
    xgb_clf = xgb.DMatrix(X, y, missing=-999.0,
    weight=df['test_Weight'])
    ```

4. Set additional hyperparameters.

    The hyperparameters that follow are defaults provided by XGBoost for the competition:

    a) Initialize a blank dictionary called `param`:

    ```
    param = {}
    ```

    b) Define the objective as `'binary:logitraw'`.

    This means a binary model is created from logistic regression probabilities. This objective defines the model as a classifier and allows a ranking of the target column, which is required of submissions for this particular Kaggle competition:

    ```
    param['objective'] = 'binary:logitraw'
    ```

    c) Scale the positive examples using the background weights divided by the signal weights. This will help the model perform better on the test set:

    ```
    param['scale_pos_weight'] = b/s
    ```

    d) The learning rate, `eta`, is given as 0.1:

    ```
    param['eta'] = 0.1
    ```

    e) `max_depth` is given as 6:

    ```
    param['max_depth'] = 6
    ```

f) Set the scoring method as `'auc'` for display purposes:

```
param['eval_metric'] = 'auc'
```

Although the AMS score will be printed, the evaluation metric is given as `auc`, which stands for **Area Under Curve**. `auc` is the true positive versus false positive curve that is perfect when it equals 1. Similar to accuracy, `auc` is a standard scoring metric for classification, although it's often superior to accuracy since accuracy is limited for imbalanced datasets, as discussed in *Chapter 7, Discovering Exoplanets with XGBoost*.

5. Create a list of parameters that includes the preceding items, along with the evaluation metric (`auc`) and `ams@0.15`, XGBoost's implementation of the AMS score using a 15% threshold:

```
plst = list(param.items())+[('eval_metric', 'ams@0.15')]
```

6. Create a watchlist that includes the initialized classifier and `'train'` so that you can view scores as the trees continue to boost:

```
watchlist = [ (xg_clf, 'train') ]
```

7. Set the number of boosting rounds to `120`:

```
num_round = 120
```

8. Train and save the model. Train the model by placing the parameter list, the classifier, the number of rounds, and the watchlist as inputs. Save the model using the `save_model` method so that you do not have to go through a time-consuming training process a second time. Then, run the code and watch how the scores improve as the trees are boosted:

```
print ('loading data end, start to boost trees')
bst = xgb.train( plst, xgmat, num_round, watchlist )
bst.save_model('higgs.model')
print ('finish training')
```

The end of your results should have the following output:

```
[110] train-auc:0.94505 train-ams@0.15:5.84830
[111] train-auc:0.94507 train-ams@0.15:5.85186
[112] train-auc:0.94519 train-ams@0.15:5.84451
[113] train-auc:0.94523 train-ams@0.15:5.84007
[114] train-auc:0.94532 train-ams@0.15:5.85800
```

```
[115] train-auc:0.94536  train-ams@0.15:5.86228
[116] train-auc:0.94550  train-ams@0.15:5.91160
[117] train-auc:0.94554  train-ams@0.15:5.91842
[118] train-auc:0.94565  train-ams@0.15:5.93729
[119] train-auc:0.94580  train-ams@0.15:5.93562
finish training
```

Congratulations on building an XGBoost classifier that can predict Higgs boson decay!

The model performs with 94.58 percent auc, and an AMS of 5.9. As far as the AMS is concerned, the top values of the competition were in the upper threes. This model achieves an AMS of around 3.6 when submitted with the test data.

The model that you just built was provided as a baseline by Tanqi Chen for XGBoost users during the competition. The winner of the competition, Gabor Melis, used this baseline to build his model. As can be seen from viewing the winning solution at https://github.com/melisgl/higgsml and clicking on **xgboost-scripts**, changes made to the baseline model are not significant. Melis, like most Kaggle competitors, also performed feature engineering to add more relevant columns to the data, a practice we will address in *Chapter 9, XGBoost Kaggle Masters*.

It is possible to build and train your own model after the deadline and submit it through Kaggle. For Kaggle competitions, submissions must be ranked, properly indexed, and delivered with the Kaggle API topics that require further explanation. If you want to submit models for the actual competition, the XGBoost ranking code, which you may find helpful, is available at https://github.com/dmlc/xgboost/blob/master/demo/kaggle-higgs/higgs-pred.py.

Summary

In this chapter, you learned how XGBoost was designed to improve the accuracy and speed of gradient boosting with missing values, sparse matrices, parallel computing, sharding, and blocking. You learned the mathematical derivation behind the XGBoost objective function that determines the parameters for gradient descent and regularization. You built XGBClassifier and XGBRegressor templates from classic scikit-learn datasets, obtaining very good scores. Finally, you built the baseline model provided by XGBoost for the Higgs Challenge that led to the winning solution and lifted XGBoost into the spotlight.

Now that you have a solid understanding of the overall narrative, design, parameter selection, and model-building templates of XGBoost, in the next chapter, you will fine-tune XGBoost's hyperparameters to achieve optimal scores.

6
XGBoost Hyperparameters

XGBoost has many hyperparameters. XGBoost base learner hyperparameters incorporate all decision tree hyperparameters as a starting point. There are gradient boosting hyperparameters, since XGBoost is an enhanced version of gradient boosting. Hyperparameters unique to XGBoost are designed to improve upon accuracy and speed. However, trying to tackle all XGBoost hyperparameters at once can be dizzying.

In *Chapter 2, Decision Trees in Depth*, we reviewed and applied base learner hyperparameters such as `max_depth`, while in *Chapter 4, From Gradient Boosting to XGBoost*, we applied important XGBoost hyperparameters, including `n_estimators` and `learning_rate`. We will revisit these hyperparameters in this chapter in the context of XGBoost. Additionally, we will also learn about novel XGBoost hyperparameters such as `gamma` and a technique called **early stopping**.

In this chapter, to gain proficiency in fine-tuning XGBoost hyperparameters, we will cover the following main topics:

- Preparing data and base models
- Tuning core XGBoost hyperparameters
- Applying early stopping
- Putting it all together

Technical requirements

The code for this chapter can be found at `https://github.com/PacktPublishing/Hands-On-Gradient-Boosting-with-XGBoost-and-Scikit-learn/tree/master/Chapter06`.

Preparing data and base models

Before introducing and applying XGBoost hyperparameters, let's prepare by doing the following:

- Getting the **heart disease dataset**
- Building an `XGBClassifier` model
- Implementing `StratifiedKFold`
- Scoring a **baseline XGBoost model**
- Combining `GridSearchCV` with `RandomizedSearchCV` to form one powerful function

Good preparation is essential for gaining accuracy, consistency, and speed when fine-tuning hyperparameters.

The heart disease dataset

The dataset used throughout this chapter is the heart disease dataset originally presented in *Chapter 2, Decision Trees in Depth*. We have chosen the same dataset to maximize the time spent doing hyperparameter fine-tuning, and to minimize the time spent on data analysis. Let's begin the process:

1. Go to `https://github.com/PacktPublishing/Hands-On-Gradient-Boosting-with-XGBoost-and-Scikit-learn/tree/master/Chapter06` to load `heart_disease.csv` into a DataFrame and display the first five rows. Here is the code:

```
import pandas as pd
df = pd.read_csv('heart_disease.csv')
df.head()
```

The result should look as follows:

	age	sex	cp	trestbps	chol	fbs	restecg	thalach	exang	oldpeak	slope	ca	thal	target
0	63	1	3	145	233	1	0	150	0	2.3	0	0	1	1
1	37	1	2	130	250	0	1	187	0	3.5	0	0	2	1
2	41	0	1	130	204	0	0	172	0	1.4	2	0	2	1
3	56	1	1	120	236	0	1	178	0	0.8	2	0	2	1
4	57	0	0	120	354	0	1	163	1	0.6	2	0	2	1

Figure 6.1 – The first five rows

The last column, **target**, is the target column, where **1** indicates presence, meaning the patient has a heart disease, and **2** indicates absence. For detailed information on the other columns, visit `https://archive.ics.uci.edu/ml/datasets/ Heart+Disease` at the UCI Machine Learning Repository, or see *Chapter 2, Decision Trees in Depth*.

2. Now, check `df.info()` to ensure that the data is all numerical with no null values:

```
df.info()
```

Here is the output:

```
<class 'pandas.core.frame.DataFrame'>
RangeIndex: 303 entries, 0 to 302
Data columns (total 14 columns):
 #   Column    Non-Null Count   Dtype
---  ------    --------------   -----
 0   age       303 non-null     int64
 1   sex       303 non-null     int64
 2   cp        303 non-null     int64
 3   trestbps  303 non-null     int64
 4   chol      303 non-null     int64
 5   fbs       303 non-null     int64
 6   restecg   303 non-null     int64
 7   thalach   303 non-null     int64
 8   exang     303 non-null     int64
 9   oldpeak   303 non-null     float64
 10  slope     303 non-null     int64
 11  ca        303 non-null     int64
```

```
 12   thal        303 non-null      int64
 13   target      303 non-null      int64
dtypes: float64(1), int64(13)
memory usage: 33.3 KB
```

Since all data points are non-null and numerical, the data is machine learning-ready. It's time to build a classifier.

XGBClassifier

Before tuning hyperparameters, let's build a classifier so that we can obtain a baseline score as a starting point.

To build an XGBoost classifier, follow these steps:

1. Download XGBClassifier and accuracy_score from their respective libraries. The code is as follows:

```
from xgboost import XGBClassifier
from sklearn.metrics import accuracy_score
```

2. Declare X as the predictor columns and y as the target column, where the last row is the target column:

```
X = df.iloc[:, :-1]
y = df.iloc[:, -1]
```

3. Initialize XGBClassifier with the booster='gbtree' and objective='binary:logistic' defaults along with random_state=2:

```
model = XGBClassifier(booster='gbtree',
objective='binary:logistic', random_state=2)
```

The 'gbtree' booster, the base learner, is a gradient boosted tree. The 'binary:logistic' objective is standard for binary classification in determining the loss function. Although XGBClassifier includes these values by default, we include them here to gain familiarity in preparation of modifying them in later chapters.

4. To score the baseline model, import `cross_val_score` and numpy to fit, score, and display results:

```
from sklearn.model_selection import cross_val_score
import numpy as np
scores = cross_val_score(model, X, y, cv=5)
print('Accuracy:', np.round(scores, 2))
print('Accuracy mean: %0.2f' % (scores.mean()))
```

The accuracy score is as follows:

```
Accuracy: [0.85 0.85 0.77 0.78 0.77]
Accuracy mean: 0.81
```

An accuracy score of 81% is an excellent starting point, considerably higher than the 76% cross-validation obtained by `DecisionTreeClassifier` in *Chapter 2, Decision Trees in Depth*.

We used `cross_val_score` here, and we will use `GridSearchCV` to tune hyperparameters. Next, let's find a way to ensure that the test folds are the same using `StratifiedKFold`.

StratifiedKFold

When fine-tuning hyperparameters, `GridSearchCV` and `RandomizedSearchCV` are the standard options. An issue from *Chapter 2, Decision Trees in Depth*, is that `cross_val_score` and `GridSearchCV`/`RandomizedSearchCV` do not split data the same way.

One solution is to use `StratifiedKFold` whenever cross-validation is used.

A stratified fold includes the same percentage of target values in each fold. If a dataset contains 60% 1s and 40% 0s in the target column, each stratified test set contains 60% 1s and 40% 0s. When folds are random, it's possible that one test set contains a 70-30 split while another contains a 50-50 split of target values.

> **Tip**
>
> When using `train_test_split`, the shuffle and stratify parameters use defaults to stratify the data for you. See `https://scikit-learn.org/stable/modules/generated/sklearn.model_selection.train_test_split.html` for general information.

To use `StratifiedKFold`, do the following:

1. Implement `StratifiedKFold` from `sklearn.model_selection`:

```
from sklearn.model_selection import StratifiedKFold
```

2. Next, define the number of folds as `kfold` by selecting `n_splits=5`, `shuffle=True`, and `random_state=2` as the `StratifiedKFold` parameters. Note that `random_state` provides a consistent ordering of indices, while `shuffle=True` allows rows to be initially shuffled:

```
kfold = StratifiedKFold(n_splits=5, shuffle=True, random_
state=2)
```

The `kfold` variable can now be used inside `cross_val_score`, `GridSeachCV`, and `RandomizedSearchCV` to ensure consistent results.

Now, let's return to `cross_val_score` using `kfold` so that we have an appropriate baseline for comparison.

Baseline model

Now that we have a method for obtaining consistent folds, it's time to score an official baseline model using `cv=kfold` inside `cross_val_score`. The code is as follows:

```
scores = cross_val_score(model, X, y, cv=kfold)
print('Accuracy:', np.round(scores, 2))
print('Accuracy mean: %0.2f' % (scores.mean()))
```

The accuracy score is as follows:

```
Accuracy: [0.72 0.82 0.75 0.8 0.82]
Accuracy mean: 0.78
```

The score has gone down. What does this mean?

It's important not to become too invested in obtaining the highest possible score. In this case, we trained the same XGBClassifier model on different folds and obtained different scores. This shows the importance of being consistent with test folds when training models, and why the score is not necessarily the most important thing. Although when choosing between models, obtaining the best possible score is an optimal strategy, the difference in scores here reveals that the model is not necessarily better. In this case, the two models have the same hyperparameters, and the difference in scores is attributed to the different folds.

The point here is to use the same folds to obtain new scores when fine-tuning hyperparameters with GridSearchCV and RandomizedSearchCV so that the comparison of scores is fair.

Combining GridSearchCV and RandomizedSearchCV

GridSearchCV searches all possible combinations in a hyperparameter grid to find the best results. RandomizedSearchCV selects 10 random hyperparameter combinations by default. RandomizedSearchCV is typically used when GridSearchCV becomes unwieldy because there are too many hyperparameter combinations to exhaustively check each one.

Instead of writing two separate functions for GridSearchCV and RandomizedSearchCV, we will combine them into one streamlined function with the following steps:

1. Import GridSearchCV and RandomizedSearchCV from sklearn.model_ selection:

    ```
    from sklearn.model_selection import GridSearchCV,
    RandomizedSearchCV
    ```

2. Define a grid_search function with the params dictionary as input, along with random=False:

    ```
    def grid_search(params, random=False):
    ```

3. Initialize an XGBoost classifier using the standard defaults:

    ```
    xgb = XGBClassifier(booster='gbtree',
    objective='binary:logistic', random_state=2)
    ```

4. If `random=True`, initialize `RandomizedSearchCV` with `xgb` and the `params` dictionary. Set `n_iter=20` to allow 20 random combinations instead of 10. Otherwise, initialize `GridSearchCV` with the same inputs. Make sure to set `cv=kfold` for consistent results:

```
if random:
    grid = RandomizedSearchCV(xgb, params, cv=kfold,
n_iter=20, n_jobs=-1)

else:
    grid = GridSearchCV(xgb, params, cv=kfold, n_
jobs=-1)
```

5. Fit X and y to the `grid` model:

```
grid.fit(X, y)
```

6. Obtain and print `best_params_`:

```
best_params = grid.best_params_
print("Best params:", best_params)
```

7. Obtain and print `best_score_`:

```
best_score = grid.best_score_
print("Training score: {:.3f}".format(best_score))
```

The `grid_search` function can now be used to fine-tune all hyperparameters.

Tuning XGBoost hyperparameters

There are many XGBoost hyperparameters, some of which have been introduced in previous chapters. The following table summarizes key XGBoost hyperparameters, most of which we cover in this book.

> **Note**
> The XGBoost hyperparameters presented here are not meant to be exhaustive, but they are meant to be comprehensive. For a complete list of hyperparameters, read the official documentation, *XGBoost Parameters*, at `https://xgboost.readthedocs.io/en/latest/parameter.html`.

Following the table, further explanations and examples are provided:

Name	Default	Range	Effect	Notes/Tips
n_estimators	100	[1, inf)	Increasing may improve scores with large data.	The number of trees in the ensemble.
learning_rate alias:eta	0.3	[0, inf)	Decreasing prevents overfitting.	Shrinks the tree weights in each round of boosting.
max_depth	6	[0, inf)	Decreasing prevents overfitting.	The depth of the tree. 0 is an option in a loss-guided growing policy.
gamma alias: min_split_loss	0	[0, inf)	Increasing prevents overfitting.	Low values, usually lower than 10, are standard.
min_child_weight	1	[0, inf)	Increasing prevents overfitting.	The minimum sum of weights required for a node to split.
subsample	1	(0, 1]	Decreasing prevents overfitting.	Limits the percentage of training rows for each boosting round.
colsample_bytree	1	(0, 1]	Decreasing prevents overfitting.	Limits the percentage of training columns for each boosting round.
colsample_bylevel	1	(0, 1]	Decreasing prevents overfitting.	Limits the percentage of columns for each depth level of the tree.
colsample_bynode	1	(0, 1]	Decreasing prevents overfitting.	Limits the percentage of columns to evaluate splits.
scale_pos_weight	1	(0, inf)	Sum(negatives)/ Sum(positives) balances data.	Used for imbalanced datasets. See *Chapter 5, XGBoost Unveiled*, and *Chapter 7, Discovering Exoplanets with XGBoost*.
max_delta_step	0	[0, inf)	Increasing prevents overfitting.	Only recommended for extremely imbalanced datasets.
lambda	1	[0, inf)	Increasing prevents overfitting.	L2 regularization of weights.
alpha	0	[0, inf)	Increasing prevents overfitting.	L1 regularization of weights.
missing	None	(-inf, inf)	Finds optimal null values.	Replace null values with numerical value like -999.0, then set equal to -999.0. See Chapter 5, XGBoost Unveiled.

Figure 6.2 – XGBoost hyperparameter table

Now that the key XGBoost hyperparameters have been presented, let's get to know them better by tuning them one at a time.

Applying XGBoost hyperparameters

The XGBoost hyperparameters presented in this section are frequently fine-tuned by machine learning practitioners. After a brief explanation of each hyperparameter, we will test standard variations using the `grid_search` function defined in the previous section.

n_estimators

Recall that `n_estimators` provides the number of trees in the ensemble. In the case of XGBoost, `n_estimators` is the number of trees trained on the residuals.

Initialize a grid search of `n_estimators` with the default of `100`, then double the number of trees through `800` as follows:

```
grid_search(params={'n_estimators':[100, 200, 400, 800]})
```

The output is as follows:

```
Best params: {'n_estimators': 100}
Best score: 0.78235
```

Since our dataset is small, increasing `n_estimators` did not produce better results. One strategy for finding an ideal value of `n_estimators` is discussed in the *Applying early stopping* section in this chapter.

learning_rate

`learning_rate` shrinks the weights of trees for each round of boosting. By lowering `learning_rate`, more trees are required to produce better scores. Lowering `learning_rate` prevents overfitting because the size of the weights carried forward is smaller.

A default value of `0.3` is used, though previous versions of scikit-learn have used `0.1`. Here is a starting range for `learning_rate` as placed inside our `grid_search` function:

```
grid_search(params={'learning_rate':[0.01, 0.05, 0.1, 0.2, 0.3,
0.4, 0.5]})
```

The output is as follows:

```
Best params: {'learning_rate': 0.05}
Best score: 0.79585
```

Changing the learning rate has resulted in a slight increase. As described in *Chapter 4, From Gradient Boosting to XGBoost*, lowering `learning_rate` may be advantageous when n_estimators goes up.

max_depth

`max_depth` determines the length of the tree, equivalent to the number of rounds of splitting. Limiting `max_depth` prevents overfitting because the individual trees can only grow as far as `max_depth` allows. XGBoost provides a default `max_depth` value of six:

```
grid_search(params={'max_depth':[2, 3, 5, 6, 8]})
```

The output is as follows:

```
Best params: {'max_depth': 2}
Best score: 0.79902
```

Changing `max_depth` from 6 to 2 gave a better score. The lower value for `max_depth` means variance has been reduced.

gamma

Known as a **Lagrange multiplier**, `gamma` provides a threshold that nodes must surpass before making further splits according to the loss function. There is no upper limit to the value of gamma. The default is 0, and anything over 10 is considered very high. Increasing gamma results in a more conservative model:

```
grid_search(params={'gamma':[0, 0.1, 0.5, 1, 2, 5]})
```

The output is as follows:

```
Best params: {'gamma': 0.5}
Best score: 0.79574
```

Changing gamma from 0 to 0.5 has resulted in a slight improvement.

min_child_weight

`min_child_weight` refers to the minimum sum of weights required for a node to split into a child. If the sum of the weights is less than the value of `min_child_weight`, no further splits are made. `min_child_weight` reduces overfitting by increasing its value:

```
grid_search(params={'min_child_weight':[1, 2, 3, 4, 5]})
```

The output is as follows:

```
Best params: {'min_child_weight': 5}
Best score: 0.81219
```

A slight adjustment to `min_child_weight` gives the best results yet.

subsample

The `subsample` hyperparameter limits the percentage of training instances (rows) for each boosting round. Decreasing `subsample` from 100% reduces overfitting:

```
grid_search(params={'subsample':[0.5, 0.7, 0.8, 0.9, 1]})
```

The output is as follows:

```
Best params: {'subsample': 0.8}
Best score: 0.79579
```

The score has improved by a slight amount once again, indicating a small presence of overfitting.

colsample_bytree

Similar to `subsample`, `colsample_bytree` randomly selects particular columns according to the given percentage. `colsample_bytree` is useful for limiting the influence of columns and reducing variance. Note that `colsample_bytree` takes a percentage as input, not the number of columns:

```
grid_search(params={'colsample_bytree':[0.5, 0.7, 0.8, 0.9,
1]})
```

The output is as follows:

```
Best params: {'colsample_bytree': 0.7}
Best score: 0.79902
```

Gains here are minimal at best. You are encouraged to try `colsample_bylevel` and `colsample_bynode` on your own. `colsample_bylevel` randomly selects columns for each tree depth, and `colsample_bynode` randomly selects columns when evaluating each tree split.

Fine-tuning hyperparameters is an art and a science. As with both disciplines, varied approaches work. Next, we will look into early stopping as a specific strategy for fine-tuning `n_estimators`.

Applying early stopping

Early stopping is a general method to limit the number of training rounds in iterative machine learning algorithms. In this section, we look at `eval_set`, `eval_metric`, and `early_stopping_rounds` to apply early stopping.

What is early stopping?

Early stopping provides a limit to the number of rounds that iterative machine learning algorithms train on. Instead of predefining the number of training rounds, early stopping allows training to continue until n consecutive rounds fail to produce any gains, where n is a number decided by the user.

It doesn't make sense to only choose multiples of 100 when looking for `n_estimators`. It's possible that the best value is 737 instead of 700. Finding a value this precise manually can be tiring, especially when hyperparameter adjustments may require changes down the road.

With XGBoost, a score may be determined after each boosting round. Although scores go up and down, eventually scores will level off or move in the wrong direction.

A peak score is reached when all subsequent scores fail to provide any gains. You determine the peak after 10, 20, or 100 training rounds fail to improve upon the score. You choose the number of rounds.

In early stopping, it's important to give the model sufficient time to fail. If the model stops too early, say, after five rounds of no improvement, the model may miss general patterns that it could pick up on later. As with deep learning, where early stopping is used frequently, gradient boosting needs sufficient time to find intricate patterns within data.

For XGBoost, `early_stopping_rounds` is the key parameter for applying early stopping. If `early_stopping_rounds=10`, the model will stop training after 10 consecutive training rounds fail to improve the model. Similarly, if `early_stopping_rounds=100`, training continues until 100 consecutive rounds fail to improve the model.

Now that you understand what early stopping is, let's take a look at `eval_set` and `eval_metric`.

eval_set and eval_metric

early_stopping_rounds is not a hyperparameter, but a strategy for optimizing the n_estimators hyperparameter.

Normally when choosing hyperparameters, a test score is given after all boosting rounds are complete. To use early stopping, we need a test score after each round.

eval_metric and eval_set may be used as parameters for .fit to generate test scores for each training round. eval_metric provides the scoring method, commonly 'error' for classification, and 'rmse' for regression. eval_set provides the test to be evaluated, commonly X_test and y_test.

The following six steps display an evaluation metric for each round of training with the default n_estimators=100:

1. Split the data into training and test sets:

    ```
    from sklearn.model_selection import train_test_split
    X_train, X_test, y_train, y_test = train_test_split(X, y,
    random_state=2)
    ```

2. Initialize the model:

    ```
    model = XGBClassifier(booster='gbtree',
    objective='binary:logistic', random_state=2)
    ```

3. Declare eval_set:

    ```
    eval_set = [(X_test, y_test)]
    ```

4. Declare eval_metric:

    ```
    eval_metric = 'error'
    ```

5. Fit the model with eval_metric and eval_set:

    ```
    model.fit(X_train, y_train, eval_metric=eval_metric,
    eval_set=eval_set)
    ```

6. Check the final score:

    ```
    y_pred = model.predict(X_test)
    accuracy = accuracy_score(y_test, y_pred)
    print("Accuracy: %.2f%%" % (accuracy * 100.0))
    ```

Here is the truncated output:

```
[0]    validation_0-error:0.15790
[1]    validation_0-error:0.10526
[2]    validation_0-error:0.11842
[3]    validation_0-error:0.13158
[4]    validation_0-error:0.11842
...
[96]   validation_0-error:0.17105
[97]   validation_0-error:0.17105
[98]   validation_0-error:0.17105
[99]   validation_0-error:0.17105
Accuracy: 82.89%
```

Do not get too excited about the score as we have not used cross-validation. In fact, we know that StratifiedKFold cross-validation gives a mean accuracy of 78% when n_estimators=100. The disparity in scores comes from the difference in test sets.

early_stopping_rounds

early_stopping_rounds is an optional parameter to include with eval_metric and eval_set when fitting a model.

Let's try early_stopping_rounds=10.

The previous code is repeated with early_stopping_rounds=10 added in:

```
model = XGBClassifier(booster='gbtree',
objective='binary:logistic', random_state=2)
eval_set = [(X_test, y_test)]
eval_metric='error'
model.fit(X_train, y_train, eval_metric="error", eval_set=eval_
set, early_stopping_rounds=10, verbose=True)
y_pred = model.predict(X_test)
accuracy = accuracy_score(y_test, y_pred)
print("Accuracy: %.2f%%" % (accuracy * 100.0))
```

The output is as follows:

```
[0]  validation_0-error:0.15790
Will train until validation_0-error hasn't improved in 10
rounds.
```

```
[1]  validation_0-error:0.10526
[2]  validation_0-error:0.11842
[3]  validation_0-error:0.13158
[4]  validation_0-error:0.11842
[5]  validation_0-error:0.14474
[6]  validation_0-error:0.14474
[7]  validation_0-error:0.14474
[8]  validation_0-error:0.14474
[9]  validation_0-error:0.14474
[10] validation_0-error:0.14474
[11] validation_0-error:0.15790
Stopping. Best iteration:
[1]  validation_0-error:0.10526
```

```
Accuracy: 89.47%
```

The result may come as a surprise. Early stopping reveals that n_estimators=2 gives the best result, which may be an account of the test fold.

Why only two trees? By only giving the model 10 rounds to improve upon accuracy, it's possible that patterns within the data have not yet been discovered. However, the dataset is very small, so it's possible that two boosting rounds gives the best possible result.

A more thorough approach is to use larger values, say, n_estimators = 5000 and early_stopping_rounds=100.

By setting early_stopping_rounds=100, you are guaranteed to reach the default of 100 boosted trees presented by XGBoost.

Here is the code that gives a maximum of 5,000 trees and that will stop after 100 consecutive rounds fail to find any improvement:

```
model = XGBClassifier(random_state=2, n_estimators=5000)
eval_set = [(X_test, y_test)]
eval_metric="error"
model.fit(X_train, y_train, eval_metric=eval_metric, eval_
set=eval_set, early_stopping_rounds=100)
y_pred = model.predict(X_test)
accuracy = accuracy_score(y_test, y_pred)
print("Accuracy: %.2f%%" % (accuracy * 100.0))
```

Here is the truncated output:

```
[0]  validation_0-error:0.15790
Will train until validation_0-error hasn't improved in 100
rounds.
[1]  validation_0-error:0.10526
[2]  validation_0-error:0.11842
[3]  validation_0-error:0.13158
[4]  validation_0-error:0.11842
...
[98] validation_0-error:0.17105
[99] validation_0-error:0.17105
[100]         validation_0-error:0.17105
[101]         validation_0-error:0.17105
Stopping. Best iteration:
[1]  validation_0-error:0.10526


Accuracy: 89.47%
```

After 100 rounds of boosting, the score provided by two trees remains the best.

As a final note, consider that early stopping is particularly useful for large datasets when it's unclear how high you should aim.

Now, let's use the results from early stopping with all the hyperparameters previously tuned to generate the best possible model.

Combining hyperparameters

It's time to combine all the components of this chapter to improve upon the 78% score obtained through cross-validation.

As you know, there is no one-size-fits-all approach to hyperparameter fine-tuning. One approach is to input all hyperparameter ranges with `RandomizedSearchCV`. A more systematic approach is to tackle hyperparameters one at a time, using the best results for subsequent iterations. All approaches have advantages and limitations. Regardless of strategy, it's essential to try multiple variations and make adjustments when the data comes in.

One hyperparameter at a time

Using a systematic approach, we add one hyperparameter at a time, aggregating results along the way.

n_estimators

Even though the n_estimators value of 2 gave the best result, it's worth trying a range on the grid_search function, which uses cross-validation:

```
grid_search(params={'n_estimators':[2, 25, 50, 75, 100]})
```

The output is as follows:

```
Best params: {'n_estimators': 50}
Best score: 0.78907
```

It's no surprise that n_estimators=50, between the previous best value of 2, and the default of 100, gives the best result. Since cross-validation was not used in early stopping, the results here are different.

max_depth

The max_depth hyperparameter determines the length of each tree. Here is a nice range:

```
grid_search(params={'max_depth':[1, 2, 3, 4, 5, 6, 7, 8], 'n_
estimators':[50]})
```

The output is as follows:

```
Best params: {'max_depth': 1, 'n_estimators': 50}
Best score: 0.83869
```

This is a very substanial gain. A tree with a depth of 1 is called a **decision tree stump**. We have gained four percentage points from our baseline model by adjusting just two hyperparameters.

A limitation with the approach of keeping the top values is that we may miss out on better combinations. Perhaps n_estimators=2 or n_esimtators=100 gives better results in conjunction with max_depth. Let's find out:

```
grid_search(params={'max_depth':[1, 2, 3, 4, 6, 7, 8], 'n_
estimators':[2, 50, 100]})
```

The output is as follows:

```
Best params: {'max_depth': 1, 'n_estimators': 50}
Best score: 0.83869
```

`n_estimators=50` and `max_depth=1` still give the best results, so we will use them going forward, returning to our early stopping analysis later.

learning_rate

Since `n_esimtators` is reasonably low, adjusting `learning_rate` may improve results. Here is a standard range:

```
grid_search(params={'learning_rate':[0.01, 0.05, 0.1, 0.2, 0.3,
0.4, 0.5], 'max_depth':[1], 'n_estimators':[50]})
```

The output is as follows:

```
Best params: {'learning_rate': 0.3, 'max_depth': 1, 'n_
estimators': 50}
Best score: 0.83869
```

This is the same score as previously obtained. Note that a `learning_rate` value of 0.3 is the default value provided by XGBoost.

min_child_weight

Let's see whether adjusting the sum of weights required to split into child nodes increases the score:

```
grid_search(params={'min_child_weight':[1, 2, 3, 4, 5], 'max_
depth':[1], 'n_estimators':[50]})
```

The output is as follows:

```
Best params: {'max_depth': 1, 'min_child_weight': 1, 'n_
estimators': 50}
Best score: 0.83869
```

In this case, the best score is the same. Note that 1 is the default for `min_child_weight`.

subsample

If reducing variance is beneficial, `subsample` may work by limiting the percentage of samples. In this case, however, there are only 303 samples to begin with, and a small number of samples makes it difficult to adjust hyperparameters to improve scores. Here is the code:

```
grid_search(params={'subsample':[0.5, 0.6, 0.7, 0.8, 0.9, 1],
'max_depth':[1], 'n_estimators':[50]})
```

The output is as follows:

```
Best params: {'max_depth': 1, 'n_estimators': 50, 'subsample':
1}
Best score: 0.83869
```

Still no gains. At this point, you may be wondering whether new gains would have continued with `n_esimtators=2`.

Let's find out by using a comprehensive grid search of the values used thus far.

```
grid_search(params={'subsample':[0.5, 0.6, 0.7, 0.8, 0.9, 1],
                    'min_child_weight':[1, 2, 3, 4, 5],
                    'learning_rate':[0.1, 0.2, 0.3, 0.4, 0.5],
                    'max_depth':[1, 2, 3, 4, 5],
                    'n_estimators':[2]})
```

The output is as follows:

```
Best params: {'learning_rate': 0.5, 'max_depth': 2, 'min_child_
weight': 4, 'n_estimators': 2, 'subsample': 0.9}
Best score: 0.81224
```

It's not surprising that a classifier with only two trees performs worse. Even though the initial scores were better, it does not go through enough iterations for the hyperparameters to make significant adjustments.

Hyperparameter adjustments

When shifting directions with hyperparameters, `RandomizedSearchCV` is useful due to the extensive range of inputs.

Here is a range of hyperparameter values combining new inputs with previous knowledge. Limiting ranges with `RandomizedSearchCV` increases the odds of finding the best combination. Recall that `RandomizedSearchCV` is useful when the total number of combinations is too time-consuming for a grid search. There are 4,500 possible combinations with the following options:

```
grid_search(params={'subsample':[0.5, 0.6, 0.7, 0.8, 0.9, 1],
                    'min_child_weight':[1, 2, 3, 4, 5],
                    'learning_rate':[0.1, 0.2, 0.3, 0.4, 0.5],
                    'max_depth':[1, 2, 3, 4, 5, None],
                    'n_estimators':[2, 25, 50, 75, 100]},
                    random=True)
```

The output is as follows:

```
Best params: {'subsample': 0.6, 'n_estimators': 25, 'min_child_
weight': 4, 'max_depth': 4, 'learning_rate': 0.5}
Best score: 0.82208
```

This is interesting. Different values are obtaining good results.

We use the hyperparameters from the best score going forward.

Colsample

Now, let's try `colsample_bytree`, `colsample_bylevel`, and `colsample_bynode`, in that order.

colsample_bytree

Let's start with `colsample_bytree`:

```
grid_search(params={'colsample_bytree':[0.5, 0.6, 0.7, 0.8,
0.9, 1], 'max_depth':[1], 'n_estimators':[50]})
```

The output is as follows:

```
Best params: {'colsample_bytree': 1, 'max_depth': 1, 'n_
estimators': 50}
Best score: 0.83869
```

The score has not improved. Next, try `colsample_bylevel`.

colsample_bylevel

Use the following code to try out `colsample_bylevel`:

```
grid_search(params={'colsample_bylevel':[0.5, 0.6, 0.7, 0.8,
0.9, 1],'max_depth':[1], 'n_estimators':[50]})
```

The output is as follows:

```
Best params: {'colsample_bylevel': 1, 'max_depth': 1, 'n_
estimators': 50}
Best score: 0.83869
```

Still no gain.

It seems that we are peaking out with the shallow dataset. Let's try a different approach. Instead of using `colsample_bynode` alone, let's tune all colsamples together.

colsample_bynode

Try the following code:

```
grid_search(params={'colsample_bynode':[0.5, 0.6, 0.7, 0.8,
0.9, 1], 'colsample_bylevel':[0.5, 0.6, 0.7, 0.8, 0.9,
1], 'colsample_bytree':[0.5, 0.6, 0.7, 0.8, 0.9, 1], 'max_
depth':[1], 'n_estimators':[50]})
```

The output is as follows:

```
Best params: {'colsample_bylevel': 0.9, 'colsample_bynode':
0.5, 'colsample_bytree': 0.8, 'max_depth': 1, 'n_estimators':
50}
Best score: 0.84852
```

Outstanding. Working together, the colsamples have combined to deliver the highest score yet, 5 percentage points higher than the original.

gamma

The last hyperparameter that we will attempt to fine-tune is gamma. Here is a range of gamma values designed to reduce overfitting:

```
grid_search(params={'gamma':[0, 0.01, 0.05, 0.1, 0.5,
1, 2, 3], 'colsample_bylevel':[0.9], 'colsample_
bytree':[0.8], 'colsample_bynode':[0.5], 'max_depth':[1], 'n_
estimators':[50]})
```

The output is as follows:

```
Best params: {'colsample_bylevel': 0.9, 'colsample_bynode':
0.5, 'colsample_bytree': 0.8, 'gamma': 0, 'max_depth': 1, 'n_
estimators': 50}
Best score: 0.84852
```

gamma remains at the default value of 0.

Since our best score is over five percentage points higher than the original, no small feat with XGBoost, we will stop here.

Summary

In this chapter, you prepared for hyperparameter fine-tuning by establishing a baseline XGBoost model using StratifiedKFold. Then, you combined GridSearchCV and RandomizedSearchCV to form one powerful function. You learned the standard definitions, ranges, and applications of key XGBoost hyperparameters, in addition to a new technique called early stopping. You synthesized all functions, hyperparameters, and techniques to fine-tune the heart disease dataset, gaining an impressive five percentage points from the default XGBoost classifier.

XGBoost hyperparameter fine-tuning takes time to master, and you are well on your way. Fine-tuning hyperparameters is a key skill that separates machine learning experts from machine learning novices. Knowledge of XGBoost hyperparameters is not just useful, it's essential to get the most out of the machine learning models that you build.

Congratulations on completing this important chapter.

Next, we present a case study of XGBoost regression from beginning to end, highlighting the power, range, and applications of XGBClassifier.

7
Discovering Exoplanets with XGBoost

In this chapter, you will journey through the stars in an attempt to discover exoplanets with `XGBClassifier` as your guide.

The reason for this chapter is twofold. The first is that it's important to gain practice in a top-to-bottom study using XGBoost since for all practical purposes, that is what you will normally do with XGBoost. Although you may not discover exoplanets with XGBoost on your own, the strategies that you implement here, which include choosing the correct scoring metric and carefully fine-tuning hyperparameters with that scoring metric in mind, apply to any practical use of XGBoost. The second reason for this particular case study is that it's essential for all machine learning practitioners to be proficient at competently handling imbalanced datasets, which is the key theme of this particular chapter.

Specifically, you will gain new skills in using the **confusion matrix** and the **classification report**, understanding **precision versus recall**, resampling data, applying `scale_pos_weight`, and more. Getting the best results from `XGBClassifier` will require careful analysis of the imbalanced data and clear expectations of the goal at hand. In this chapter, `XGBClassifier` is the centerpiece of a top-to-bottom study analyzing light data to predict exoplanets in the universe.

In this chapter, we cover the following main topics:

- Searching for exoplanets
- Analyzing the confusion matrix
- Resampling imbalanced data
- Tuning and scaling XGBClassifier

Technical requirements

The code for this chapter may be found at `https://github.com/PacktPublishing/Hands-On-Gradient-Boosting-with-XGBoost-and-Scikit-learn/tree/master/Chapter07`.

Searching for exoplanets

In this section, we'll begin the search for exoplanets by analyzing the Exoplanets dataset. We'll provide historical context for the discovery of exoplanets before attempting to detect them via plotting and observing light graphs. Plotting time series is a valuable machine learning skill that may be used to gain insights into any time series datasets. Finally, we'll make initial predictions using machine learning before revealing a glaring shortcoming.

Historical background

Astronomers have been gathering information from light since antiquity. With the advent of the telescope, astronomical knowledge surged in the 17th century. The combination of telescopes and mathematical models empowered 18th-century astronomers to predict planetary locations and eclipses within our own solar system with great precision.

In the 20th century, astronomical research continued with more advanced technology and more complex mathematics. Planets revolving around other stars, called exoplanets, were discovered in the habitable zone. A planet in the habitable zone means that the exoplanet's location and size are comparable to Earth, and therefore it's a candidate for harboring liquid water and life.

These exoplanets are not viewed directly via telescopes, rather they are inferred through periodic changes in starlight. An object that periodically revolves around a star that is large enough to block a detectable fraction of starlight is by definition a planet. Discovering exoplanets from starlight requires measuring light fluctuations over extended intervals of time. Since the change in light is often very minute, it's not easy to determine whether an exoplanet is actually present.

In this chapter, we are going to predict whether stars have exoplanets with XGBoost.

The Exoplanet dataset

You previewed the Exoplanet dataset in *Chapter 4, From Gradient Boosting to XGBoost*, to uncover the time advantage that XGBoost has over comparable ensemble methods for large datasets. In this chapter, we will take a deeper look at the Exoplanet dataset.

This Exoplanet dataset is taken from *NASA Kepler Space Telescope, Campaign 3, Summer 2016*. Information about the data source is available on Kaggle at https://www.kaggle.com/keplersmachines/kepler-labelled-time-series-data. Of all the stars in the dataset, 5,050 do not have exoplanets, while 37 have exoplanets.

The 300+ columns and 5,000+ rows equal 1.5 million plus entries. When multiplied by 100 XGBoost trees, this is 150 million plus data points. To expedite matters, we start with a subset of the data. Starting with a subset is a common practice when dealing with large datasets, to save time.

pd.read_csv contains an nrows parameter, used to limit the number of rows. Note that nrows=n selects the first *n* rows of the dataset. Depending on the data structure, additional code may be required to ensure that the subset is representative of the whole. Let's get started.

Import pandas, then load exoplanets.csv with nrows=400. Then view the data:

```
import pandas as pd
df = pd.read_csv('exoplanets.csv', nrows=400)
df.head()
```

The output should appear as follows:

	LABEL	FLUX.1	FLUX.2	FLUX.3	FLUX.4	FLUX.5	FLUX.6	FLUX.7	FLUX.8	FLUX.9	...	FLUX.3188	FLUX.3189	FLUX.3190	FLUX.3191	FLUX.3192
0	2	93.85	83.81	20.10	-26.98	-39.56	-124.71	-135.18	-96.27	-79.89	...	-78.07	-102.15	-102.15	25.13	48.57
1	2	-38.88	-33.83	-58.54	-40.09	-79.31	-72.81	-86.55	-85.33	-83.97	...	-3.28	-32.21	-32.21	-24.89	-4.86
2	2	532.64	535.92	513.73	496.92	456.45	466.00	464.50	486.39	436.56	...	-71.69	13.31	13.31	-29.89	-20.88
3	2	326.52	347.39	302.35	298.13	317.74	312.70	322.33	311.31	312.42	...	5.71	-3.73	-3.73	30.05	20.03
4	2	-1107.21	-1112.59	-1118.95	-1095.10	-1057.55	-1034.48	-998.34	-1022.71	-989.57	...	-594.37	-401.66	-401.66	-357.24	-443.76

5 rows × 3198 columns

Figure 7.1 – Exoplanet DataFrame

The large number of columns (**3198**) listed underneath the DataFrame makes sense. When looking for periodic changes in light, you need enough data points to find periodicity. The revolutions of planets within our own solar system range from 88 days (Mercury) to 165 years (Neptune). If exoplanets are to be detected, data points must be examined frequently enough so as not to miss the transit of the planet when the planet orbits in front of the star.

Since there are only 37 exoplanet stars, it's important to know how many exoplanet stars are contained in the subset.

The .value_counts() method determines the number of each value in a particular column. Since we are interested in the LABEL column, the number of exoplanet stars may be found using the following code:

```
df['LABEL'].value_counts()
```

The output is as follows:

```
1     363
2      37
Name: LABEL, dtype: int64
```

All exoplanet stars are included in our subset. As .head() reveals, the exoplanet stars are at the beginning.

Graphing the data

The expectation is that when an exoplanet blocks light from a star, the light flux goes down. If drops in flux occur periodically, an exoplanet is likely the reason since, by definition, a planet is a large object orbiting a star.

Let's visualize the data by graphing:

1. Import `matplotlib`, `numpy`, and `seaborn`, then set `seaborn` to the dark grid as follows:

```
import matplotlib.pyplot as plt
import numpy as np
import seaborn as sns
sns.set()
```

When plotting light fluctuations, the LABEL column is not of interest. The LABEL column will be our target column for machine learning.

> **Tip**
>
> `seaborn` is recommended to improve your `matplotlib` graphs. The `sns.set()` default provides a nice light-gray background with a white grid. Furthermore, many standard graphs, such as `plt.hist()`, look more aesthetically pleasing with this Seaborn default in place. For more information on Seaborn, check out `https://seaborn.pydata.org/`.

2. Now, let's split the data into X, the predictor columns (which we will graph), and y, the target column. Note that for the Exoplanet dataset, the target column is the first column, not the last:

```
X = df.iloc[:,1:]
y = df.iloc[:,0]
```

3. Now write a function called `light_plot`, which takes as input the index of the data (the row) that plots all data points as *y* coordinates (the light flux), and the number of observations as *x* coordinates. Use appropriate labels for the graph as follows:

```
def light_plot(index):
    y_vals = X.iloc[index]
    x_vals = np.arange(len(y_vals))
    plt.figure(figsize=(15,8))
    plt.xlabel('Number of Observations')
    plt.ylabel('Light Flux')
    plt.title('Light Plot ' + str(index), size=15)
    plt.plot(x_vals, y_vals)
    plt.show()
```

4. Now, call the function to plot the first index. This star has been classified as an exoplanet star:

```
light_plot(0)
```

Here is the expected graph for our first light plot:

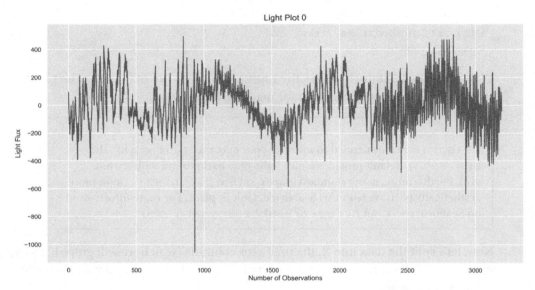

Figure 7.2 – Light plot 0. Periodic drops in light are present

There are clear drops in the data that occur periodically. However, concluding that an exoplanet is present is not obvious from this graph alone.

5. By comparison, contrast this plot with the 37th index, the first non-exoplanet star in the dataset:

```
light_plot(37)
```

Here is the expected graph for the 37th index:

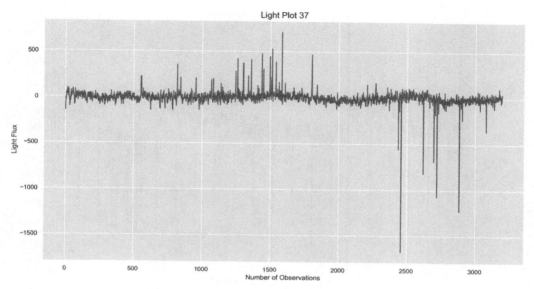

Figure 7.3 – Light plot 37

Increases and decreases in light are present, but not over the entire range.

There are clear drops in the data, but they are not periodic throughout the graph. The frequency of the drops does not recur consistently. Based on this evidence alone, it's not enough to determine the presence of an exoplanet.

6. Here is the second light plot of an exoplanet star:

```
light_plot(1)
```

Here is the expected graph for the first index:

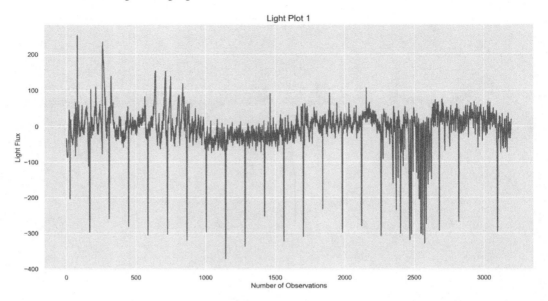

Figure 7.4 – Clear periodic drops indicate the presence of an exoplanet

The plot shows clear periodicity with large drops in light flux making an exoplanet extremely likely! If all the plots were this clear, machine learning would be unnecessary. As the other plots reveal, concluding that an exoplanet is present is usually not this clear.

The purpose here is to highlight the data and the difficulty of classifying exoplanets based on visual graphs alone. Astronomers use different methods to classify exoplanets, and machine learning is one such method.

Although this dataset is a time series, the goal is not to predict light flux for the next unit of time, but rather to classify the star based on all the data. In this respect, machine learning classifiers may be used to predict whether a given star hosts an exoplanet. The idea is to train the classifier on the provided data, which may in turn be used to predict exoplanets on new data. In this chapter, we attempt to classify the exoplanets within the data using XGBClassifier. Before we move on to classify the data, we must first prepare the data.

Preparing data

We witnessed in the previous section that not all graphs are clear enough to determine the existence of an exoplanet. This is where machine learning may be of great benefit. To begin, let's prepare the data for machine learning:

1. First, we need the dataset to be numerical with no null values. Check the data types and null values using `df.info()`:

```
df.info()
```

Here is the expected output:

```
<class 'pandas.core.frame.DataFrame'>
RangeIndex: 400 entries, 0 to 399
Columns: 3198 entries, LABEL to FLUX.3197
dtypes: float64(3197), int64(1)
memory usage: 9.8 MB
```

The subset contains 3,197 floats, and 1 int, so all columns are numerical. No information is provided about null values due to the large number of columns.

2. We can use the `.sum()` method twice on `.null()` to sum all null values, once to sum the null values in each column, and the second time to sum all columns:

```
df.isnull().sum().sum()
```

The expected output is as follows:

```
0
```

Since there are no null values and the data is numerical, we will proceed with machine learning.

Initial XGBClassifier

To start building an initial XGBClassifier, take the following steps:

1. Import `XGBClassifier` and `accuracy_score`:

```
from xgboost import XGBClassifier
from sklearn.metrics import accuracy_score
```

2. Split the model into a training and test set:

```
from sklearn.model_selection import train_test_split
X_train, X_test, y_train, y_test = train_test_split(X, y,
random_state=2)
```

3. Build and score the model using `booster='gbtree'`,
    `objective='binary:logistic'`, and `random_state=2` as parameters:

```
model = XGBClassifier(booster='gbtree',
objective='binary:logistic', random_state=2)
model.fit(X_train, y_train)
y_pred = model.predict(X_test)
score = accuracy_score(y_pred, y_test)
print('Score: ' + str(score))
```

The score is as follows:

```
Score: 0.89
```

Correctly classifying 89% of stars seems like a good starting point, but there is one glaring issue.

Can you figure it out?

Imagine that you present your model to your astronomy professor. Assuming your professor is well-trained in data analysis, your professor would respond, "I see that you obtained 89% accuracy, but exoplanets represent 10% of the data, so how do you know your results aren't better than a model that predicts no exoplanets 100% of the time?"

Therein lies the issue. If the model determines that no stars contain exoplanets, its accuracy will be approximately 90% since 9 out of 10 stars do not contain exoplanets.

With imbalanced data, accuracy isn't enough.

Analyzing the confusion matrix

A confusion matrix is a table that summarizes the correct and incorrect predictions of a classification model. The confusion matrix is ideal for analyzing imbalanced data because it provides more information on which predictions are correct, and which predictions are wrong.

For the Exoplanet subset, here is the expected output for a perfect confusion matrix:

```
array([[88,  0],
       [ 0,  12]])
```

When all positive entries are on the left diagonal, the model has 100% accuracy. A perfect confusion matrix here predicts 88 non-exoplanet stars and 12 exoplanet stars. Notice that the confusion matrix does not provide labels, but in this case, labels may be inferred based on the size.

Before getting into further detail, let's see the actual confusion matrix using scikit-learn.

confusion_matrix

Import `confusion_matrix` from `sklearn.metrics` as follows:

```
from sklearn.metrics import confusion_matrix
```

Run `confusion_matrix` with `y_test` and `y_pred` as inputs (variables obtained in the previous section), making sure to put `y_test` first:

```
confusion_matrix(y_test, y_pred)
```

The output is as follows:

```
array([[86,  2],
       [9,  3]])
```

The numbers on the diagonals of the confusion matrix reveal 86 correct non-exoplanet-star predictions and only 3 correct exoplanet star predictions.

In the upper-right corner of the matrix, the number 2 reveals that two non-exoplanet-stars were misclassified as exoplanet stars. Similarly, in the bottom-left corner of the matrix, the number 9 reveals that 9 exoplanet stars were misclassified as non-exoplanet-stars.

When analyzed horizontally, 86 of 88 non-exoplanet stars were correctly classified, while only 3 of 12 exoplanet stars were correctly classified.

As you can see, the confusion matrix reveals important details of the model's predictions that an accuracy score is unable to pick up on.

classification_report

The various percentages from the numbers revealed in the confusion matrix in the previous section are contained within a classification report. Let's view the classification report:

1. Import `classification_report` from `sklearn.metrics`:

    ```
    from sklearn.metrics import classification_report
    ```

2. Place `y_test` and `y_pred` inside `clasification_report`, making sure to put `y_test` first. Then place `classification_report` inside the global print function to keep the output aligned and easy to read:

    ```
    print(classification_report(y_test, y_pred))
    ```

Here is the expected output:

	precision	recall	f1-score	support
1	0.91	0.98	0.94	88
2	0.60	0.25	0.35	12
accuracy			0.89	100
macro avg	0.75	0.61	0.65	100
weighted avg	0.87	0.89	0.87	100

It's important to understand what the preceding scores mean, so let's review them one at a time.

Precision

Precision gives the predictions of the positive cases (2s) that are actually correct. It's technically defined in terms of true positives and false positives.

True positives

Here are a definition and example of true positives:

- Definition – Number of labels correctly predicted as positive.
- Example – 2s are correctly predicted as 2s.

False positives

Here are a definition and example of false positives:

- Definition – Number of positive labels incorrectly predicted as negative.

- Example – For exoplanet stars, 2s are incorrectly predicted as 1s.

The definition of precision is most often referred to in its mathematical form as follows:

$$precision = \frac{TP}{TP + FP}$$

Here TP stands for true positive and FP stands for false positive.

In the Exoplanet dataset, we have the following two mathematical forms:

$$precision \, of \, exoplanet \, stars = \frac{3}{3 + 2} = 0.6$$

and

$$precision \, of \, nonexpolanet \, stars = \frac{86}{86 + 9} = 0.91.$$

Precision gives the percentage of correct predictions for each target class. Now let's review other key scoring metrics that the classification report reveals.

Recall

Recall gives you the percentage of positive cases that your predictions uncovered. Recall is the number of true positives divided by the true positives plus false negatives.

False negatives

Here are a definition and example of false negatives:

- Definition – Number of labels incorrectly predicted as negative.

- Example – For exoplanet star predictions, 2s are incorrectly predicted as 1s.

In mathematical form, this looks as follows:

$$recall = \frac{TP}{TP + FN}$$

Here TP stands for true positive and FN stands for false negative.

In the Exoplanet dataset, we have the following:

$$recall\ of\ exoplanet\ stars = \frac{3}{3+9} = 0.25$$

and

$$recall\ of\ nonexoplanet\ stars = \frac{86}{86+2} = 0.98$$

Recall tells you how many of the positive cases were found. In the exoplanet case, only 25% of exoplanets have been found.

F1 score

The F1 score is the harmonic mean between precision and recall. The harmonic mean is used because precision and recall are based on different denominators and the harmonic mean evens them out. When precision and recall are equally important, the F1 score is best. Note that the F1 score ranges from 0 to 1 with 1 being the highest.

Alternative scoring methods

Precision, recall, and the F1 score are alternative scoring methods provided by scikit-learn. A list of standard scoring methods may be found in the official documentation at `https://scikit-learn.org/stable/modules/model_evaluation.html`.

> **Tip**
>
> Accuracy is often not the best choice for classification datasets. Another popular scoring method is `roc_auc_score`, the area under the curve of the receiving operator characteristic. As with most classification scoring methods, the closer to 1, the better the results. See `https://scikit-learn.org/stable/modules/generated/sklearn.metrics.roc_auc_score.html#sklearn.metrics.roc_auc_score` for more information.

When choosing a scoring method, it's critical to understand the goal. The goal in the Exoplanet dataset is to find exoplanets. This is obvious. What is not obvious is how to select the best scoring method to achieve the desired results.

Imagine two different scenarios:

- Scenario 1: Of the 4 exoplanet stars the machine learning model predicts, 3 are actually exoplanet stars: 3/4 = 75% precision.

- Scenario 2: Of the 12 exoplanet stars, the model correctly predicts 8 exoplanet stars (8/12 = 66% recall).

Which is more desirable?

The answer is that it depends. Recall is ideal for flagging potential positive cases (exoplanets) with the goal of finding them all. Precision is ideal for ensuring that the predictions (exoplanets) are indeed positive.

Astronomers are unlikely to announce that an exoplanet has been discovered just because a machine learning model says so. They are more likely to carefully examine potential exoplanet stars before confirming or refuting the claim based on additional evidence.

Assuming that the goal of the machine learning model is to find as many exoplanets as possible, recall is an excellent choice. Why? Recall tells us how many of the 12 exoplanet stars have been found (2/12, 5/12, 12/12). Let's try to find them all.

> **Precision note**
>
> A higher percentage of precision does not indicate more exoplanet stars. For instance, a recall of 1/1 is 100%, but it only finds one exoplanet.

recall_score

As indicated in the previous section, we will proceed with recall as the scoring method for the Exoplanet dataset to find as many exoplanets as possible. Let's begin:

1. Import recall_score from sklearn.metrics:

   ```
   from sklearn.metrics import recall_score
   ```

   By default, recall_score reports the recall score of the positive class, typically labeled 1. It is unusual for the positive class to be labeled 2 and for the negative class to be labeled 1 as is the case with the Exoplanet dataset.

2. To obtain the recall_score value of exoplanet stars, input y_test and y_pred as parameters for recall_score along with pos_label=2:

   ```
   recall_score(y_test, y_pred, pos_label=2)
   ```

The score of exoplanet stars is as follows:

```
0.25
```

This is the same percentage given by the classification report under the recall score of 2, which is the exoplanet stars. Going forward, instead of using `accuracy_score`, we will use `recall_score` with the preceding parameters as our scoring metric.

Next, let's learn about resampling, an important strategy for improving the scores of imbalanced datasets.

Resampling imbalanced data

Now that we have an appropriate scoring method to discover exoplanets, it's time to explore strategies such as resampling, undersampling, and oversampling for correcting the imbalanced data causing the low recall score.

Resampling

One strategy to counteract imbalanced data is to resample the data. It's possible to undersample the data by reducing rows of the majority class and to oversample the data by repeating rows of the minority class.

Undersampling

Our exploration began by selecting 400 rows from 5,087. This is an example of undersampling since the subset contains fewer rows than the original.

Let's write a function that allows us to undersample the data by any number of rows. This function should return the recall score so that we can see how undersampling changes the results. We will begin with the scoring function.

The scoring function

The following function takes XGBClassifier and the number of rows as input and produces the confusion matrix, classification report, and recall score of exoplanet stars as output.

Here are the steps:

1. Define a function, `xgb_clf`, that takes `model`, the machine learning model, and `nrows`, the number of rows, as input:

    ```
    def xgb_clf(model, nrows):
    ```

2. Load the DataFrame with `nrows`, then split the data into `X` and `y` and training and test sets:

```
df = pd.read_csv('exoplanets.csv', nrows=nrows)
X = df.iloc[:,1:]
y = df.iloc[:,0]
X_train, X_test, y_train, y_test = train_test_
split(X, y, random_state=2)
```

3. Initialize the model, fit the model to the training set, and score it with the test set using `y_test`, `y_pred`, and `pos_label=2` for `recall_score` as input:

```
model.fit(X_train, y_train)
y_pred = xg_clf.predict(X_test)
score = recall_score(y_test, y_pred, pos_label=2)
```

4. Print the confusion matrix and classification report, and return the score:

```
print(confusion_matrix(y_test, y_pred))
print(classification_report(y_test, y_pred))
return score
```

Now, we can undersample the number of rows and see how the scores change.

Undersampling nrows

Let's start by doubling `nrows` to `800`. This is still undersampling since the original dataset has `5087` rows:

```
xgb_clf(XGBClassifier(random_state=2), nrows=800)
```

This is the expected output:

```
[[189    1]
 [  9    1]]
```

	precision	recall	f1-score	support
1	0.95	0.99	0.97	190
2	0.50	0.10	0.17	10
accuracy			0.95	200
macro avg	0.73	0.55	0.57	200

weighted avg	0.93	0.95	0.93	200

```
0.1
```

Despite the near-perfect recall for non-exoplanet stars, the confusion matrix reveals that only 1 of 10 exoplanet stars have been recalled.

Next, decrease `nrows` from `400` to `200`:

```
xgb_clf(XGBClassifier(random_state=2), nrows=200)
```

This is the expected output:

```
[[37  0]
 [ 8  5]]
```

	precision	recall	f1-score	support
1	0.82	1.00	0.90	37
2	1.00	0.38	0.56	13
accuracy			0.84	50
macro avg	0.91	0.69	0.73	50
weighted avg	0.87	0.84	0.81	50

This is a little better. By decreasing n_rows the recall has gone up.

Let's see what happens if we balance the classes precisely. Since there are 37 exoplanet-stars, 37 non-exoplanet stars balance the data.

Run the `xgb_clf` function with `nrows=74`:

```
xgb_clf(XGBClassifier(random_state=2), nrows=74)
```

This is the expected output:

```
[[6 2]
 [5 6]]
```

	precision	recall	f1-score	support
1	0.55	0.75	0.63	8
2	0.75	0.55	0.63	11

accuracy			0.63	19
macro avg	0.65	0.65	0.63	19
weighted avg	0.66	0.63	0.63	19

```
0.545454545454545454
```

These results are respectable, even though the subset is much smaller.

Next, let's see what happens when we apply the strategy of oversampling.

Oversampling

Another resampling technique is oversampling. Instead of eliminating rows, oversampling adds rows by copying and redistributing the positive cases.

Although the original dataset has over 5,000 rows, we continue to use `nrows=400` as our starting point to expedite the process.

When `nrows=400`, the ratio of positive to negative cases is 10 to 1. We need 10 times as many positive cases to obtain a balance.

Our strategy is as follows:

- Create a new DataFrame that copies the positive cases nine times.
- Concatenate a new DataFrame with the original to obtain a 10-10 ratio.

Before proceeding, a warning is in order. If the data is resampled before splitting it into training and test sets, the recall score will be inflated. Can you see why?

When resampling, nine copies will be made of the positive cases. After splitting this data into training and test sets, copies are likely contained in both sets. So, the test set will contain most of the same data points as the training set.

The appropriate strategy is to split the data into a training and test set first and then to resample the data. As done previously, we can use X_train, X_test, y_train, and y_test. Let's start:

1. Merge X_train and y_train on the left and right index with pd.merge as follows:

```
df_train = pd.merge(y_train, X_train, left_index=True,
right_index=True)
```

2. Create a DataFrame, `new_df`, using `np.repeat` that includes the following:

   a) The values of the positive cases: `df_train[df_train['LABEL']==2.values`.

   b) The number of copies – in this case, 9

   c) The `axis=0` parameter to specify that we are working with columns:

   ```
   new_df = pd.DataFrame(np.repeat(df_train[df_
   train['LABEL']==2].values,9,axis=0))
   ```

3. Copy the column names:

   ```
   new_df.columns = df_train.columns
   ```

4. Concatenate the DataFrames:

   ```
   df_train_resample = pd.concat([df_train, new_df])
   ```

5. Verify that `value_counts` is as expected:

   ```
   df_train_resample['LABEL'].value_counts()
   ```

   The expected output is as follows:

   ```
   1.0     275
   2.0     250
   Name: LABEL, dtype: int64
   ```

6. Split X and y using the resampled DataFrame:

   ```
   X_train_resample = df_train_resample.iloc[:,1:]
   y_train_resample = df_train_resample.iloc[:,0]
   ```

7. Fit the model on the resampled training set:

   ```
   model = XGBClassifier(random_state=2)
   model.fit(X_train_resample, y_train_resample)
   ```

8. Score the model with X_test and y_test. Include the confusion matrix and classification report in your result:

   ```
   y_pred = model.predict(X_test)
   score = recall_score(y_test, y_pred, pos_label=2)
   print(confusion_matrix(y_test, y_pred))
   ```

```
print(classification_report(y_test, y_pred))
print(score)
```

The score is as follows:

```
[[86  2]
 [ 8  4]]
              precision    recall  f1-score   support

           1       0.91      0.98      0.95        88
           2       0.67      0.33      0.44        12

    accuracy                           0.90       100
   macro avg       0.79      0.66      0.69       100
weighted avg       0.89      0.90      0.88       100

0.3333333333333333
```

By appropriately holding out a test set to begin with, oversampling achieves 33.3% recall, a score that is twice as strong as the 17% obtained earlier, although still much too low.

> **Tip**
> **SMOTE** is a popular resampling library that may be imported from `imblearn`, which must be downloaded to use. I achieved the same results as SMOTE using the preceding resampling code.

Since resampling has produced modest gains at best, it's time to adjust the hyperparameters of XGBoost.

Tuning and scaling XGBClassifier

In this section, we will fine-tune and scale XGBClassifier to obtain the best possible `recall_score` value for the Exoplanets dataset. First, you will adjust weights using `scale_pos_weight`, then you will run grid searches to find the best combination of hyperparameters. In addition, you will score models for different subsets of the data before consolidating and analyzing the results.

Adjusting weights

In *Chapter 5*, *XGBoost Unveiled*, you used the `scale_pos_weight` hyperparameter to counteract imbalances in the Higgs boson dataset. `Scale_pos_weight` is a hyperparameter used to scale the *positive* weight. The emphasis here on *positive* is important because XGBoost assumes that a target value of 1 is *positive* and a target value of 0 is *negative*.

In the Exoplanet dataset, we have been using the default 1 as negative and 2 as positive as provided by the dataset. We will now switch to 0 as negative and 1 as positive using the `.replace()` method.

replace

The `.replace()` method may be used to reassign values. The following code replaces 1 with 0 and 2 with 1 in the LABEL column:

```
df['LABEL'] = df['LABEL'].replace(1, 0)
df['LABEL'] = df['LABEL'].replace(2, 1)
```

If the two lines of code were reversed, all column values would end up as 0 since all 2s would become 1s, and then all 1s would become 0s. In programming, order matters!

Verify the counts using the `value_counts` method:

```
df['LABEL'].value_counts()
```

Here is the expected output:

```
0     363
1     37
Name: LABEL, dtype: int64
```

The positive cases are now labeled 1 and the negative cases are labeled 0.

scale_pos_weight

It's time to build a new `XGBClassifier` with `scale_pos_weight=10` to account for the imbalance in the data:

1. Split the new DataFrame into X, the predictor columns, and y, the target columns:

    ```
    X = df.iloc[:,1:]
    y = df.iloc[:,0]
    ```

2. Split the data into training and test sets:

```
X_train, X_test, y_train, y_test = train_test_split(X, y,
random_state=2)
```

3. Build, fit, predict, and score XGBClassifier with scale_pos_weight=10. Print out the confusion matrix and the classification report to view the complete results:

```
model = XGBClassifier(scale_pos_weight=10, random_
state=2)
model.fit(X_train, y_train)
y_pred = model.predict(X_test)
score = recall_score(y_test, y_pred)
print(confusion_matrix(y_test, y_pred))
print(classification_report(y_test, y_pred))
print(score)
```

Here is the expected output:

```
[[86  2]
 [ 8  4]]
```

	precision	recall	f1-score	support
0	0.91	0.98	0.95	88
1	0.67	0.33	0.44	12
accuracy			0.90	100
macro avg	0.79	0.66	0.69	100
weighted avg	0.89	0.90	0.88	100

```
0.3333333333333333
```

The results are the same as our resampling method from the previous section.

The oversampling method that we implemented from scratch gives the same predictions as XGBClassifier with scale_pos_weight.

Tuning XGBClassifier

It's time to see whether hyperparameter fine-tuning can increase precision.

It's standard to use GridSearchCV and RandomizedSearchCV when fine-tuning hyperparameters. Both require cross-validation of two or more folds. We have yet to implement cross-validation since our initial models did not perform well and it's computationally expensive to test multiple folds on large datasets.

A balanced approach is to use GridSearchCV and RandomizedSearchCV with two folds to save time. To ensure consistent results, StratifiedKFold (*Chapter 6, XGBoost Hyperparameters*) is recommended. We will begin with the baseline model.

The baseline model

Here are the steps to build a baseline model that implements the same k-fold cross-validation as grid searches:

1. Import GridSearchCV, RandomizedSearchCV, StratifiedKFold, and cross_val_score:

    ```
    from sklearn.model_selection import GridSearchCV,
    RandomizedSearchCV, StratifiedKFold, cross_val_score
    ```

2. Intialize StratifiedKFold as kfold with n_splits=2 and shuffle=True:

    ```
    kfold = StratifiedKFold(n_splits=2, shuffle=True, random_
    state=2)
    ```

3. Initialize XGBClassifier with scale_pos_weight=10 since there are 10 times as many negative cases as positive cases:

    ```
    model = XGBClassifier(scale_pos_weight=10, random_
    state=2)
    ```

4. Score the model using cross_val_score with cv=kfold and score='recall' as parameters, then display the scores:

    ```
    scores = cross_val_score(model, X, y, cv=kfold,
    scoring='recall')
    print('Recall: ', scores)
    print('Recall mean: ', scores.mean())
    ```

    The scores are as follows:

    ```
    Recall:  [0.10526316 0.27777778]
    Recall mean:  0.1915204678362573
    ```

The scores are a little worse with cross-validation. When there are very few positive cases, it makes a difference which rows end up in the training and test sets. Different implementations of `StratifiedKFold` and `train_test_split` may lead to different results.

grid_search

We'll now implement a variation of the `grid_search` function from *Chapter 6, XGBoost Hyperparameters*, to fine-tune hyperparameters:

1. The new function takes the same dictionary of parameters as input, along with a random option that uses `RandomizedSearchCV`. In addition, `X` and `y` are provided as default parameters for use with other subsets and the scoring method is recall as follows:

```python
def grid_search(params, random=False, X=X, y=y,
model=XGBClassifier(random_state=2)):
    xgb = model
    if random:
        grid = RandomizedSearchCV(xgb, params, cv=kfold,
n_jobs=-1, random_state=2, scoring='recall')
    else:
        grid = GridSearchCV(xgb, params, cv=kfold, n_
jobs=-1, scoring='recall')
    grid.fit(X, y)
    best_params = grid.best_params_
    print("Best params:", best_params)
    best_score = grid.best_score_
    print("Best score: {:.5f}".format(best_score))
```

2. Let's run the grid searches excluding defaults to try and improve scores. Here are some initial grid searches along with their results:

a) Grid search 1:

```python
grid_search(params={'n_estimators':[50, 200, 400, 800]})
```

Results:

```
Best params: {'n_estimators': 50}
Best score: 0.19152
```

b) Grid search 2:

```
grid_search(params={'learning_rate':[0.01, 0.05, 0.2,
0.3]})
```

Results:

```
Best params: {'learning_rate': 0.01}
```
```
Best score: 0.40351
```

c) Grid search 3:

```
grid_search(params={'max_depth':[1, 2, 4, 8]})
```

Results:

```
Best params: {'max_depth': 2}
```
```
Best score: 0.24415
```

d) Grid search 4:

```
grid_search(params={'subsample':[0.3, 0.5, 0.7, 0.9]})
```

Results:

```
Best params: {'subsample': 0.5}
```
```
Best score: 0.21637
```

e) Grid search 5:

```
grid_search(params={'gamma':[0.05, 0.1, 0.5, 1]})
```

Results:

```
Best params: {'gamma': 0.05}
```
```
Best score: 0.24415
```

3. Changing `learning_rate`, `max_depth`, and gamma has resulted in gains. Let's try to combine them by narrowing the range:

```
grid_search(params={'learning_rate':[0.001, 0.01, 0.03],
'max_depth':[1, 2], 'gamma':[0.025, 0.05, 0.5]})
```

The score is as follows:

```
Best params: {'gamma': 0.025, 'learning_rate': 0.001,
'max_depth': 2}
```
```
Best score: 0.53509
```

4. It's also worth trying `max_delta_step`, which XGBoost only recommends for imbalanced datasets. The default is 0 and increasing the steps results in a more conservative model:

```
grid_search(params={'max_delta_step':[1, 3, 5, 7]})
```

The score is as follows:

```
Best params: {'max_delta_step': 1}
Best score: 0.24415
```

5. As a final strategy, we combine `subsample` with all the column samples in a random search:

```
grid_search(params={'subsample':[0.3, 0.5, 0.7, 0.9, 1],
'colsample_bylevel':[0.3, 0.5, 0.7, 0.9, 1],
'colsample_bynode':[0.3, 0.5, 0.7, 0.9, 1],
'colsample_bytree':[0.3, 0.5, 0.7, 0.9, 1]}, random=True)
```

The score is as follows:

```
Best params: {'subsample': 0.3, 'colsample_bytree': 0.7,
'colsample_bynode': 0.7, 'colsample_bylevel': 1}
Best score: 0.35380
```

Instead of continuing with this subset of data that contains 400 rows, let's switch to the balanced subset (undersampled) that contains 74 rows to compare results.

The balanced subset

The balanced subset of 74 rows has the least amount of data points. It's also the fastest to test.

X and y need to be explicitly defined since they were last used for the balanced subset inside a function. The new definitions for X_short and y_short are given as follows:

```
X_short = X.iloc[:74, :]
y_short = y.iloc[:74]
```

After a few grid searches, combining `max_depth` and `colsample_bynode` gave the following results:

```
grid_search(params={'max_depth':[1, 2, 3], 'colsample_
bynode':[0.5, 0.75, 1]}, X=X_short, y=y_short,
model=XGBClassifier(random_state=2))
```

The score is as follows:

```
Best params: {'colsample_bynode': 0.5, 'max_depth': 2}
Best score: 0.65058
```

This is an improvement.

It's time to try hyperparameter fine-tuning on all the data.

Fine-tuning all the data

The issue with implementing the grid_search function on all the data is time. Now that we are at the end, it's time to run the code and take breaks as the computer sweats:

1. Read all the data into a new DataFrame, df_all:

    ```
    df_all = pd.read_csv('exoplanets.csv')
    ```

2. Replace the 1s with 0s and the 2s with 1s:

    ```
    df_all['LABEL'] = df_all['LABEL'].replace(1, 0)
    df_all['LABEL'] = df_all['LABEL'].replace(2, 1)
    ```

3. Split the data into X and y:

    ```
    X_all = df_all.iloc[:,1:]
    y_all = df_all.iloc[:,0]
    ```

4. Verify value_counts of the 'LABEL' column:

    ```
    df_all['LABEL'].value_counts()
    ```

    The output is as follows:

    ```
    0     5050
    1       37
    Name: LABEL, dtype: int64
    ```

5. Scale the weights by dividing the negative class by the positive class:

    ```
    weight = int(5050/37)
    ```

6. Score a baseline model for all the data with XGBClassifier and scale_pos_weight=weight:

    ```
    model = XGBClassifier(scale_pos_weight=weight, random_state=2)
    ```

```
scores = cross_val_score(model, X_all, y_all, cv=kfold,
scoring='recall')
```
```
print('Recall:', scores)
```
```
print('Recall mean:', scores.mean())
```

The output is as follows:

```
Recall: [0.10526316 0.          ]
```
```
Recall mean: 0.05263157894736842
```

This score is awful. Presumably, the classifier is scoring a high percentage of accuracy, despite the low recall.

7. Let's try optimizing hyperparameters based on the most successful results thus far:

```
grid_search(params={'learning_rate':[0.001, 0.01]},
X=X_all, y=y_all, model=XGBClassifier(scale_pos_
weight=weight, random_state=2))
```

The score is as follows:

```
Best params: {'learning_rate': 0.001}
```
```
Best score: 0.26316
```

This is much better than the initial score with all the data.

Let's try combining hyperparameters:

```
grid_search(params={'max_depth':[1,
2],'learning_rate':[0.001]}, X=X_all, y=y_all,
model=XGBClassifier(scale_pos_weight=weight, random_
state=2))
```

The score is as follows:

```
Best params: {'learning_rate': 0.001, 'max_depth': 2}
```
```
Best score: 0.53509
```

This is better, though not as strong as the undersampled dataset scored earlier.

With the score on all the data starting lower and taking more time, a question naturally arises. Are the machine learning models better on the smaller subsets for the Exoplanet dataset?

Let's find out.

Consolidating results

It's tricky to consolidate results with different datasets. We have been working with the following subsets:

- 5,050 rows – approx. 54% recall

- 400 rows – approx. 54% recall

- 74 rows – approx. 68% recall

The best results obtained have included `learning_rate=0.001`, `max_depth=2`, and `colsample_bynode=0.5`.

Let's train a model on *all 37 exoplanet stars*. This means the test results will come from data points that the model has already trained on. Normally, this is not a good idea. In this case, however, the positive cases are very few and it may be instructive to see how the smaller subsets test on the positive cases it has not seen before.

The following function takes X, y, and the machine learning model as input. The model is fit on the data provided, then predictions are made on the entire dataset. Finally, `recall_score`, `confusion matrix`, and `classification report` are all printed:

```
def final_model(X, y, model):
    model.fit(X, y)
    y_pred = model.predict(X_all)
    score = recall_score(y_all, y_pred,)
    print(score)
    print(confusion_matrix(y_all, y_pred,))
    print(classification_report(y_all, y_pred))
```

Let's run the function for each of our three subsets. Of the three strongest hyperparameters, it turns out that `colsample_bynode` and `max_depth` give the best results.

Let's start with the smallest number of rows, where the number of exoplanet stars and non-exoplanet stars match.

74 rows

Let's begin with 74 rows:

```
final_model(X_short, y_short, XGBClassifier(max_depth=2,
colsample_by_node=0.5, random_state=2))
```

The output is as follows:

```
1.0
[[3588 1462]
 [   0   37]]
              precision    recall  f1-score   support

           0       1.00      0.71      0.83      5050
           1       0.02      1.00      0.05        37

    accuracy                           0.71      5087
   macro avg       0.51      0.86      0.44      5087
weighted avg       0.99      0.71      0.83      5087
```

All 37 exoplanet stars were correctly identified, but 1,462 non-exoplanet stars were misclassified! Despite 100% recall, the precision is 2%, and the F1 score is 5%. Low precision and a low F1 score are a risk when tuning for recall only. In practice, an astronomer would have to sort through 1,462 potential exoplanet stars to find 37. This is unacceptable.

Now let's see what happens when we train on 400 rows.

400 rows

In the case of 400 rows, we use the `scale_pos_weight=10` hyperparameter to balance the data:

```
final_model(X, y, XGBClassifier(max_depth=2, colsample_
bynode=0.5, scale_pos_weight=10, random_state=2))
```

The output is as follows:

```
1.0
[[4901  149]
 [   0   37]]
              precision    recall  f1-score   support

           0       1.00      0.97      0.99      5050
           1       0.20      1.00      0.33        37
```

	precision	recall	f1-score	support
accuracy			0.97	5087
macro avg	0.60	0.99	0.66	5087
weighted avg	0.99	0.97	0.98	5087

Again, all 37 exoplanet stars were correctly classified for 100% recall, but 149 non-exoplanet stars were incorrectly classified, for a precision of 20%. In this case, an astronomer would need to sort through 186 stars to find the 37 exoplanet stars.

Finally, let's train on all the data.

5,050 rows

In the case of all the data, set `scale_pos_weight` equal to the `weight` variable, as previously defined:

```
final_model(X_all, y_all, XGBClassifier(max_depth=2, colsample_
bynode=0.5, scale_pos_weight=weight, random_state=2))
```

The output is as follows:

```
1.0
[[5050    0]
 [   0   37]]
```

	precision	recall	f1-score	support
0	1.00	1.00	1.00	5050
1	1.00	1.00	1.00	37
accuracy			1.00	5087
macro avg	1.00	1.00	1.00	5087
weighted avg	1.00	1.00	1.00	5087

Amazing. All predictions, recall and precision, are 100% perfect. In this highly desirable case, an astronomer would find all of the exoplanet stars without having to sift through any bad data.

Keep in mind, however, that these scores are based on the training data, not on unseen test data, which is mandatory to build a strong model. In other words, although the model fits the training data perfectly, it's unlikely to generalize this well to new data. These numbers, however, are valuable.

Based on this result, since the machine learning model performs impressively on the training set and modestly at best on the test set, the variance is likely too high. Additionally, more trees and more rounds of fine-tuning may be required to pick up on nuanced patterns within the data.

Analyzing results

When scored on the training set, the tuned models delivered perfect recall but varied considerably on the precision. Here are the takeaways:

- Using precision without recall or the F1 score can result in suboptimal models. By using the classification report, more details are revealed.

- Over-emphasizing high scores from small subsets is not advised.

- When test scores are low, but training scores are high on imbalanced datasets, deeper models with extensive hyperparameter fine-tuning is advised.

A survey of kernels, publicly displayed notebooks put forward by Kaggle users, at `https://www.kaggle.com/keplersmachines/kepler-labelled-time-series-data/kernels` for the Exoplanet dataset reveals the following:

- Many users fail to understand that a high accuracy score is easy to obtain and virtually meaningless with highly imbalanced data.

- Users posting precision are generally posting from 50 to 70 percent, and users posting recall are posting 60 to 100 percent (a user with 100% recall has 55% precision), indicating the challenges and limitations of this dataset.

When you present your results to your astronomy professor, wiser to the limitations of imbalanced data, you conclude that your model performs with 70% recall at best, and that 37 exoplanet stars are not enough to build a robust machine learning model to find life on other planets. Your XGBClassifier, however, will allow astronomers and others trained in data analysis to use machine learning to decide which stars to focus on in the universe to discover the next exoplanets in orbit.

Summary

In this chapter, you surveyed the universe with the Exoplanet dataset to discover new planets, and potentially new life. You built multiple XGBClassifiers to predict when exoplanet stars are the result of periodic changes in light. With only 37 exoplanet stars and 5,050 non-exoplanet stars, you corrected the imbalanced data by undersampling, oversampling, and tuning XGBoost hyperparameters including `scale_pos_weight`.

You analyzed results using the confusion matrix and the classification report. You learned key differences between various classification scoring metrics, and why for the Exoplanet dataset accuracy is virtually worthless, while a high recall is ideal, especially when combined with high precision for a good F1 score. Finally, you realized the limitations of machine learning models when the data is extremely varied and imbalanced.

After this case study, you have the necessary background and skills to fully analyze imbalanced datasets with XGBoost using `scale_pos_weight`, hyperparameter fine-tuning, and alternative classification scoring metrics.

In the next chapter, you will greatly expand your range of XGBoost by applying alternative XGBoost base learners beyond gradient boosted trees. Although gradient boosted trees are often the best option, XGBoost comes equipped with linear base learners, dart base learners, and even random forests, all coming next!

Section 3: Advanced XGBoost

Building advanced XGBoost models takes practice, analysis, and experimentation. In this section, you will experiment with and fine-tune alternative base learners, learn innovative tips and tricks from Kaggle masters—including stacking and advanced feature engineering—and practice building robust models ready for industry deployment using sparse matrices, customized transformers, and pipelines.

This section comprises the following chapters:

- *Chapter 8, XGBoost Alternative Base Learners*
- *Chapter 9, XGBoost Kaggle Masters*
- *Chapter 10, XGBoost Model Deployment*

8
XGBoost Alternative Base Learners

In this chapter, you will analyze and apply different **base learners** in XGBoost. In XGBoost, base learners are the individual models, most commonly trees, that are iterated upon for each boosting round. Along with the default decision tree, which XGBoost defines as `gbtree`, additional options for base learners include `gblinear` and `dart`. Furthermore, XGBoost has its own implementations of random forests as base learners and as tree ensemble algorithms that you will experiment with in this chapter.

By learning how to apply alternative base learners, you will greatly extend your range with XGBoost. You will have the capacity to build many more models and you will learn new approaches to developing linear, tree-based, and random forest machine learning algorithms. The goal of the chapter is to give you proficiency in building XGBoost models with alternative base learners so that you can leverage advanced XGBoost options to find the best possible model for a range of situations.

In this chapter, we cover the following main topics:

- Exploring alternative base learners
- Applying `gblinear`
- Comparing `dart`
- Finding XGBoost random forests

Technical requirements

The code and datasets for this chapter may be found at `https://github.com/PacktPublishing/Hands-On-Gradient-Boosting-with-XGBoost-and-Scikit-learn/tree/master/Chapter08`.

Exploring alternative base learners

The base learner is the machine learning model that XGBoost uses to build the first model in its ensemble. The word *base* is used because it's the model that comes first, and the word *learner* is used because the model iterates upon itself after learning from the errors.

Decision trees have emerged as the preferred base learners for XGBoost on account of the excellent scores that boosted trees consistently produce. The popularity of decision trees extends beyond XGBoost to other ensemble algorithms such as random forests and **extremely randomized trees**, which you can preview in the scikit-learn documentation under `ExtraTreesClassifier` and `ExtraTreesRegressor` (`https://scikit-learn.org/stable/modules/ensemble.html`).

In XGBoost, the default base learner, known as `gbtree`, is one of several base learners. There is also `gblinear`, a gradient boosted linear model, and `dart`, a variation of decision trees that includes a dropout technique based on neural networks. Furthermore, there are XGBoost random forests. In the next section, we will explore the differences between these base learners before applying them in subsequent sections.

gblinear

Decision trees are optimal for **non-linear data** as they can easily access points by splitting the data as many times as needed. Decision trees are often preferable as base learners because real data is usually non-linear.

There may be cases, however, where a **linear model** is ideal. If the real data has a linear relationship, a decision tree is probably not the best option. For this scenario, XGBoost provides `gblinear` as an option for a **linear base learner**.

The general idea behind boosted linear models is the same as boosted tree models. A base model is built, and each subsequent model is trained upon the residuals. At the end, the individual models are summed for the final result. The primary distinction with linear base learners is that each model in the ensemble is linear.

Like **Lasso** and **Ridge**, variations of linear regression that add regularization terms (see *Chapter 1, Machine Learning Landscape*), gblinear also adds regularization terms to linear regression. Tianqi Chin, the founder and developer of XGBoost commented on GitHub that multiple rounds of boosting gblinear may be used *to get back a single lasso regression* (https://github.com/dmlc/xgboost/issues/332).

gblinear may also be used for classification problems via **logistic regression**. This works because logistic regression is also built by finding optimal coefficients (weighted inputs), as in **linear regression**, and summed via the **sigmoid equation** (see *Chapter 1, Machine Learning Landscape*).

We will explore the details and applications of gblinear in the *Applying gblinear* section in this chapter. For now, let's learn about dart.

DART

Dropouts meet Multiple Additive Regression Trees, simply known as **DART**, was introduced in 2015 by K. V. Rashmi from UC Berkeley and Ran Gilad-Bachrach from Microsoft in the following paper: http://proceedings.mlr.press/v38/korlakaivinayak15.pdf.

Rashmi and Gilad-Bachrach highlight **Multiple Additive Regression Trees (MART)** as a successful model that suffers from too much dependency on earlier trees. Instead of focusing on **shrinkage**, a standard penalization term, they use the **dropout** technique from **neural networks**. Simply put, the dropout technique eliminates nodes (mathematical points) from each layer of learning in a neural network, thereby reducing overfitting. In other words, the dropout technique slows down the learning process by eliminating information from each round.

In DART, in each new round of boosting, instead of summing the residuals from all previous trees to build a new model, DART selects a random sample of previous trees and normalizes the leaves by a scaling factor $1/k$ where k is the number of trees dropped.

DART is a variation of decision trees. The XGBoost implementation of DART is similar to gbtree with additional hyperparameters to accommodate dropouts.

For the mathematical details of DART, reference the original paper highlighted in the first paragraph of this section.

You will practice building machine learning models with DART base learners in the *Comparing dart* section later in this chapter.

XGBoost random forests

The final option that we'll explore in this section is XGBoost random forests. Random forests may be implemented as base learners by setting `num_parallel_trees` equal to an integer greater than 1, and as class options within XGBoost defined as `XGBRFRegressor` and `XGBRFClassifier`.

Keep in mind that gradient boosting was designed to improve upon the errors of relatively weak base learners, not strong base learners like random forests. Nevertheless, there may be fringe cases where random forest base learners can be advantageous so it's a nice option to have.

As an additional bonus, XGBoost provides `XGBRFRegressor` and `XGBRFClassifier` as random forest machine learning algorithms that are not base learners, but algorithms in their own right. These algorithms work in a similar manner as scikit-learn's random forests (see *Chapter 3*, *Bagging with Random Forests*). The primary difference is that XGBoost includes default hyperparameters to counteract overfitting and their own methods for building individual trees. XGBoost random forests have been in the experimental stage, but they are starting to outperform scikit-learn's random forests as of late 2020 as you willwill see in this chapter.

In the final section of this chapter, we will experiment with XGBoost's random forests, both as base learners and as models in their own right.

Now that you have an overview of XGBoost base learners, let's apply them one at a time.

Applying gblinear

It's challenging to find real-world datasets that work best with linear models. It's often the case that real data is messy and more complex models like tree ensembles produce better scores. In other cases, linear models may generalize better.

The success of machine learning algorithms depends on how they perform with real-world data. In the next section, we will apply `gblinear` to the Diabetes dataset first and then to a linear dataset by construction.

Applying gblinear to the Diabetes dataset

The Diabetes dataset is a regression dataset of 442 diabetes patients provided by scikit-learn. The prediction columns include age, sex, **BMI (body mass index)**, **BP (blood pressure)**, and five serum measurements. The target column is the progression of the disease after 1 year. You can read about the dataset in the original paper here: `http://web.stanford.edu/~hastie/Papers/LARS/LeastAngle_2002.pdf`.

Scikit-learn's datasets are already split into predictor and target columns for you. They are preprocessed for machine learning with X, the predictor columns, and y, the target column, loaded separately.

Here is the full list of imports that you will need to work with this dataset and the rest of this chapter:

```
import pandas as pd
import numpy as np
from sklearn.datasets import load_diabetes
from sklearn.model_selection import cross_val_score
from xgboost import XGBRegressor, XGBClassifier,
XGBRFRegressor, XGBRFClassifier
from sklearn.ensemble import RandomForestRegressor,
RandomForestClassifier
from sklearn.linear_model import LinearRegression,
LogisticRegression
from sklearn.linear_model import Lasso, Ridge
from sklearn.model_selection import GridSearchCV
from sklearn.model_selection import KFold
from sklearn.metrics import mean_squared_error as MSE
```

Let's begin! To use the Diabetes dataset, do the following:

1. You first need to define X and y using `load_diabetes` with the `return_X_y` parameter set equal to `True`:

    ```
    X, y = load_diabetes(return_X_y=True)
    ```

    The plan is to use `cross_val_score` and `GridSearchCV`, so let's create folds in advance to obtain consistent scores. In *Chapter 6, XGBoost Hyperparameters*, we used `StratifiedKFold`, which stratifies the target column, ensuring that each test set includes the same number of classes.

    This approach works for classification, but not for regression, where the target column takes on continuous values and classes are not involved. `KFold` achieves a similar goal without stratification by creating consistent splits in the data.

2. Now, shuffle the data and use 5 splits with `KFold` using the following parameters:

    ```
    kfold = KFold(n_splits=5, shuffle=True, random_state=2)
    ```

3. Build a function with `cross_val_score` that takes a machine learning model as input and returns the mean score of 5 folds as the output, making sure to set `cv=kfold`:

```
def regression_model(model):
    scores = cross_val_score(model, X, y, scoring='neg_
mean_squared_error', cv=kfold)
    rmse = (-scores)**0.5
    return rmse.mean()
```

4. To use `gblinear` as the base model, just set `booster='gblinear'` for `XGBRegressor` inside the regression function:

```
regression_model(XGBRegressor(booster='gblinear'))
```

The score is as follows:

```
55.4968907398679
```

5. Let's check this score against other linear models including `LinearRegression`, `Lasso`, which uses **L1** or **absolute value regularization**, and `Ridge`, which uses **L2** or **Euclidean distance regularization**:

a) `LinearRegression` is as follows:

```
regression_model(LinearRegression())
```

The score is as follows:

```
55.50927267834351
```

b) `Lasso` is as follows:

```
regression_model(Lasso())
```

The score is as follows:

```
62.64900771743497
```

c) `Ridge` is as follows:

```
regression_model(Ridge())
```

The score is as follows:

```
58.83525077919004
```

As you can see, `XGBRegressor` with `gblinear` as the base learner performs the best, along with `LinearRegression`.

6. Now place `booster='gbtree'` inside `XGBRegressor`, which is the default base learner:

```
regression_model(XGBRegressor(booster='gbtree'))
```

The score is as follows:

```
65.96608419624594
```

As you can see, the `gbtree` base learner does not perform nearly as well as the `gblinear` base learner in this case indicating that a linear model is ideal.

Let's see if we can modify hyperparameters to make some gains with `gblinear` as the base learner.

gblinear hyperparameters

It's important to understand the differences between `gblinear` and `gbtree` when adjusting hyperparameters. Many of the XGBoost hyperparameters presented in *Chapter 6, XGBoost Hyperparameters*, are tree hyperparameters and do not apply to `gblinear`. For instance, `max_depth` and `min_child_weight` are hyperparameters specifically designed for trees.

The following list is a summary of XGBoost `gblinear` hyperparameters that are designed for linear models.

reg_lambda

Scikit-learn uses `reg_lambda` instead of `lambda`, which is a reserved keyword for lambda functions in Python. This is the standard L2 regularization used by `Ridge`. Values close to 0 tend to work best:

- *Default: 0*
- *Range: [0, inf)*
- *Increasing prevents overfitting*
- *Alias: lambda*

reg_alpha

Scikit-learn accepts both `reg_alpha` and `alpha`. This is the standard L1 regularization used by `Lasso`. Values close to 0 tend to work best:

- *Default: 0*
- *Range: [0, inf)*

- *Increasing prevents overfitting*
- *Alias: alpha*

updater

This is the algorithm that XGBoost uses to build the linear model during each round of boosting. `shotgun` uses `hogwild` parallelism with coordinate descent to produce a non-deterministic solution. By contrast, `coord_descent` is ordinary coordinate descent with a deterministic solution:

- *Default: shotgun*
- *Range: shotgun, coord_descent*

> **Note**
> *Coordinate descent* is a machine learning term defined as minimizing the error by finding the gradient one coordinate at a time.

feature_selector

`feature_selector` determines how the weights are selected with the following options:

a) `cyclic` – cycles through features iteratively

b) `shuffle` – cyclic with random feature-shuffling in each round

c) `random` – the coordinate selector during coordinate descent is random

d) `greedy` – time-consuming; selects the coordinate with the greatest gradient magnitude

e) `thrifty` – approximately greedy, reorders features according to weight changes

- *Default: cyclic*
- *Range must be used in conjunction with updater as follows:*

a) `shotgun`: `cyclic`, `shuffle`

b) `coord_descent`: `random`, `greedy`, `thrifty`

> **Note**
> `greedy` will be computationally expensive for large datasets, but the number of features that `greedy` considers may be reduced by changing the parameter `top_k` (see the following).

top_k

top_k is the number of features that greedy and thrifty select from during coordinate descent:

- *Default: 0 (all features)*
- *Range: [0, max number of features]*

> **Note**
>
> For more information on XGBoost gblinear hyperparameters consult the official XGBoost documentation page at https://xgboost. readthedocs.io/en/latest/parameter.html#parameters-for-linear-booster-booster-gblinear.

gblinear grid search

Now that you are familiar with the range of hyperparameters that gblinear may use, let's use GridSearchCV in a customized grid_search function to find the best ones:

1. Here is a version of our grid_search function from *Chapter 6, XGBoost Hyperparameters*:

```
def grid_search(params,
reg=XGBRegressor(booster='gblinear')):
    grid_reg = GridSearchCV(reg, params, scoring='neg_
mean_squared_error', cv=kfold)
    grid_reg.fit(X, y)
    best_params = grid_reg.best_params_
    print("Best params:", best_params)
    best_score = np.sqrt(-grid_reg.best_score_)
    print("Best score:", best_score)
```

2. Let's start by modifying alpha with a standard range:

```
grid_search(params={'reg_alpha':[0.001, 0.01, 0.1, 0.5,
1, 5]})
```

The output is as follows:

```
Best params: {'reg_alpha': 0.01}
Best score: 55.485310447306425
```

The score is about the same, with a very slight improvement.

3. Next, let's modify `reg_lambda` with the same range:

```
grid_search(params={'reg_lambda':[0.001, 0.01, 0.1, 0.5,
1, 5]})
```

The output is as follows:

```
Best params: {'reg_lambda': 0.001}
Best score: 56.17163554152289
```

This score here is very similar but slightly worse.

4. Now let's use `feature_selector` in tandem with `updater`. By default, `updater=shotgun` and `feature_selector=cyclic`. When `updater=shotgun`, the only other option for `feature_selector` is `shuffle`.

Let's see if `shuffle` can perform better than `cyclic`:

```
grid_search(params={'feature_selector':['shuffle']})
```

The output is as follows:

```
Best params: {'feature_selector': 'shuffle'}
Best score: 55.531684115240594
```

In this case, `shuffle` does not perform better.

5. Now let's change `updater` to `coord_descent`. As a result, `feature_selector` may take on `random`, `greedy`, or `thrifty`. Try all `feature_selector` alternatives in `grid_search` by entering the following code:

```
grid_search(params={'feature_selector':['random',
'greedy', 'thrifty'], 'updater':['coord_descent'] })
```

The output is as follows:

```
Best params: {'feature_selector': 'thrifty', 'updater':
'coord_descent'}
Best score: 55.48798105805444
This is a slight improvement from the base score.
```

The final hyperparameter to check is `top_k`, which defines the number of features that `greedy` and `thrifty` check during coordinate descent. A range from 2 to 9 is acceptable since there are 10 features in total.

6. Enter a range for `top_k` inside `grid_search` for `greedy` and `thrifty` to find the best option:

```
grid_search(params={'feature_selector':['greedy',
'thrifty'], 'updater':['coord_descent'], 'top_k':[3, 5,
7, 9]})
```

The output is as follows:

```
Best params: {'feature_selector': 'thrifty', 'top_k': 3,
'updater': 'coord_descent'}
Best score: 55.478623763746256
```

This is the best score yet.

Before moving on, note that additional hyperparameters that are not limited to trees, such as `n_estimators` and `learning_rate`, may be used as well.

Now let's see how `gblinear` works on a dataset that is linear by construction.

Linear datasets

One way to ensure that a dataset is linear is by construction. We can choose a range of X values, say 1 to 99, and multiply them by a scaling factor with some randomness involved.

Here are the steps to construct a linear dataset:

1. Set the range of X values from 1 to 100:

```
X = np.arange(1,100)
```

2. Declare a random seed using NumPy to ensure the consistency of the results:

```
np.random.seed(2)
```

3. Create an empty list defined as y:

```
y = []
```

4. Loop through X, multiplying each entry by a random number from -0.2 to 0.2:

```
for i in X:
        y.append(i * np.random.uniform(-0.2, 0.2))
```

5. Transform y to a numpy array for machine learning:

```
y = np.array(y)
```

6. Reshape X and y so that they contain as many rows as members in the array and one column since columns are expected as machine learning inputs with scikit-learn:

```
X = X.reshape(X.shape[0], 1)
y = y.reshape(y.shape[0], 1)
```

We now have a linear dataset that includes randomness in terms of X and y.

Let's run the regression_model function again with gblinear as the base learner:

```
regression_model(XGBRegressor(booster='gblinear',
objective='reg:squarederror'))
```

The score is as follows:

```
6.214946302686011
```

Now run the regression_model function with gbtree as the base learner:

```
regression_model(XGBRegressor(booster='gbtree',
objective='reg:squarederror'))
```

The score is as follows:

```
9.37235946501318
```

As you can see, gblinear performs much better in our constructed linear dataset.

For good measure, let's try LinearRegression on the same dataset:

```
regression_model(LinearRegression())
```

The score is as follows:

```
6.214962315808842
```

In this case, gblinear performs slightly better, perhaps negligibly, scoring 0.00002 points lower than LinearRegression.

Analyzing gblinear

gblinear is a compelling option, but it should only be used when you have reason to believe that a linear model may perform better than a tree-based model. gblinear did outperform LinearRegression in the real and constructed datasets by a very slight margin. Within XGBoost, gblinear is a strong option for a base learner when datasets are large and linear. gblinear is an option for classification datasets as well, an option that you will apply in the next section.

Comparing dart

The base learner dart is similar to gbtree in the sense that both are gradient boosted trees. The primary difference is that dart removes trees (called dropout) during each round of boosting.

In this section, we will apply and compare the base learner dart to other base learners in regression and classification problems.

DART with XGBRegressor

Let's see how dart performs on the Diabetes dataset:

1. First, redefine X and y using load_diabetes as before:

    ```
    X, y = load_diabetes(return_X_y=True)
    ```

2. To use dart as the XGBoost base learner, set the XGBRegressor parameter booster='dart' inside the regression_model function:

    ```
    regression_model(XGBRegressor(booster='dart',
    objective='reg:squarederror'))
    ```

    The score is as follows:

    ```
    65.96444746130739
    ```

The dart base learner gives the same result as the gbtree base learner down to two decimal places. The similarity of results is on account of the small dataset and the success of the gbtree default hyperparameters to prevent overfitting without requiring the dropout technique.

Let's see how dart performs compared to gbtree on a larger dataset with classification.

dart with XGBClassifier

You have used the Census dataset in multiple chapters throughout this book. A clean version of the dataset that we modified in *Chapter 1, Machine Learning Landscape*, has been pre-loaded for you along with the code for *Chapter 8, XGBoost Alternative Base Learners*, at https://github.com/PacktPublishing/Hands-On-Gradient-Boosting-with-XGBoost-and-Scikit-learn/tree/master/Chapter08. Let's now begin to test how dart performs on a larger dataset:

1. Load the Census dataset into a DataFrame and split the predictor and target columns into X and y using the last index (-1) as the target column:

```
df_census = pd.read_csv('census_cleaned.csv')
X_census = df_census.iloc[:, :-1]
y_census = df_census.iloc[:, -1]
```

2. Define a new classification function that uses cross_val_score with the machine learning model as input and the mean score as output similar to the regression function defined earlier in this chapter:

```
def classification_model(model):
    scores = cross_val_score(model, X_census, y_census, scoring='accuracy', cv=kfold)
    return scores.mean()
```

3. Now call the function twice using XGBClassifier with booster='gbtree' and booster='dart' to compare results. Note that the run time will be longer since the dataset is larger:

a) Let's first call XGBClassifier with booster='gbtree':

```
classification_model(XGBClassifier(booster='gbtree'))
```

The score is as follows:

```
0.8701208195968675
```

b) Now, let's call XGBClassifier with booster='dart':

```
classification_model(XGBClassifier(booster='dart')
```

The score is as follows:

```
0.8701208195968675
```

This is surprising. `dart` gives the exact same result as `gbtree` for all 16 decimal places! It's unclear whether trees have been dropped or the dropping of trees has had zero effect.

We can adjust hyperparameters to ensure that trees are dropped, but first, let's see how `dart` compares to `gblinear`. Recall that `gblinear` also works for classification by using the sigmoid function to scale weights as with logistic regression:

1. Call the `classification_model` function with `XGBClassifier` and set `booster='gblinear'`:

    ```
    classification_model(XGBClassifier(booster='gblinear'))
    ```

    The score is as follows:

    ```
    0.8501275704120015
    ```

    This linear base learner does not perform as well as the tree base learners.

2. Let's see how `gblinear` compares with logistic regression. Since the dataset is large, it's best to adjust logistic regression's `max_iter` hyperparameter from `100` to `1000` to allow more time for convergence and to silence warnings. Note that increasing `max_iter` increases the accuracy in this case:

    ```
    classification_model(LogisticRegression(max_iter=1000))
    ```

    The score is as follows:

    ```
    0.8008968643699182
    ```

`gblinear` maintains a clear edge over logistic regression in this case. It's worth underscoring that XGBoost's `gblinear` option in classification provides a viable alternative to logistic regression.

Now that you have seen how `dart` compares with `gbtree` and `gblinear` as a base learner, let's modify `dart`'s hyperparameters.

DART hyperparameters

`dart` includes all `gbtree` hyperparameters along with its own set of additional hyperparameters designed to adjust the percentage, frequency, and probability of dropout trees. See the XGBoost documentation at `https://xgboost.readthedocs.io/en/latest/parameter.html#additional-parameters-for-dart-booster-booster-dart` for detailed information.

The following sections are a summary of XGBoost hyperparameters that are unique to `dart`.

sample_type

The options for `sample_type` include `uniform`, which drops trees uniformly, and `weighted`, which drops trees in proportion to their weights:

- *Default: "uniform"*
- *Range: ["uniform", "weighted"]*
- *Determines how dropped trees are selected*

normalize_type

The options for `normalize_type` include `tree`, where new trees have the same weight as dropped trees, and `forest`, where new trees have the same weight as the sum of dropped trees:

- *Default: "tree"*
- *Range: ["tree", "forest"]*
- *Calculates weights of trees in terms of dropped trees*

rate_drop

`rate_drop` allows the user to set exactly how many trees are dropped percentage-wise:

- *Default: 0.0*
- *Range: [0.0, 1.0]*
- *Percentage of trees that are dropped*

one_drop

When set to `1`, `one_drop` ensures that at least one tree is always dropped during the boosting round:

- *Default: 0*
- *Range: [0, 1]*
- *Used to ensure drops*

skip_drop

`skip_drop` gives the probability of skipping the dropout entirely. In the official documentation, XGBoost says that `skip_drop` has a higher priority than `rate_drop` or `one_drop`. By default, each tree is dropped with the same probability so there is a probability that no trees are dropped for a given boosting round. `skip_drop` allows this probability to be updated to control the number of dropout rounds:

- *Default: 0.0*
- *Range: [0.0, 1.0]*
- *Probability of skipping the dropout*

Now let's modify `dart` hyperparameters to differentiate scores.

Modifying dart hyperparameters

To ensure that at least one tree in each boosting round is dropped, we can set `one_drop=1`. Do this with the Census dataset via the `classification_model` function now:

```
classification_model(XGBClassifier(booster='dart', one_drop=1))
```

The result is as follows:

```
0.8718714338474818
```

This is an improvement by a tenth of a percentage point, indicating that dropping at least one tree per boosting round can be advantageous.

Now that we are dropping trees to change scores, let's return to the smaller and faster Diabetes dataset to modify the remaining hyperparameters:

1. Using the `regression_model` function, change `sample_type` from `uniform` to `weighted`:

    ```
    regression_model(XGBRegressor(booster='dart',
    objective='reg:squarederror', sample_type='weighted'))
    ```

    The score is as follows:
    ```
    65.96444746130739
    ```

    This is 0.002 points better than the `gbtree` model scored earlier.

2. Change `normalize_type` to `forest` to include the sum of trees when updating weights:

```
regression_model(XGBRegressor(booster='dart',
objective='reg:squarederror', normalize_type='forest'))
```

The score is as follows:

```
65.96444746130739
```

There is no change in the score, which may happen with a shallow dataset.

3. Change `one_drop` to `1` guaranteeing that at least one tree is dropped each boosting round:

```
regression_model(XGBRegressor(booster='dart',
objective='reg:squarederror', one_drop=1))
```

The score is as follows:

```
61.81275131335009
```

This is a clear improvement, gaining four full points.

When it comes to `rate_drop`, the percentage of trees that will be dropped, a range of percentages may be used with the `grid_search` function as follows:

```
grid_search(params={'rate_drop':[0.01, 0.1, 0.2, 0.4]},
reg=XGBRegressor(booster='dart', objective='reg:squarederror',
one_drop=1))
```

The results are as follows:

```
Best params: {'rate_drop': 0.2}
Best score: 61.07249602732062
```

This is the best result yet.

We can implement a similar range with `skip_drop`, which gives the probability that a given tree is *not* dropped:

```
grid_search(params={'skip_drop':[0.01, 0.1, 0.2, 0.4]},
reg=XGBRegressor(booster='dart', objective='reg:squarederror'))
```

The results are as follows:

```
Best params: {'skip_drop': 0.1}
Best score: 62.879753748627635
```

This is a good score, but `skip_drop` has resulted in no substantial gains.

Now that you see how `dart` works in action, let's analyze the results.

Analyzing dart

`dart` provides a compelling option within the XGBoost framework. Since `dart` accepts all `gbtree` hyperparameters, it's easy to change the base learner from `gbtree` to `dart` when modifying hyperparameters. In effect, the advantage is that you can experiment with new hyperparameters including `one_drop`, `rate_drop`, `normalize`, and others to see if you can make additional gains. `dart` is definitely worth trying as a base learner in your research and model-building with XGBoost.

Now that you have a good understanding of `dart`, it's time to move on to random forests.

Finding XGBoost random forests

There are two strategies to implement random forests within XGBoost. The first is to use random forests as the base learner, the second is to use XGBoost's original random forests, `XGBRFRegressor` and `XGBRFClassifier`. We start with our original theme, random forests as alternative base learners.

Random forests as base learners

There is not an option to set the booster hyperparameter to a random forest. Instead, the hyperparameter `num_parallel_tree` may be increased from its default value of `1` to transform `gbtree` (or `dart`) into a boosted random forest. The idea here is that each boosting round will no longer consist of one tree, but a number of parallel trees, which in turn make up a forest.

The following is a quick summary of the XGBoost hyperparameter `num_parallel_tree`.

num_parallel_tree

`num_parallel_tree` gives the number of trees, potentially more than 1, that are built during each boosting round:

- *Default: 1*
- *Range: [1, inf)*
- *Gives number of trees boosted in parallel*
- *Value greater than 1 turns booster into random forest*

By including multiple trees per round, the base learner is no longer a tree, but a forest. Since XGBoost includes the same hyperparameters as random forests, the base learner is appropriately classified as a random forest when `num_parallel_tree` exceeds 1.

Let's see how XGBoost random forest base learners work in practice:

1. Call `regression_model` with `XGBRegressor` and set `booster='gbtree'`. Additionally, set `num_parallel_tree=25` meaning that each boosted round consists of a forest of 25 trees:

    ```
    regression_model(XGBRegressor(booster='gbtree',
    objective='reg:squarederror', num_parallel_tree=25))
    ```

    The score is as follows:

    ```
    65.96604877151103
    ```

    The score is respectable, and in this case, it's nearly the same as boosting a single `gbtree`. The reason is that gradient boosting is designed to learn from the mistakes of the previous trees. By starting with a robust random forest, there is little to be learned and the gains are minimal at best.

    Understanding the fundamental point that gradient boosting's strength as an algorithm comes from the learning process is essential. It makes sense, therefore, to try a much smaller value for `num_parallel_tree`, such as 5.

2. Set `num_parallel_tree=5` inside the same regression model:

    ```
    regression_model(XGBRegressor(booster='gbtree',
    objective='reg:squarederror', num_parallel_tree=5))
    ```

    The score is as follows:

    ```
    65.96445649315855
    ```

    Technically, this score is 0.002 points better than the score produced by a forest of 25 trees. Although the improvement is not much, generally speaking, when building XGBoost random forests, low values of `num_parallel_tree` are better.

Now that you have seen how random forests may be implemented as base learners within XGBoost, it's time to build random forests as original XGBoost models.

Random forests as XGBoost models

In addition to `XGBRegressor` and `XGBClassifier`, `XGBoost` also comes with `XGBRFRegressor` and `XGBRFClassifier` to build random forests.

According to the official XGBoost documentation at `https://xgboost.readthedocs.io/en/latest/tutorials/rf.html`, the random forest scikit-learn wrapper is still in the experimentation stage and the defaults may be changed at any time. At the time of writing, in 2020, the following `XGBRFRegressor` and `XGBRFClassifier` defaults are included.

n_estimators

Use `n_estimators` and not `num_parallel_tree` when using `XGBRFRegressor` or `XGBRFClassifier` to build a random forest. Keep in mind that when using `XGBRFRegressor` and `XGBRFClassifier`, you are not gradient boosting but bagging trees in one round only as is the case with a traditional random forest:

- *Default: 100*
- *Range: [1, inf)*
- *Automatically converted to num_parallel_tree for random forests*

learning_rate

`learning_rate` is generally designed for models that learn, including boosters, not `XGBRFRegressor` or `XGBRFClassifier` since they consist of one round of trees. Nevertheless, changing `learning_rate` from 1 will change the scores, so modifying this hyperparameter is generally not advised:

- *Default: 1*
- *Range: [0, 1]*

subsample, colsample_by_node

Scikit-learn's random forest keeps these defaults at 1, making the default `XGBRFRegressor` and `XGBRFClassifier` less prone to overfitting. This is the primary difference between the XGBoost and scikit-learn random forest default implementations:

- *Defaults: 0.8*
- *Range: [0, 1]*
- *Decreasing helps prevent overfitting*

Now, let's see how XGBoost's random forests work in practice:

1. First, place `XGBRFRegressor` inside of the `regression_model` function:

   ```
   regression_
   model(XGBRFRegressor(objective='reg:squarederror'))
   ```

   The score is as follows:

   ```
   59.447250741400595
   ```

   This score is a little better than the `gbtree` model presented earlier, and a little worse than the best linear models presented in this chapter.

2. As a comparison, let's see how `RandomForestRegressor` performs by placing it inside the same function:

   ```
   regression_model(RandomForestRegressor())
   ```

   The score is as follows:

   ```
   59.46563031802505
   ```

   This score is slightly worse than `XGBRFRegressor`.

Now let's compare the XGBoost random forest with scikit-learn's standard random forest using the larger Census dataset for classification:

1. Place `XGBRFClassifier` inside of the `classification_model` function to see how well it predicts user income:

   ```
   classification_model(XGBRFClassifier())
   ```

   The score is as follows:

   ```
   0.856085650471878
   ```

   This is a good score, a little off the mark from `gbtree`, which previously gave 87%.

2. Now place `RandomForestClassifier` inside the same function to compare results:

   ```
   classification_model(RandomForestClassifier())
   ```

   The score is as follows:

   ```
   0.8555328202034789
   ```

   This is slightly worse than XGBoost's implementation.

Since XGBoost's random forests are still in the developmental stage, we'll stop here and analyze the results.

Analyzing XGBoost random forests

You can try a random forest as your XGBoost base learner anytime by increasing num_parallel_tree to a value greater than 1. Although, as you have seen in this section, boosting is designed to learn from weak models, not strong models, so values for num_parallel_tree should remain close to 1. Trying random forests as base learners should be used sparingly. If boosting single trees fails to produce optimal scores, random forest base learners are an option.

Alternatively, the XGBoost random forest's XGBRFRegressor and XGBRFClassifier may be implemented as alternatives to scikit-learn's random forests. XGBoost's new XGBRFRegressor and XGBRFClassifier outperformed scikit-learn's RandomForestRegressor and RandomForestClassifier, although the comparison was very close. Given the overall success of XGBoost in the machine learning community, it's definitely worth using XGBRFRegressor and XGBRFClassifier as viable options going forward.

Summary

In this chapter, you greatly extended your range of XGBoost by applying all XGBoost base learners, including gbtree, dart, gblinear, and random forests, to regression and classification datasets. You previewed, applied, and tuned hyperparameters unique to base learners to improve scores. Furthermore, you experimented with gblinear using a linearly constructed dataset and with XGBRFRegressor and XGBRFClassifier to build XGBoost random forests without any boosting whatsoever. Now that you have worked with all base learners, your comprehension of the range of XGBoost is at an advanced level.

In the next chapter, you will analyze tips and tricks from Kaggle masters to advance your XGBoost skills even further!

9
XGBoost Kaggle Masters

In this chapter, you will learn valuable tips and tricks from **Kaggle Masters** who used XGBoost to win Kaggle competitions. Although we will not enter a Kaggle competition here, the skills that you will gain can apply to building stronger machine learning models in general. Specifically, you will learn why an extra **hold-out set** is critical, how to **feature engineer** new columns of data with **mean encoding**, how to implement `VotingClassifier` and `VotingRegressor` to build non-correlated machine learning ensembles, and the advantages of **stacking** a final model.

In this chapter, we will cover the following main topics:

- Exploring Kaggle competitions
- Engineering new columns of data
- Building non-correlated ensembles
- Stacking final models

Technical requirements

The code for this chapter can be found at `https://github.com/PacktPublishing/Hands-On-Gradient-Boosting-with-XGBoost-and-Scikit-learn/tree/master/Chapter09`.

Exploring Kaggle competitions

> *"I used only XGBoost (tried others but none of them performed well enough to end up in my ensemble)."*
>
> *– Qingchen Wang, Kaggle Winner*

(`https://www.cnblogs.com/yymn/p/4847130.html`)

In this section, we will investigate Kaggle competitions by looking at a brief history of Kaggle competitions, how they are structured, and the importance of a hold-out/test set as distinguished from a validation/test set.

XGBoost in Kaggle competitions

XGBoost built its reputation as the leading machine learning algorithm on account of its unparalleled success in winning Kaggle competitions. XGBoost often appeared in winning ensembles along with deep learning models such as **neural networks**, in addition to winning outright. A sample list of XGBoost Kaggle competition winners appears on the *Distributed (Deep) Machine Learning Community* web page at `https://github.com/dmlc/xgboost/tree/master/demo#machine-learning-challenge-winning-solutions`. For a list of more XGBoost Kaggle competition winners, it's possible to sort through *Winning solutions of Kaggle competitions* (`https://www.kaggle.com/sudalairajkumar/winning-solutions-of-kaggle-competitions`) to research the winning models.

> **Note**
> While XGBoost is regularly featured among the winners, other machine learning models make appearances as well.

As mentioned in *Chapter 5*, *XGBoost Unveiled*, Kaggle competitions are machine learning competitions where machine learning practitioners compete against one another to obtain the best possible score and win cash prizes. When XGBoost exploded onto the scene in 2014 during the *Higgs Boson Machine Learning Challenge*, it immediately jumped the leaderboard and became one of the most preferred machine learning algorithms in Kaggle competitions.

Between 2014 and 2018, XGBoost consistently outperformed the competition on tabular data—data organized in rows and columns as contrasted with unstructured data such as images or text, where neural networks had an edge. With the emergence of **LightGBM** in 2017, a lightning-fast Microsoft version of gradient boosting, XGBoost finally had some real competition with tabular data.

The following introductory paper, *LightGBM: A Highly Efficient Gradient Boosting Decision Tree*, written by eight authors, is recommended for an introduction to LightGBM: `https://papers.nips.cc/paper/6907-lightgbm-a-highly-efficient-gradient-boosting-decision-tree.pdf`.

Implementing a great machine algorithm such as XGBoost or LightGBM in Kaggle competitions isn't enough. Similarly, fine-tuning a model's hyperparameters often isn't enough. While individual model predictions are important, it's equally important to engineer new data and to combine optimal models to attain higher scores.

The structure of Kaggle competitions

It's worth understanding the structure of Kaggle competitions to gain insights into why techniques such as non-correlated ensemble building and stacking are widespread. Furthermore, exploring the structure of Kaggle competitions will give you confidence in entering Kaggle competitions down the road if you choose to pursue that route.

> **Tip**
>
> Kaggle recommends *Housing Prices: Advanced Regression Techniques*, `https://www.kaggle.com/c/house-prices-advanced-regression-techniques`, for machine learning students looking to transition beyond the basics to advanced competitions. This is one of many knowledge-based competitions that do not offer cash prizes.

Kaggle competitions exist on the Kaggle website. Here is the website from *Avito Context Ad Clicks* from 2015 won by XGBoost user Owen Zhang: `https://www.kaggle.com/c/avito-context-ad-clicks/overview`. Several XGBoost Kaggle competition winners, Owen Zhang included, are from 2015, indicating XGBoost's circulation before Tianqi Chin's landmark paper, *XGBoost: A Scalable Tree Boosting System* published in 2016: `https://arxiv.org/pdf/1603.02754.pdf`.

Here is the top of the *Avito Context Ad Clicks* website:

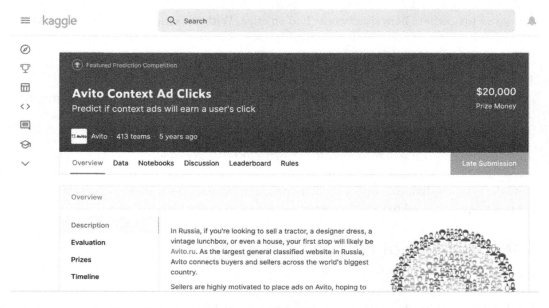

Figure 9.1 – Avito Context Ad Clicks Kaggle competition website

This overview page explains the competition as follows:

- Additional links next to **Overview** (highlighted in blue) include **Data**, where you access data for the competition.

- **Notebooks**, where Kagglers post solutions and starter notebooks.

- **Discussion**, where Kagglers post and answer questions.

- **Leaderboard**, where the top scores are displayed.

- **Rules**, which explains how the competition works.

- Additionally, note the **Late Submission** link on the far-right side, which indicates that submissions are still acceptable even though the competition is over, a general Kaggle policy.

To download the data, you need to enter the competition by signing up for a free account. The data is typically split into two datasets, `training.csv`, the training set used to build a model, and `test.csv`, the test set used to score the model. After submitting a model, you earn a score on the public leaderboard. At the competition's end, a final model is submitted against a private test set to determine the winning solution.

Hold-out sets

It's important to make the distinction between building machine learning models for Kaggle competitions and building them on your own. Up to this point, we have split datasets into training and test sets to ensure that our models generalize well. In Kaggle competitions, however, models must be tested in a competitive environment. For that reason, data from the test set remains hidden.

Here are the differences between Kaggle's training set and test set:

- `training.csv`: This is where you train and score models on your own. This training set should be split into its own training and test sets using `train_test_split` or `cross_val_score` to build models that generalize well to new data. The test sets used during training are often referred to as **validation sets** since they validate the models.

- `test.csv`: This is a separate hold-out set. You don't use the test set until you have a final model ready to test on data it has never seen before. The purpose of the hidden test set is to maintain the integrity of the competition. The test data is hidden from participants and the results are only revealed after participants submit a model.

It's always good practice to keep a test set aside when building a model for research or industry. When a model is tested using data it has already seen, the model risks overfitting the test set, a possibility that often arises in Kaggle competitions when competitors obsess over improving their position in the public leaderboard by few thousandths of a percent.

Kaggle competitions intersect with the real world regarding this hold-out set. The purpose of building machine learning models is to make accurate predictions using unknown data. For example, if a model gives 100% accuracy on the training set, but only gives 50% accuracy on unknown data, the model is basically worthless.

This distinction, between validating models on test sets and testing models on hold-out sets, is very important.

Here is a general approach for validating and testing machine learning models on your own:

1. **Split data into a training set and a hold-out set**: Keep the hold-out set away and resist the temptation to look at it.

2. **Split the training set into a training and test set or use cross-validation**: Fit new models on the training set and validate the model, going back and forth to improve scores.

3. **After obtaining a final model, test it on the hold-out set**: This is the real test of the model. If the score is below expectations, return to *step 2* and repeat. Do not—and this is important—use the hold-out set as the new validation set, going back and forth adjusting hyperparameters. When this happens, the model is adjusting itself to match the hold-out set, which defeats the purpose of a hold-out set in the first place.

In Kaggle competitions, adjusting the machine learning model too closely to the test set will not work. Kaggle often splits test sets into an additional public and private component. The public test set gives participants a chance to score their models and work on improvements, adjusting and resubmitting along the way. The private test set is not revealed until the last day of the competition. Although rankings are displayed for the public test set, competition winners are announced based on the results of the unseen test set.

Winning a Kaggle competition requires getting the best possible score on the private test set. In Kaggle competitions, every percentage point matters. The need for this kind of precision, sometimes scoffed at by the industry, has led to innovative machine learning practices to improve scores. Understanding these techniques, as presented in this chapter, can lead to stronger models and a deeper understanding of machine learning overall.

Engineering new columns

"Almost always I can find open source code for what I want to do, and my time is much better spent doing research and feature engineering."

– *Owen Zhang, Kaggle Winner*

```
(https://medium.com/kaggle-blog/profiling-top-kagglers-owen-
zhang-currently-1-in-the-world-805b941dbb13)
```

Many Kagglers and data scientists have confessed to spending considerable time on research and feature engineering. In this section, we will use `pandas` to engineer new columns of data.

What is feature engineering?

Machine learning models are as good as the data that they train on. When data is insufficient, building a robust machine learning model is impossible.

A more revealing question is whether the data can be improved. When new data is extracted from other columns, these new columns of data are said to be *engineered*.

Feature engineering is the process of developing new columns of data from the original columns. The question is not whether you should implement feature engineering, but how much feature engineering you should implement.

Let's practice feature engineering on a dataset predicting the cab fare of **Uber** and **Lyft** rides.

Uber and Lyft data

In addition to hosting competitions, Kaggle hosts a large number of datasets that include public datasets such as the following one, which predicts Uber and Lyft cab prices: `https://www.kaggle.com/ravi72munde/uber-lyft-cab-prices`:

1. To get started, first import all the libraries and modules needed for this section and silence the warnings:

```
import pandas as pd
import numpy as np
from sklearn.model_selection import cross_val_score
from xgboost import XGBClassifier, XGBRFClassifier
from sklearn.ensemble import RandomForestClassifier,
StackingClassifier
from sklearn.linear_model import LogisticRegression
from sklearn.model_selection import train_test_split,
StratifiedKFold
from sklearn.metrics import accuracy_score
from sklearn.ensemble import VotingClassifier
import warnings
warnings.filterwarnings('ignore')
```

2. Next, load the `'cab_rides.csv'` CSV file and view the first five rows. Limit nrows to 10000 to expedite computations. There are 600,000+ rows in total:

```
df = pd.read_csv('cab_rides.csv', nrows=10000)
df.head()
```

Here is the expected output:

	distance	cab_type	time_stamp	destination	source	price	surge_multiplier	id	product_id	name
0	0.44	Lyft	1544952607890	North Station	Haymarket Square	5.0	1.0	424553bb-7174-41ea-aeb4-fe06d4f4b9d7	lyft_line	Shared
1	0.44	Lyft	1543284023677	North Station	Haymarket Square	11.0	1.0	4bd23055-6827-41c6-b23b-3c491f24e74d	lyft_premier	Lux
2	0.44	Lyft	1543366822198	North Station	Haymarket Square	7.0	1.0	981a3613-77af-4620-a42a-0c0866077d1e	lyft	Lyft
3	0.44	Lyft	1543553582749	North Station	Haymarket Square	26.0	1.0	c2d88af2-d278-4bfd-a8d0-29ca77cc5512	lyft_luxsuv	Lux Black XL
4	0.44	Lyft	1543463360223	North Station	Haymarket Square	9.0	1.0	e0126e1f-8ca9-4f2e-82b3-50505a09db9a	lyft_plus	Lyft XL

Figure 9.2 – Cab rides dataset

This display reveals a wide range of columns, including categorical features and a timestamp.

Null values

As always, check for null values before making any computations:

1. Recall that df.info() also provides information about column types:

```
df.info()
```

The output is as follows:

```
<class 'pandas.core.frame.DataFrame'>
RangeIndex: 10000 entries, 0 to 9999
Data columns (total 10 columns):
 #   Column           Non-Null Count   Dtype
---  ------           --------------   -----
 0   distance         10000 non-null   float64
 1   cab_type         10000 non-null   object
 2   time_stamp       10000 non-null   int64
 3   destination      10000 non-null   object
 4   source           10000 non-null   object
 5   price            9227 non-null    float64
 6   surge_multiplier 10000 non-null   float64
 7   id               10000 non-null   object
 8   product_id       10000 non-null   object
 9   name             10000 non-null   object
dtypes: float64(3), int64(1), object(6)
memory usage: 781.4+ KB
```

As you can see from the output, null values exist in the price column since there are less than 10,000 non-null floats.

2. It's worth checking the null values to see whether more information can be gained about the data:

```
df[df.isna().any(axis=1)]
```

Here are the first five rows of the output:

	distance	cab_type	time_stamp	destination	source	price	surge_multiplier	id	product_id	name
18	1.11	Uber	1543673584211	West End	North End	NaN	1.0	fa5fb705-03a0-4eb9-82d9-7fe80872f754	8cf7e821-f0d3-49c6-8eba-e679c0ebcf6a	Taxi
31	2.48	Uber	1543794776318	South Station	Beacon Hill	NaN	1.0	eee70d94-6706-4b95-a8ce-0e34f0fa8f37	8cf7e821-f0d3-49c6-8eba-e679c0ebcf6a	Taxi
40	2.94	Uber	1543523885298	Fenway	North Station	NaN	1.0	7f47ff53-7cf2-4a6a-8049-83c90e042593	8cf7e821-f0d3-49c6-8eba-e679c0ebcf6a	Taxi
60	1.16	Uber	1544731816318	West End	North End	NaN	1.0	43abdbe4-ab9e-4f39-afdc-31cfa375dc25	8cf7e821-f0d3-49c6-8eba-e679c0ebcf6a	Taxi
69	2.67	Uber	1543583283653	Beacon Hill	North End	NaN	1.0	80db1c49-9d51-4575-a4f4-1ec23b4d3e31	8cf7e821-f0d3-49c6-8eba-e679c0ebcf6a	Taxi

Figure 9.3 – Null values in the cab rides dataset

As you can see, there is nothing particularly glaring about these rows. It could be that the price of the ride was never recorded.

3. Since `price` is the target column, these rows can be deleted with `dropna` using the `inplace=True` parameter to ensure that drops occur within the DataFrame:

```
df.dropna(inplace=True)
```

You can verify that no null values are present by using `df.na()` or `df.info()` one more time.

Feature engineering time columns

Timestamp columns often represent **Unix time**, which is the number of milliseconds since January 1st, 1970. Specific time data can be extracted from the timestamp column that may help predict cab fares, such as the month, hour of the day, whether it is rush hour, and so on:

1. First, convert the timestamp column into a time object using `pd.to_datetime`, and then view the first five rows:

```
df['date'] = pd.to_datetime(df['time_stamp'])
df.head()
```

Here is the expected output:

	distance	cab_type	time_stamp	destination	source	price	surge_multiplier	id	product_id	name	date
0	0.44	Lyft	1544952607890	North Station	Haymarket Square	5.0	1.0	424553bb-7174-41ea-aeb4-fe06d4f4b9d7	lyft_line	Shared	1970-01-01 00:25:44.952607890
1	0.44	Lyft	1543284023677	North Station	Haymarket Square	11.0	1.0	4bd23055-6827-41c6-b23b-3c491f24e74d	lyft_premier	Lux	1970-01-01 00:25:43.284023677
2	0.44	Lyft	1543366822198	North Station	Haymarket Square	7.0	1.0	981a3613-77af-4620-a42a-0c0866077d1e	lyft	Lyft	1970-01-01 00:25:43.366822198
3	0.44	Lyft	1543553582749	North Station	Haymarket Square	26.0	1.0	c2d88af2-d278-4bfd-a8d0-29ca77cc5512	lyft_luxsuv	Lux Black XL	1970-01-01 00:25:43.553582749
4	0.44	Lyft	1543463360223	North Station	Haymarket Square	9.0	1.0	e0126e1f-8ca9-4f2e-82b3-50505a09db9a	lyft_plus	Lyft XL	1970-01-01 00:25:43.463360223

Figure 9.4 – The cab rides dataset after time_stamp conversion

Something is wrong with this data. It doesn't take much domain expertise to know that Lyft and Uber were not around in 1970. The extra decimal places are a clue that the conversion is incorrect.

2. After trying several multipliers to make an appropriate conversion, I discovered that `10**6` gives the appropriate results:

```
df['date'] = pd.to_datetime(df['time_stamp']*(10**6))
df.head()
```

Here is the expected output:

	distance	cab_type	time_stamp	destination	source	price	surge_multiplier	id	product_id	name	date
0	0.44	Lyft	1544952607890	North Station	Haymarket Square	5.0	1.0	424553bb-7174-41ea-aeb4-fe06d4f4b9d7	lyft_line	Shared	2018-12-16 09:30:07.890
1	0.44	Lyft	1543284023677	North Station	Haymarket Square	11.0	1.0	4bd23055-6827-41c6-b23b-3c491f24e74d	lyft_premier	Lux	2018-11-27 02:00:23.677
2	0.44	Lyft	1543366822198	North Station	Haymarket Square	7.0	1.0	981a3613-77af-4620-a42a-0c0866077d1e	lyft	Lyft	2018-11-28 01:00:22.198
3	0.44	Lyft	1543553582749	North Station	Haymarket Square	26.0	1.0	c2d88af2-d278-4bfd-a8d0-29ca77cc5512	lyft_luxsuv	Lux Black XL	2018-11-30 04:53:02.749
4	0.44	Lyft	1543463360223	North Station	Haymarket Square	9.0	1.0	e0126e1f-8ca9-4f2e-82b3-50505a09db9a	lyft_plus	Lyft XL	2018-11-29 03:49:20.223

Figure 9.5 – The cab rides dataset after 'date' conversion

3. With a datetime column, you can extract new columns, such as `month`, `hour`, and `day of week`, after importing `datetime`, as follows:

```
import datetime as dt
df['month'] = df['date'].dt.month
df['hour'] = df['date'].dt.hour
df['dayofweek'] = df['date'].dt.dayofweek
```

Now, you can use these columns to feature engineer more columns, such as whether it's the weekend or rush hour.

4. The following function determines whether a day of the week is a weekend by checking whether `'dayofweek'` is equivalent to 5 or 6, which represent Saturday or Sunday, according to the official documentation: `https://pandas.pydata.org/pandas-docs/stable/reference/api/pandas.Series.dt.weekday.html`:

```
def weekend(row):
    if row['dayofweek'] in [5,6]:
        return 1
    else:
        return 0
```

5. Next, apply the function to the DataFrame as a new column, df['weekend'], as follows:

```
df['weekend'] = df.apply(weekend, axis=1)
```

6. The same strategy can be implemented to create a rush hour column by seeing whether the hour is between 6–10 AM (hours 6–10) and 3–7 PM (hours 15–19):

```
def rush_hour(row):
    if (row['hour'] in [6,7,8,9,15,16,17,18]) &
        (row['weekend'] == 0):
            return 1
    else:
        return 0
```

7. Now, apply the function to a new 'rush_hour' column:

```
df['rush_hour'] = df.apply(rush_hour, axis=1)
```

8. The last five rows show variation in the new columns, as df.tail() reveals:

```
df.tail()
```

Here is an excerpt from the output revealing the new columns:

me_stamp	destination	source	price	surge_multiplier	id	product_id	name	date	month	hour	dayofweek	weekend	rush_hour
04379037	Fenway	North Station	11.5	1.0	934d2fbe-f978-4495-9786-da7b4dd21107	997acbb5-e102-41e1-b155-9df7de0a73f2	UberPool	2018-11-29 15:12:59.037	11	15	3	0	1
00477997	Fenway	North Station	26.0	1.0	af8fd57c-fe7c-4584-bd1f-beef1a53ad42	6c84fd89-3f11-4782-9b50-97c468b19529	Black	2018-12-03 01:27:57.997	12	1	0	0	0
07083241	Fenway	North Station	19.5	1.0	b3c5db97-554b-47bf-908b-3ac880e86103	6f72dfc5-27f1-42e8-84db-ccc7a75f6969	UberXL	2018-11-28 12:11:23.241	11	12	2	0	0
96813623	Fenway	North Station	36.5	1.0	fcb35184-9047-43f7-8909-f62a7b17b6cf	6d318bcc-22a3-4af6-bddd-b409bfce1546	Black SUV	2018-12-15 18:00:13.623	12	18	5	1	0
12781166	Theatre District	Northeastern University	7.0	1.0	7f0e8caf-e057-41eb-bdef-27eb14c88122	lyft_line	Shared	2018-12-03 04:53:01.166	12	4	0	0	0

Figure 9.6 – The last five rows of the cab rides dataset after feature engineering

The process of extracting and engineering new time columns can continue.

> **Note**
>
> When engineering a lot of new columns, it's worth checking to see whether new features are strongly correlated. The correlation of data will be explored later in this chapter.

Now that you understand the practice of feature engineering time columns, let's feature engineer categorical columns.

Feature engineering categorical columns

Previously, we used `pd.get_dummies` to convert categorical columns into numerical columns. Scikit-learn's `OneHotEncoder` feature is another option designed to transform categorical data into 0s and 1s using sparse matrices, a technique that you will apply in *Chapter 10, XGBoost Model Deployment*. While converting categorical data into numerical data using either of these options is standard, alternatives exist.

Although 0s and 1s make sense as numerical values for categorical columns, since 0 indicates absence and 1 indicates presence, it's possible that other values may deliver better results.

One strategy would be to convert categorical columns into their frequencies, which equates to the percentage of times each category appears within the given column. So, instead of a column of categories, each category is converted into its percentage within the column.

Let's view the steps to convert categorical values into numerical values next.

Engineering frequency columns

To engineer a categorical column, such as `'cab_type'`, first view the number of values for each category:

1. Use the `.value_counts()` method to see the frequency of types:

    ```
    df['cab_type'].value_counts()
    ```

    The result is as follows:

    ```
    Uber    4654
    Lyft    4573
    Name: cab_type, dtype: int64
    ```

2. Use `groupby` to place the counts in a new column. `df.groupby(column_name)` is groupby, while `[column_name].transform` specifies the column to be transformed followed by the aggregate in parentheses:

```
df['cab_freq'] = df.groupby('cab_type')['cab_type'].
transform('count')
```

3. Divide the new column by the total number of rows to obtain the frequency:

```
df['cab_freq'] = df['cab_freq']/len(df)
```

4. Verify that changes have been made as expected:

```
df.tail()
```

Here is an excerpt from the output showing the new columns:

destination	source	price	surge_multiplier	id	product_id	name	date	month	hour	dayofweek	weekend	rush_hour	cab_freq
Fenway	North Station	11.5	1.0	934d2fbe-f978-4495-9786-da7b4dd21107	997acbb5-e102-41e1-b155-9df7de0a73f2	UberPool	2018-11-29 15:12:59.037	11	15	3	0	1	0.504389
Fenway	North Station	26.0	1.0	af8fd57c-fe7c-4584-bd1f-beef1a53ad42	6c84fd89-3f11-4782-9b50-97c468b19529	Black	2018-12-03 01:27:57.997	12	1	0	0	0	0.504389
Fenway	North Station	19.5	1.0	b3c5db97-554b-47bf-908b-3ac880e86103	6f72dfc5-27f1-42e8-84db-ccc7a75f6969	UberXL	2018-11-28 12:11:23.241	11	12	2	0	0	0.504389
Fenway	North Station	36.5	1.0	fcb35184-9047-43f7-8909-f62a7b17b6cf	6d318bcc-22a3-4af6-bddd-b409bfce1546	Black SUV	2018-12-15 18:00:13.623	12	18	5	1	0	0.504389
Theatre District	Northeastern University	7.0	1.0	7f0e8caf-e057-41eb-bdef-27eb14c88122	lyft_line	Shared	2018-12-03 04:53:01.166	12	4	0	0	0	0.495611

Figure 9.7 – The cab rides dataset after engineering the frequency of cabs

The cab frequency now displays the expected output.

Kaggle tip – mean encoding

We will conclude this section with a competition-tested approach to feature engineering called **mean encoding** or **target encoding**.

Mean encoding transforms categorical columns into numerical columns based on the mean target variable. For instance, if the color orange led to seven target values of 1 and three target values of 0, the mean encoded column would be 7/10 = 0.7. Since there is data leakage while using the target values, additional regularization techniques are required.

Data leakage occurs when information between training and test sets, or predictor and target columns, are shared. The risk here is that the target column is being directly used to influence the predictor columns, which is generally a bad idea in machine learning. Nevertheless, mean encoding has been shown to produce outstanding results. It can work when datasets are deep, and the distribution of mean values are approximately the same for incoming data. Regularization is an extra precaution taken to reduce the possibility of overfitting.

Fortunately, scikit-learn provides `TargetEncoder` to handle mean conversions for you:

1. First, import `TargetEndoder` from `category_encoders`. If this does not work, install `category_encoders` using the following code:

   ```
   pip install --upgrade category_encoders
   from category_encoders.target_encoder import
   TargetEncoder
   ```

2. Next, initialize `encoder`, as follows:

   ```
   encoder = TargetEncoder()
   ```

3. Finally, introduce a new column and apply mean encoding using the `fit_transform` method on the encoder. Include the column that is being changed and the target column as parameters:

   ```
   df['cab_type_mean'] = encoder.fit_transform(df['cab_type'], df['price'])
   ```

4. Now, verify that the changes are as expected:

   ```
   df.tail()
   ```

Here is an excerpt of the output with the new column in view:

source	price	surge_multiplier	id	product_id	name	date	month	hour	dayofweek	weekend	rush_hour	cab_freq	cab_type_mean
North Station	11.5	1.0	934d2fbe-f978-4495-9786-da7b4dd21107	997acbb5-e102-41e1-b155-9df7de0a73f2	UberPool	2018-11-29 15:12:59.037	11	15	3	0	1	0.504389	15.743446
North Station	26.0	1.0	af8fd57c-fe7c-4584-bd1f-beef1a53ad42	6c84fd89-3f11-4782-9b50-97c468b19529	Black	2018-12-03 01:27:57.997	12	1	0	0	0	0.504389	15.743446
North Station	19.5	1.0	b3c5db97-554b-47bf-908b-3ac880e86103	6f72dfc5-27f1-42e8-84db-ccc7a75f6969	UberXL	2018-11-28 12:11:23.241	11	12	2	0	0	0.504389	15.743446
North Station	36.5	1.0	fcb35184-9047-43f7-8909-f62a7b17b6cf	6d318bcc-22a3-4af6-bddd-b409bfce1546	Black SUV	2018-12-15 18:00:13.623	12	18	5	1	0	0.504389	15.743446
theastern Jniversity	7.0	1.0	7f0e8caf-e057-41eb-bdef-27eb14c88122	lyft_line	Shared	2018-12-03 04:53:01.166	12	4	0	0	0	0.495611	16.916357

Figure 9.8 – The cab rides dataset after mean encoding

The far-right column, `cab_type_mean`, is as expected.

For more information on mean encoding, refer to this Kaggle study: `https://www.kaggle.com/vprokopev/mean-likelihood-encodings-a-comprehensive-study`.

The idea here is not to say that mean encoding is better than one-hot encoding, but rather that mean encoding is a proven technique that has done well in Kaggle competitions and may be worth implementing to try and improve scores.

More feature engineering

There is no reason to stop here. More feature engineering may include statistical measures on other columns using `groupby` and additional encoders. Other categorical columns, such as the destination and arrival columns, may be converted to latitude and longitude and then to new measures of distance, such as the taxicab distance or the **Vincenty** distance, which takes spherical geometry into account.

In Kaggle competitions, participants may engineer thousands of new columns hoping to gain a few extra decimal places of accuracy. If you have a high number of engineered columns, you can select the most significant ones using `.feature_importances_`, as outlined in *Chapter 2, Decision Trees in Depth*. You can also eliminate highly correlated columns (explained in the next section, *Building non-correlated ensembles*).

For this particular cab rides dataset, there is an additional CSV file that includes the weather. But what if there wasn't a weather file? You could always research the weather data from the provided dates and include the weather data on your own.

Feature engineering is an essential skill for any data scientist to build robust models. The strategies covered here are only a fraction of the options that exist. Feature engineering involves research, experimentation, domain expertise, standardizing columns, feedback on the machine learning performance of new columns, and narrowing down the final columns at the end.

Now that you understand the various strategies for feature engineering, let's move on to building non-correlated ensembles.

Building non-correlated ensembles

"In our final model, we had XGBoost as an ensemble model, which included 20 XGBoost models, 5 random forests, 6 randomized decision tree models, 3 regularized greedy forests, 3 logistic regression models, 5 ANN models, 3 elastic net models and 1 SVM model."

– Song, Kaggle Winner

(`https://hunch243.rssing.com/chan-68612493/all_p1.html`)

The winning models of Kaggle competitions are rarely individual models; they are almost always ensembles. By ensembles, I do not mean boosting or bagging models, such as random forests or XGBoost, but pure ensembles that include any distinct models, including XGBoost, random forests, and others.

In this section, we will combine machine learning models into non-correlated ensembles to gain accuracy and reduce overfitting.

Range of models

The Wisconsin Breast Cancer dataset, used to predict whether a patient has breast cancer, has 569 rows and 30 columns, and can be viewed at `https://scikit-learn.org/stable/modules/generated/sklearn.datasets.load_breast_cancer.html?highlight=load_breast_cancer`.

Here are the steps to prepare and score the dataset using several classifiers:

1. Import the `load_breast_cancer` dataset from scikit-learn so that we can quickly start building models:

    ```
    from sklearn.datasets import load_breast_cancer
    ```

2. Assign the predictor columns to X and the target column to y by setting the
   `return_X_y=True` parameter:

```
X, y = load_breast_cancer(return_X_y=True)
```

3. Prepare 5-fold cross-validation using `StratifiedKFold` for consistency:

```
kfold = StratifiedKFold(n_splits=5)
```

4. Now, build a simple classification function that takes a model as input and returns
   the mean cross-validation score as output:

```
def classification_model(model):
    scores = cross_val_score(model, X, y, cv=kfold)
    return scores.mean()
```

5. Get the scores of several default classifiers, including XGBoost, along with its
   alternative base learners, a random forest, and logistic regression:

   a) Score with XGBoost:

```
classification_model(XGBClassifier())
```

   The score is as follows:

```
0.9771619313771154
```

   b) Score with `gblinear`:

```
classification_model(XGBClassifier(booster='gblinear'))
```

   The score is as follows:

```
0.5782952957615277
```

   c) Score with `dart`:

```
classification_model(XGBClassifier(booster='dart', one_
drop=True))
```

   The score is as follows:

```
0.9736376339077782
```

   Note that for the dart booster, we set `one_drop=True` to ensure that trees are
   actually dropped.

   d) Score with `RandomForestClassifier`:

```
classification_model(RandomForestClassifier(random_
state=2))
```

The score is as follows:

```
0.9666356155876418
```

e) Score with `LogisticRegression`:

```
classification_model(LogisticRegression(max_iter=10000))
```

The score is as follows:

```
0.9490451793199813
```

Most models perform respectably, with the XGBoost classifier obtaining the highest score. The `gblinear` base learner did not perform particularly well, however, so we will not use it going forward.

In practice, each of these models should be tuned. Since we have already covered hyperparameter tuning in multiple chapters, that option is not pursued here. Nevertheless, knowledge of hyperparameters can give confidence in trying a quick model with some adjusted values. For instance, as done in the following code, lowering `max_depth` to `2`, increasing `n_estimators` to `500`, and making sure that `learning_rate` is set to `0.1` may be attempted on XGBoost:

```
classification_model(XGBClassifier(max_depth=2, n_
estimators=500, learning_rate=0.1))
```

The score is as follows:

```
0.9701133364384411
```

This is a very good score. Although it's not the highest, it may be of value in our ensemble.

Now that we have a variety of models, let's learn about the correlations between them.

Correlation

The purpose of this section is not to select all models for the ensemble, but rather to select the non-correlated models.

First, let's understand what **correlation** represents.

Correlation is a statistical measure between -1 and 1 that indicates the strength of the linear relationship between two sets of points. A correlation of 1 is a perfectly straight line, while a correlation of 0 shows no linear relationship whatsoever.

Some visuals on correlation should make things clear. The following visuals are taken from Wikipedia's *Correlation and Dependence* page at `https://en.wikipedia.org/wiki/Correlation_and_dependence`:

- Scatter plots with listed correlations look as follows:

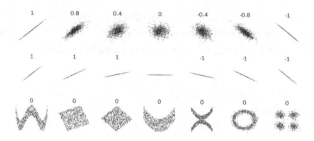

Figure 9.9 – Listed Correlations

- Anscombe's quartet – four scatter plots with a correlation of **0.816** – looks as follows:

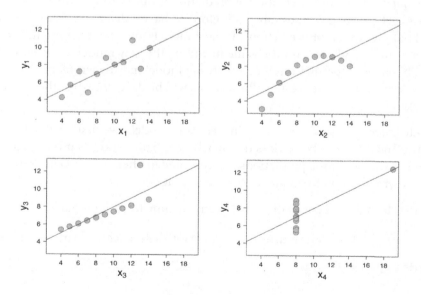

Figure 9.10 – Correlation of 0.816

License information

By Anscombe.svg: Schutz (label using subscripts): Avenue – Anscombe.svg, CC BY-SA 3.0, `https://commons.wikimedia.org/w/index.php?curid=9838454`

The first example shows that the higher the correlation, the closer the dots generally are to a straight line. The second example shows that data points of the same correlation can differ widely. In other words, correlation provides valuable information, but it doesn't tell the whole story.

Now that you understand what correlation means, let's apply correlation to building machine learning ensembles.

Correlation in machine learning ensembles

Now we choose which models to include in our ensemble.

A high correlation between machine learning models is undesirable in an ensemble. But why?

Consider the case of two classifiers with 1,000 predictions each. If these classifiers all make the same predictions, no new information is gained from the second classifier, making it superfluous.

Using a *majority rules* implementation, a prediction is only wrong if the majority of classifiers get it wrong. It's desirable, therefore, to have a diversity of models that score well but give different predictions. If most models give the same predictions, the correlation is high, and there is little value in adding the new model to the ensemble. Finding differences in predictions where a strong model may be wrong gives the ensemble the chance to produce better results. Predictions will be different when the models are non-correlated.

To compute correlations between machine learning models, we first need data points to compare. The different data points that machine learning models produce are their predictions. After obtaining predictions, we concatenate them into a DataFrame, and then apply the `.corr` method to obtain all correlations at once.

Here are the steps to find correlations between machine learning models:

1. Define a function that returns predictions for each machine learning model:

```
def y_pred(model):
    model.fit(X_train, y_train)
    y_pred = model.predict(X_test)
```

```
    score = accuracy_score(y_pred, y_test)
    print(score)
    return y_pred
```

2. Prepare the data for one-fold predictions using `train_test_split`:

```
X_train, X_test, y_train, y_test = train_test_split(X, y,
random_state=2)
```

3. Obtain the predictions of all classifier candidates using the previously defined function:

a) `XGBClassifier` uses the following:

```
y_pred_gbtree = y_pred(XGBClassifier())
```

The accuracy score is as follows:

```
0.951048951048951
```

b) `XGBClassifier` with `dart` uses the following:

```
y_pred_dart = y_pred(XGBClassifier(booster='dart', one_
drop=True))
```

The accuracy score is as follows:

```
0.951048951048951
```

c) `RandomForestClassifier` uses the following:

```
y_pred_forest = y_pred(RandomForestClassifier())
```

The accuracy score is as follows:

```
0.9370629370629371
```

d) `LogisticRegression` uses the following:

```
y_pred_logistic = y_pred(LogisticRegression(max_
iter=10000))
```

The accuracy score is as follows:

```
0.9370629370629371
```

> **Note**
>
> `max_iter` is increased in `LogisticRegression` to prevent warnings (and potentially gain accuracy).

e) `Tuned XGBClassifier` uses the following:

```
y_pred_xgb = y_pred(XGBClassifier(max_depth=2, n_
estimators=500, learning_rate=0.1))
```

The accuracy score is as follows:

```
0.965034965034965
```

4. Concatenate the predictions into a new DataFrame using `np.c` (the `c` is short for concatenation):

```
df_pred = pd.DataFrame(data= np.c_[y_pred_gbtree, y_
pred_dart, y_pred_forest, y_pred_logistic, y_pred_xgb],
columns=['gbtree', 'dart','forest', 'logistic', 'xgb'])
```

5. Run correlations on the DataFrame using the `.corr()` method:

```
df_pred.corr()
```

You should see the following output:

	gbtree	dart	forest	logistic	xgb
gbtree	1.000000	0.971146	0.884584	0.914111	0.971146
dart	0.971146	1.000000	0.913438	0.914111	0.971146
forest	0.884584	0.913438	1.000000	0.943308	0.913438
logistic	0.914111	0.914111	0.943308	1.000000	0.914111
xgb	0.971146	0.971146	0.913438	0.914111	1.000000

Figure 9.11 – Correlations between various machine learning models

As you can see, all correlations on the diagonal are `1.0` because the correlation between the model and itself must be perfectly linear. All other values are reasonably high.

There is no clear cut-off to obtain a non-correlated threshold. It ultimately depends on the values of correlation and the number of models to choose from. For this example, we could pick the next two least correlated models with our best model, `xgb`, which are the random forest and logistic regression.

Now that we have chosen our models, we will combine them into a single ensemble using the `VotingClassifier` ensemble, introduced next.

The VotingClassifier ensemble

Scikit-learn's `VotingClassifier` ensemble is designed to combine multiple classification models and select the output for each prediction using majority rules. Note that scikit-learn also comes with `VotingRegressor`, which combines multiple regression models by taking the average of each one.

Here are the steps to create an ensemble in scikit-learn:

1. Initialize an empty list:

    ```
    estimators = []
    ```

2. Initialize the first model:

    ```
    logistic_model = LogisticRegression(max_iter=10000)
    ```

3. Append the model to the list as a tuple in the form (`model_name`, `model`):

    ```
    estimators.append(('logistic', logistic_model))
    ```

4. Repeat *steps 2* and *3* as many times as desired:

    ```
    xgb_model = XGBClassifier(max_depth=2, n_estimators=500,
    learning_rate=0.1)
    estimators.append(('xgb', xgb_model))
    rf_model = RandomForestClassifier(random_state=2)
    estimators.append(('rf', rf_model))
    ```

5. Initialize `VotingClassifier` (or `VotingRegressor`) using the list of models as input:

    ```
    ensemble = VotingClassifier(estimators)
    ```

6. Score the classifier using `cross_val_score`:

    ```
    scores = cross_val_score(ensemble, X, y, cv=kfold)
    print(scores.mean())
    ```

    The score is as follows:

    ```
    0.9754075454122031
    ```

As you can see, the score has improved.

Now that you understand the purpose and technique of building non-correlated machine learning ensembles, let's move on to a similar but potentially advantageous technique called stacking.

Stacking models

> *"For stacking and boosting I use xgboost, again primarily due to familiarity and its proven results."*
>
> *– David Austin, Kaggle Winner*

(https://www.pyimagesearch.com/2018/03/26/interview-david-austin-1st-place-25000-kaggles-popular-competition/)

In this final section, we will examine one of the most powerful tricks frequently used by Kaggle winners, called stacking.

What is stacking?

Stacking combines machine learning models at two different levels: the base level, whose models make predictions on all the data, and the meta level, which takes the predictions of the base models as input and uses them to generate final predictions.

In other words, the final model in stacking does not take the original data as input, but rather takes the predictions of the base machine learning models as input.

Stacked models have found huge success in Kaggle competitions. Most Kaggle competitions have merger deadlines, where individuals and teams can join together. These mergers can lead to greater success as teams rather than individuals because competitors can build larger ensembles and stack their models together.

Note that stacking is distinct from a standard ensemble on account of the meta-model that combines predictions at the end. Since the meta-model takes predictive values as the input, it's generally advised to use a simple meta-model, such as linear regression for regression and logistic regression for classification.

Now that you have an idea of what stacking is, let's apply stacking with scikit-learn.

Stacking in scikit-learn

Fortunately, scikit-learn comes with a stacking regressor and classifier that makes the process fairly straightforward. The general idea is very similar to the ensemble model in the last section. A variety of base models are chosen, and then linear regression or logistic regression is chosen for the meta-model.

Here are the steps to use stacking with scikit-learn:

1. Create an empty list of base models:

    ```
    base_models = []
    ```

2. Append all base models to the base model list as tuples using the syntax (name, model):

    ```
    base_models.append(('lr', LogisticRegression()))
    base_models.append(('xgb', XGBClassifier()))
    base_models.append(('rf', RandomForestClassifier(random_state=2)))
    ```

    More models may be chosen when stacking since there are no majority rules limitations and linear weights adjust more easily to new data. An optimal approach is to use non-correlation as loose a guideline and to experiment with different combinations.

3. Choose a meta model, preferably linear regression for regression and logistic regression for classification:

    ```
    meta_model = LogisticRegression()
    ```

4. Initialize StackingClassifier (or StackingRegressor) using base_models for estimators and meta_model for final_estimator:

    ```
    clf = StackingClassifier(estimators=base_models, final_estimator=meta_model)
    ```

5. Validate the stacked model using cross_val_score or any other scoring method:

    ```
    scores = cross_val_score(clf, X, y, cv=kfold)
    print(scores.mean())
    ```

    The score is as follows:

    ```
    0.9789318428815401
    ```

This is the strongest result yet.

As you can see, stacking is an incredibly powerful method and outperformed the non-correlated ensemble from the previous section.

Summary

In this chapter, you learned some of the well-tested tips and tricks from the winners of Kaggle competitions. In addition to exploring Kaggle competitions and understanding the importance of a hold-out set, you gained essential practice in feature engineering time columns, feature engineering categorical columns, mean encoding, building non-correlated ensembles, and stacking. These advanced techniques are widespread among elite Kagglers, and they can give you an edge when developing machine learning models for research, competition, and industry.

In the next and final chapter, we will shift gears from the competitive world to the tech world, where we will build an XGBoost model from beginning to end using transformers and pipelines to complete a model ready for industry deployment.

10
XGBoost Model Deployment

In this final chapter on XGBoost, you will put everything together and develop new techniques to build a robust machine learning model that is industry ready. Deploying models for industry is a little different than building models for research and competitions. In industry, automation is important since new data arrives frequently. More emphasis is placed on procedure, and less emphasis is placed on gaining minute percentage points by tweaking machine learning models.

Specifically, in this chapter, you will gain significant experience with **one-hot encoding** and **sparse matrices**. In addition, you will implement and customize scikit-learn transformers to automate a machine learning pipeline to make predictions on data that is mixed with **categorical** and **numerical** columns. At the end of this chapter, your machine learning pipeline will be ready for any incoming data.

In this chapter, we cover the following topics:

- Encoding mixed data
- Customizing scikit-learn transformers
- Finalizing an XGBoost model
- Building a machine learning pipeline

Technical requirements

The code for this chapter may be found at `https://github.com/PacktPublishing/Hands-On-Gradient-Boosting-with-XGBoost-and-Scikit-learn/tree/master/Chapter10`.

Encoding mixed data

Imagine that you are working for an EdTech company and your job is to predict student grades to target services aimed at bridging the tech skills gap. Your first step is to load data that contains student grades into `pandas`.

Loading data

The Student Performance dataset, provided by your company, may be accessed by loading the `student-por.csv` file that has been imported for you.

Start by importing `pandas` and silencing warnings. Then, download the dataset and view the first five rows:

```
import pandas as pd
import warnings
warnings.filterwarnings('ignore')
df = pd.read_csv('student-por.csv')
df.head()
```

Here is the expected output:

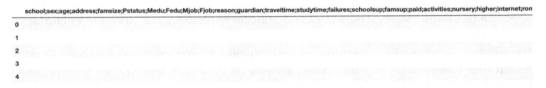

Figure 10.1 – The Student Performance dataset as is

Welcome to the world of industry, where data does not always appear as expected.

A recommended option is to view the CSV file. This can be done in Jupyter Notebooks by locating the folder for this chapter and clicking on the `student-por.csv` file.

You should see the following:

```
school;sex;age;address;famsize;Pstatus;Medu;Fedu;Mjob;Fjob;reason;guardian;traveltime;studytime;failures;schoolsup;famsup;paid;act
ivities;nursery;higher;internet;romantic;famrel;freetime;goout;Dalc;Walc;health;absences;G1;G2;G3
"GP";NULL;18;"U";"GT3";"A";4;4;"at_home";"teacher";"course";NULL;2;2;0;"yes";"no";"no";"no";"yes";"yes";"no";"no";4;3;4;1;1;3;4;"0
";"11";11
"GP";"F";NULL;"U";"GT3";"T";1;1;"at_home";"other";"course";"father";1;2;0;"no";"yes";"no";"no";"no";"yes";"yes";"no";5;3;3;1;1;3;2
;"9";"11";11
"GP";"F";15;"U";"LE3";"T";1;1;"at_home";"other";"other";"mother";1;2;0;"yes";"no";"no";"no";"yes";"yes";"yes";"no";4;3;2;2;3;3;6;"
12";"13";12
"GP";"F";15;"U";"GT3";"T";4;2;"health";"services";"home";"mother";1;3;0;"no";"yes";"no";"yes";"yes";"yes";"yes";"yes";3;2;2;1;1;5;
0;"14";"14";14
"GP";"F";16;"U";"GT3";"T";3;3;"other";"other";"home";"father";1;2;0;"no";"yes";"no";"no";"yes";"yes";"no";"no";4;3;2;1;2;5;0;"11";
"13";13
"GP";"M";16;"U";"LE3";"T";4;3;"services";"other";"reputation";"mother";1;2;0;"no";"yes";"no";"yes";"yes";"yes";"yes";"no";5;4;2;1;
2;5;6;"12";"12";13
"GP";"M";16;"U";"LE3";"T";2;2;"other";"other";"home";"mother";1;2;0;"no";"no";"no";"no";"yes";"yes";"yes";"no";4;4;4;1;1;3;0;"13";
"12";13
"GP";"F";17;"U";"GT3";"A";4;4;"other";"teacher";"home";"mother";2;2;0;"yes";"yes";"no";"no";"yes";"yes";"no";"no";4;1;4;1;1;1;2;"1
0";"13";13
"GP";"M";15;"U";"LE3";"A";3;2;"services";"other";"home";"mother";1;2;0;"no";"yes";"no";"no";"yes";"yes";"yes";"no";4;2;2;1;1;1;0;"
15";"16";17
"GP";"M";15;"U";"GT3";"T";3;4;"other";"other";"home";"mother";1;2;0;"no";"yes";"no";"yes";"yes";"yes";"yes";"no";5;5;1;1;1;5;0;"12
";"12";13
"GP";"F";15;"U";"GT3";"T";4;4;"teacher";"health";"reputation";"mother";1;2;0;"no";"yes";"no";"no";"yes";"yes";"yes";"no";3;3;3;1;2
;2;2;"14";"14";14
"GP";"F";15;"U";"GT3";"T";2;1;"services";"other";"reputation";"father";3;3;0;"no";"yes";"no";"yes";"yes";"yes";"yes";"no";5;2;2;1;
1;4;0;"10";"12";13
"GP";"M";15;"U";"LE3";"T";4;4;"health";"services";"course";"father";1;1;0;"no";"yes";"no";"yes";"yes";"yes";"yes";"no";4;3;3;1;3;5
;0;"12";"13";12
"GP";"M";15;"U";"GT3";"T";4;3;"teacher";"other";"course";"mother";2;2;0;"no";"yes";"no";"yes";"yes";"yes";"yes";"no";5;4;3;1;2;3;0;
"12";"12";13
"GP";"M";15;"U";"GT3";"A";2;2;"other";"other";"home";"other";1;3;0;"no";"yes";"no";"no";"yes";"yes";"yes";"yes";4;5;2;1;1;3;0;"14"
;"14";15
"GP";"F";16;"U";"GT3";"T";4;4;"health";"other";"home";"mother";1;1;0;"no";"yes";"no";"no";"yes";"yes";"yes";"no";4;4;4;1;2;2;6;"17
";"17";17
```

Figure 10.2 – The Student Performance CSV file

As you can see in the preceding figure, the data is separated by semi-colons. CSV stands for **Comma-Separated Values**, not **Semi-Colon-Separated Values**. Fortunately, `pandas` comes with a `sep` parameter, which stands for **separator**, that may be set to the semi-colon, (;), as follows:

```
df = pd.read_csv('student-por.csv', sep=';')
df.head()
```

Here is the expected output:

	school	sex	age	address	famsize	Pstatus	Medu	Fedu	Mjob	Fjob	...	famrel	freetime	goout	Dalc	Walc	health	absences	G1	G2	G3
0	GP	NaN	18.0	U	GT3	A	4	4	at_home	teacher	...	4	3	4	1	1	3	4	0	11	11
1	GP	F	NaN	U	GT3	T	1	1	at_home	other	...	5	3	3	1	1	3	2	9	11	11
2	GP	F	15.0	U	LE3	T	1	1	at_home	other	...	4	3	2	2	3	3	6	12	13	12
3	GP	F	15.0	U	GT3	T	4	2	health	services	...	3	2	2	1	1	5	0	14	14	14
4	GP	F	16.0	U	GT3	T	3	3	other	other	...	4	3	2	1	2	5	0	11	13	13

Figure 10.3 – The Student Performance dataset

Now that the DataFrame looks as expected, with a mix of categorical and numerical values, we must clean up the **null values**.

Clearing null values

You can view all columns of null values by calling the `.sum()` method on `df.insull()`. Here is an excerpt of the results:

```
df.isnull().sum()
school          0
sex             1
age             1
address         0
...
health          0
absences        0
G1              0
G2              0
G3              0
dtype: int64
```

You can view the rows of these columns using conditional notation by placing `df.isna().any(axis=1)` inside of brackets with `df`:

```
df[df.isna().any(axis=1)]
```

Here is the expected output:

	school	sex	age	address	famsize	Pstatus	Medu	Fedu	Mjob	Fjob	...	famrel	freetime	goout	Dalc	Walc	health	absences	G1	G2	G3
0	GP	NaN	18.0	U	GT3	A	4	4	at_home	teacher	...	4	3	4	1	1	3	4	0	11	11
1	GP	F	NaN	U	GT3	T	1	1	at_home	other	...	5	3	3	1	1	3	2	9	11	11

Figure 10.4 – The Student Performance null data

It's preferable to see the null columns in the middle, which Jupyter removes by default on account of the number of columns. This is easily corrected by setting `max columns` to `None` as follows:

```
pd.options.display.max_columns = None
```

Now, running the code again shows all the columns:

```
df[df.isna().any(axis=1)]
```

Here is an excerpt of the expected output:

	school	sex	age	address	famsize	Pstatus	Medu	Fedu	Mjob	Fjob	reason	guardian	traveltime	studytime	failures	schoolsup	famsup	paid
0	GP	NaN	18.0	U	GT3	A	4	4	at_home	teacher	course	NaN	2	2	0	yes	no	no
1	GP	F	NaN	U	GT3	T	1	1	at_home	other	course	father	1	2	0	no	yes	no

Figure 10.5 – Null data from all rows of the Student Performance dataset

As you can see, all columns including the hidden null values under `'guardian'` are now displayed.

Numerical null values may be set to -999.0, or some other value, and XGBoost will find the best replacement for you using the `missing` hyperparameter as introduced in *Chapter 5, XGBoost Unveiled.*

Here is the code to fill the `'age'` column with `-999.0`:

```
df['age'].fillna(-999.0)
```

Next, categorical columns may be filled by the mode. The mode is the most common occurrence in a column. Filling categorical columns with the mode may distort the resulting distribution, however, only if the number of null values is large. There are only two null values present, so our distribution will not be affected. Another option includes replacing categorical null values with the 'unknown' string, which may become its own column after one-hot encoding. Note that XGBoost requires numerical input, so the `missing` hyperparameter cannot be directly applied to categorical columns as of 2020.

The following code converts the `'sex'` and `'guardian'` categorical columns to `mode`:

```
df['sex'] = df['sex'].fillna(df['sex'].mode())
df['guardian'] = df['guardian'].fillna(df['guardian'].mode())
```

Since our null values were in the first two rows, we can reveal that they have been changed using `df.head()`:

```
df.head()
```

Here is the expected output:

	school	sex	age	address	famsize	Pstatus	Medu	Fedu	Mjob	Fjob	reason	guardian	traveltime	studytime	failures	schoolsup	famsup	paid
0	GP	F	18.0	U	GT3	A	4	4	at_home	teacher	course	mother	2	2	0	yes	no	no
1	GP	F	-999.0	U	GT3	T	1	1	at_home	other	course	father	1	2	0	no	yes	no
2	GP	F	15.0	U	LE3	T	1	1	at_home	other	other	mother	1	2	0	yes	no	no
3	GP	F	15.0	U	GT3	T	4	2	health	services	home	mother	1	3	0	no	yes	no
4	GP	F	16.0	U	GT3	T	3	3	other	other	home	father	1	2	0	no	yes	no

Figure 10.6 – The Student Performance dataset with the null values removed (first five rows only)

The null values have all been cleared as expected.

Next, we will convert all categorical columns to numerical columns using one-hot encoding.

One-hot encoding

Previously, we used `pd.get_dummies` to transform all categorical variables to numerical values of 0 and 1, with 0 indicating absence and 1 indicating presence. While acceptable, this approach has some shortcomings.

The first shortcoming is that `pd.get_dummies` can be computationally expensive, as you may have found when waiting for code to run in previous chapters. The second shortcoming is that `pd.get_dummies` does not translate particularly well to scikit-learn's pipelines, a concept that we will explore in the next section.

A nice alternative to `pd.get_dummies` is scikit-learn's `OneHotEncoder`. Like `pd.get_dummies`, one-hot encoding transforms all categorical values to 0 and 1, with 0 indicating absence and 1 indicating presence, but unlike `pd.get_dummies`, it is not computationally expensive. `OneHotEncoder` uses a sparse matrix instead of a dense matrix to save space and time.

Sparse matrices save space by only storing data with values that do not include 0. The same amount of information is conserved by using fewer bits.

In addition, `OneHotEncoder` is a scikit-learn transformer, which means that it's specifically designed to work in machine learning pipelines.

In past versions of scikit-learn, `OneHotEncoder` only accepted numerical input. When that was the case, an intermediate step was taken with `LabelEncoder` to first convert all categorical columns into numerical columns.

To use `OneHotEncoder` on specific columns, you may use the following steps:

1. Convert all categorical columns of the `dtype` object into a list:

    ```
    categorical_columns = df.columns[df.dtypes==object].
    tolist()
    ```

2. Import and initialize `OneHotEncoder`:

    ```
    from sklearn.preprocessing import OneHotEncoder
    ohe = OneHotEncoder()
    ```

3. Use the `fit_transform` method on the columns:

```
hot = ohe.fit_transform(df[categorical_columns])
```

4. **Optional**: convert the one-hot encoded sparse matrix into a standard array and convert it into a DataFrame for viewing:

```
hot_df = pd.DataFrame(hot.toarray())
hot_df.head()
```

Here is the expected output:

	0	1	2	3	4	5	6	7	8	9	10	11	12	13	14	15	16	17	18	19	20	21	22	23	24	25	26	27	28	29	30	31	32
0	1.0	0.0	1.0	0.0	0.0	1.0	1.0	0.0	1.0	0.0	1.0	0.0	0.0	0.0	0.0	0.0	0.0	0.0	0.0	1.0	1.0	0.0	0.0	0.0	0.0	1.0	0.0	0.0	1.0	1.0	0.0	1.0	0.0
1	1.0	0.0	1.0	0.0	0.0	1.0	1.0	0.0	0.0	1.0	1.0	0.0	0.0	0.0	0.0	0.0	0.0	1.0	0.0	0.0	1.0	0.0	0.0	0.0	1.0	0.0	0.0	1.0	0.0	0.0	1.0	1.0	0.0
2	1.0	0.0	1.0	0.0	0.0	1.0	0.0	1.0	0.0	1.0	1.0	0.0	0.0	0.0	0.0	0.0	0.0	1.0	0.0	0.0	0.0	0.0	1.0	0.0	0.0	1.0	0.0	0.0	1.0	1.0	0.0	1.0	0.0
3	1.0	0.0	1.0	0.0	0.0	1.0	1.0	0.0	0.0	1.0	0.0	1.0	0.0	0.0	0.0	0.0	0.0	1.0	0.0	0.0	1.0	0.0	0.0	0.0	1.0	0.0	1.0	0.0	0.0	1.0	1.0	0.0	
4	1.0	0.0	1.0	0.0	0.0	1.0	1.0	0.0	0.0	1.0	0.0	0.0	1.0	0.0	0.0	0.0	0.0	1.0	0.0	0.0	0.0	1.0	0.0	0.0	1.0	0.0	0.0	1.0	0.0	0.0	1.0	1.0	0.0

Figure 10.7 – DataFrame of a one-hot encoded matrix

This looks as expected, with all the values being 0 or 1.

5. If you want to see what the `hot` sparse matrix actually looks like, you can print it out as follows:

```
print(hot)
```

Here is an excerpt of the results:

```
(0, 0)       1.0
(0, 2)       1.0
(0, 5)       1.0
(0, 6)       1.0
(0, 8)       1.0
...
(648, 33) 1.0
(648, 35) 1.0
(648, 38) 1.0
(648, 40) 1.0
(648, 41) 1.0
```

As you can see, only the values of 0 have been skipped. For instance, the 0th row and the 1st column, denoted by (0, 1), has a value of 0.0 in the dense matrix, but it's skipped over in the one-hot matrix.

If you want more information about the sparse matrix, just enter the following variable:

```
hot
```

The result is as follows:

```
<649x43 sparse matrix of type '<class 'numpy.float64'>'
    with 11033 stored elements in Compressed Sparse Row
format>
```

This tells us that the matrix is 649 by 43, but only 11033 values have been stored, saving a significant amount of space. Note that for text data, which has many zeros, sparse matrices are very common.

Combining a one-hot encoded matrix and numerical columns

Now that we have a one-hot encoded sparse matrix, we must combine it with the numerical columns of the original DataFrame.

First, let's isolate the numerical columns. This may be done with the exclude=["object"] parameter as input for df.select_dtypes, which selects columns of certain types as follows:

```
cold_df = df.select_dtypes(exclude=["object"])
cold_df.head()
```

Here is the expected output:

	age	Medu	Fedu	traveltime	studytime	failures	famrel	freetime	goout	Dalc	Walc	health	absences	G1	G2	G3
0	18.0	4	4	2	2	0	4	3	4	1	1	3	4	0	11	11
1	-999.0	1	1	1	2	0	5	3	3	1	1	3	2	9	11	11
2	15.0	1	1	1	2	0	4	3	2	2	3	3	6	12	13	12
3	15.0	4	2	1	3	0	3	2	2	1	1	5	0	14	14	14
4	16.0	3	3	1	2	0	4	3	2	1	2	5	0	11	13	13

Figure 10.8 – The Student Performance dataset's numerical columns

These are the columns we are looking for.

For data of this size, we have a choice of converting the sparse matrix to a regular DataFame, as seen in the preceding screenshot, or converting this DataFrame into a sparse matrix. Let's pursue the latter, considering that DataFrames in industry can become enormous and saving space can be advantageous:

1. To convert the `cold_df` DataFrame to a compressed sparse matrix, import `csr_matrix` from `scipy.sparse` and place the DataFrame inside, as follows:

```
from scipy.sparse import csr_matrix
cold = csr_matrix(cold_df)
```

2. Finally, stack both matrices, hot and cold, by importing and using `hstack`, which combines sparse matrices horizontally:

```
from scipy.sparse import hstack
final_sparse_matrix = hstack((hot, cold))
```

3. Verify that `final_sparse_matrix` works as expected by converting the sparse matrix into a dense matrix and by displaying the DataFrame as usual:

```
final_df = pd.DataFrame(final_sparse_matrix.toarray())
final_df.head()
```

Here is the expected output:

26	27	28	29	30	31	32	33	34	35	36	37	38	39	40	41	42	43	44	45	46	47	48	49	50	51	52	53	54	55	56	57	58
0.0	0.0	1.0	1.0	0.0	1.0	0.0	1.0	0.0	0.0	1.0	0.0	1.0	1.0	0.0	1.0	0.0	18.0	4.0	4.0	2.0	2.0	0.0	4.0	3.0	4.0	1.0	1.0	3.0	4.0	0.0	11.0	11.0
0.0	1.0	0.0	0.0	1.0	1.0	0.0	1.0	0.0	1.0	0.0	0.0	1.0	0.0	1.0	1.0	0.0	-999.0	1.0	1.0	1.0	2.0	0.0	5.0	3.0	3.0	1.0	1.0	3.0	2.0	9.0	11.0	11.0
0.0	0.0	1.0	1.0	0.0	1.0	0.0	1.0	0.0	0.0	1.0	0.0	1.0	0.0	1.0	1.0	0.0	15.0	1.0	1.0	1.0	2.0	0.0	4.0	3.0	2.0	2.0	3.0	3.0	6.0	12.0	13.0	12.0
0.0	1.0	0.0	0.0	1.0	1.0	0.0	0.0	1.0	0.0	1.0	0.0	1.0	0.0	1.0	0.0	1.0	15.0	4.0	2.0	1.0	3.0	0.0	3.0	2.0	2.0	1.0	1.0	5.0	0.0	14.0	14.0	14.0
0.0	1.0	0.0	0.0	1.0	1.0	0.0	1.0	0.0	0.0	1.0	0.0	1.0	1.0	0.0	1.0	0.0	16.0	3.0	3.0	1.0	2.0	0.0	4.0	3.0	2.0	1.0	2.0	5.0	0.0	11.0	13.0	13.0

Figure 10.9 – The DataFrame of the final sparse matrix

The output is shifted to the right to show the one-hot encoded and numerical columns together.

Now that the data is ready for machine learning, let's automate the process using transformers and pipelines.

Customizing scikit-learn transformers

Now that we have a process for transforming the DataFrame into a machine learning-ready sparse matrix, it would be advantageous to generalize the process with transformers so that it can easily be repeated for new data coming in.

Scikit-learn transformers work with machine learning algorithms by using a `fit` method, which finds model parameters, and a `transform` method, which applies these parameters to data. These methods may be combined into a single `fit_transform` method that fits and transforms data in one line of code.

When used together, various transformers, including machine learning algorithms, may work together in the same pipeline for ease of use. Data is then placed in the pipeline that is fit and transformed to achieve the desired output.

Scikit-learn comes with many great transformers, such as `StandardScaler` and `Normalizer` to standardize and normalize data, respectively, and `SimpleImputer` to convert null values. You have to be careful, however, when data contains a mix of categorical and numerical columns, as is the case here. In some cases, the scikit-learn options may not be the best options for automation. In this case, it's worth creating your own transformers to do exactly what you want.

Customizing transformers

The key to creating your own transformers is to use scikit-learn's `TransformerMixin` as your superclass.

Here is a general code outline to create a customized transformer in scikit-learn:

```
class YourClass(TransformerMixin):
    def __init__(self):
        None
    def fit(self, X, y=None):
        return self
    def transform(self, X, y=None):
        # insert code to transform X
        return X
```

As you can see, you don't have to initialize anything, and `fit` can always return `self`. Simply put, you may place all your code for transforming the data under the `transform` method.

Now that you see how customization works generally, let's create a customized transformer to handle different kinds of null values.

Customizing a mixed null value imputer

Let's see how this works by creating a customized mixed null value imputer. Here, the reason for the customization is to handle different types of columns with different approaches to correcting null values.

Here are the steps:

1. Import `TransformerMixin` and define a new class with `TransformerMixin` as the superclass:

    ```
    from sklearn.base import TransformerMixin
    class NullValueImputer(TransformerMixin):
    ```

2. Initialize the class with `self` as input. It's okay if this does nothing:

    ```
    def __init__(self):
    None
    ```

3. Create a `fit` method that takes `self` and `X` as input, with `y=None`, and returns `self`:

    ```
    def fit(self, X, y=None):
    return self
    ```

4. Create a `transform` method that takes `self` and `X` as input, with `y=None`, and transforms the data by returning a new `X`, as follows:

    ```
    def transform(self, X, y=None):
    ```

    We need to handle null values separately depending on the columns.

    Here are the steps to convert null values to the mode or `-999.0`, depending upon the column type:

    a) Loop through the columns by converting them to a list:
    ```
    for column in X.columns.tolist():
    ```

    b) Within the loop, access the columns that are strings by checking which columns are of the `object` dtype:
    ```
    if column in X.columns[X.dtypes==object].tolist():
    ```

    c) Convert the null values of the string (`object`) columns to the mode:
    ```
    X[column] = X[column].fillna(X[column].mode())
    ```

d) Otherwise, fill the columns with -999.0:

```
else:
        X[column]=X[column].fillna(-999.0)
    return X
```

In the preceding code, you may have wondered why y=None is used. The reason is that y will be needed as an input when including a machine learning algorithm in the pipeline. By setting y to None, changes will only be made to the predictor columns as expected.

Now that the customized imputer has been defined, it may be used by calling the fit_transform method on the data.

Let's reset the data by establishing a new DataFrame from the CSV file and transform the null values in one line of code using the customized NullValueImputer:

```
df = pd.read_csv('student-por.csv', sep=';')
nvi = NullValueImputer().fit_transform(df)
nvi.head()
```

Here is the expected output:

	school	sex	age	address	famsize	Pstatus	Medu	Fedu	Mjob	Fjob	reason	guardian	traveltime	studytime	failures	schoolsup	famsup	paid
0	GP	F	18.0	U	GT3	A	4	4	at_home	teacher	course	mother	2	2	0	yes	no	no
1	GP	F	-999.0	U	GT3	T	1	1	at_home	other	course	father	1	2	0	no	yes	no
2	GP	F	15.0	U	LE3	T	1	1	at_home	other	other	mother	1	2	0	yes	no	no
3	GP	F	15.0	U	GT3	T	4	2	health	services	home	mother	1	3	0	no	yes	no
4	GP	F	16.0	U	GT3	T	3	3	other	other	home	father	1	2	0	no	yes	no

Figure 10.10 – The Student Performance DataFrame after NullValueImputer()

As you can see, all null values have been cleared.

Next, let's transform the data into a one-hot encoded sparse matrix as before.

One-hot encoding mixed data

We will apply similar steps here to those from the previous section by creating a customized transformer to one-hot encode the categorical columns before joining them with the numerical columns as a sparse matrix (a dense matrix is also okay for a dataset of this size):

1. Define a new class with TransformerMixin as the superclass:

```
class SparseMatrix(TransformerMixin):
```

2. Initialize the class with `self` as input. It's okay if this does nothing:

```
def __init__(self):
        None
```

3. Create a `fit` method that takes `self` and `X` as input and returns `self`:

```
def fit(self, X, y=None):
        return self
```

4. Create a `transform` method that takes `self` and `X` as input, transforms the data, and returns a new `X`:

```
def transform(self, X, y=None):
```

Here are the steps to complete the transformation; start by accessing only the categorical columns, which are of the `object` type, as follows:

a) Put the categorical columns in a list:

```
        categorical_columns= X.columns[X.
dtypes==object].tolist()
```

b) Initialize `OneHotEncoder`:

```
        ohe = OneHotEncoder()
```

c) Transform the categorical columns with `OneHotEncoder`:

```
hot = ohe.fit_transform(X[categorical_columns])
```

d) Create a DataFrame of numerical columns only by excluding strings:

```
cold_df = X.select_dtypes(exclude=["object"])
```

e) Convert the numerical DataFrame into a sparse matrix:

```
        cold = csr_matrix(cold_df)
```

f) Combine both sparse matrices into one:

```
        final_sparse_matrix = hstack((hot, cold))
```

g) Convert this into a **Compressed Sparse Row (CSR)** matrix to limit errors. Note that XGBoost requires CSR matrices, and this conversion may happen automatically depending on your version of XGBoost:

```
        final_csr_matrix = final_sparse_matrix.tocsr()
        return final_csr_matrix
```

5. Now we can transform the `nvi` data with no null values by using the powerful `fit_transform` method on `SparseMatrix`:

```
sm = SparseMatrix().fit_transform(nvi)
print(sm)
```

The expected output, given here, is truncated to save space:

```
(0,  0)     1.0
(0,  2)     1.0
(0,  5)     1.0
(0,  6)     1.0
(0,  8)     1.0
(0, 10)     1.0
  :    :
(648, 53) 4.0
(648, 54) 5.0
(648, 55) 4.0
(648, 56) 10.0
(648, 57) 11.0
(648, 58) 11.0
```

6. You can verify that the data looks as expected by converting the sparse matrix back into a dense matrix as follows:

```
sm_df = pd.DataFrame(sm.toarray())
sm_df.head()
```

Here is the expected dense output:

26	27	28	29	30	31	32	33	34	35	36	37	38	39	40	41	42	43	44	45	46	47	48	49	50	51	52	53	54	55	56	57	58
0.0	0.0	1.0	1.0	0.0	1.0	0.0	1.0	0.0	0.0	1.0	0.0	1.0	1.0	0.0	1.0	0.0	18.0	4.0	4.0	2.0	2.0	0.0	4.0	3.0	4.0	1.0	1.0	3.0	4.0	0.0	11.0	11.0
0.0	1.0	0.0	0.0	1.0	1.0	0.0	1.0	0.0	1.0	0.0	0.0	1.0	0.0	1.0	1.0	0.0	-999.0	1.0	1.0	1.0	2.0	0.0	5.0	3.0	3.0	1.0	1.0	3.0	2.0	9.0	11.0	11.0
0.0	0.0	1.0	1.0	0.0	1.0	0.0	1.0	0.0	0.0	1.0	0.0	1.0	0.0	1.0	1.0	0.0	15.0	1.0	1.0	1.0	2.0	0.0	4.0	3.0	2.0	2.0	3.0	3.0	6.0	12.0	13.0	12.0
0.0	1.0	0.0	0.0	1.0	1.0	0.0	0.0	1.0	0.0	1.0	0.0	1.0	0.0	1.0	0.0	1.0	15.0	4.0	2.0	1.0	3.0	0.0	3.0	2.0	2.0	1.0	1.0	5.0	0.0	14.0	14.0	14.0
0.0	1.0	0.0	0.0	1.0	1.0	0.0	1.0	0.0	0.0	1.0	0.0	1.0	1.0	0.0	1.0	0.0	16.0	3.0	3.0	1.0	2.0	0.0	4.0	3.0	2.0	1.0	2.0	5.0	0.0	11.0	13.0	13.0

Figure 10.11 – The sparse matrix converted into a dense matrix

This appears correct. The figure shows a value of `0.0` for the 27th column and a value of `1.0` for the 28th column. The preceding one-hot encoded output excludes (0,27) and shows a value of `1.0` for (0,28), matching the dense output.

Now that the data has been transformed, let's combine both preprocessing steps into a single pipeline.

Preprocessing pipeline

When building machine learning models, it's standard to start by separating the data into X and y. When thinking about a pipeline, it makes sense to transform X, the predictor columns, and not y, the target column. Furthermore, it's important to hold out a test set for later.

Before placing data into the machine learning pipeline, let's split the data into training and test sets and leave the test set behind. We start from the top as follows:

1. First, read the CSV file as a DataFrame:

   ```
   df = pd.read_csv('student-por.csv', sep=';')
   ```

   When choosing X and y for the Student Performance dataset, it's important to note that the last three columns all include student grades. Two potential studies are of value here:

   a) Including previous grades as predictor columns

   b) Not including previous grades as predictor columns

   Assume that your EdTech company wants to make predictions based on socioeconomic variables, not on previous grades earned, so ignore the first two grade columns indexed as -2 and -3.

2. Select the last column as y, and all columns except for the last three as X:

   ```
   y = df.iloc[:, -1]
   X = df.iloc[:, :-3]
   ```

3. Now import train_test_split and split X and y into a training and a test set:

   ```
   from sklearn.model_selection import train_test_split
   X_train, X_test, y_train, y_test = train_test_split(X, y,
   random_state=2)
   ```

Now let's build the pipeline using the following steps:

1. First import Pipeline from sklearn.pipeline:

   ```
   from sklearn.pipeline import Pipeline
   ```

2. Next, assign tuples using the syntax (name, transformer) as parameters of Pipeline in sequence:

   ```
   data_pipeline = Pipeline([('null_imputer',
   NullValueImputer()), ('sparse', SparseMatrix())])
   ```

3. Finally, transform `X_train`, our predictor columns, by placing `X_train` inside the `fit_transform` method of `data_pipeline`:

```
X_train_transformed = data_pipeline.fit_transform(X_train)
```

Now you have a numerical, sparse matrix with no null values that can be used as the predictor column for machine learning.

Furthermore, you have a pipeline that may be used to transform any incoming data in one line of code! Let's now finalize an XGBoost model to make predictions.

Finalizing an XGBoost model

It's time to build a robust XGBoost model to add to the pipeline. Go ahead and import XGBRegressor, numpy, GridSearchCV, `cross_val_score`, KFold, and `mean_squared_error` as follows:

```
import numpy as np
from sklearn.model_selection import GridSearchCV
from sklearn.model_selection import cross_val_score, KFold
from sklearn.metrics import mean_squared_error as MSE
from xgboost import XGBRegressor
```

Now let's build the model.

First XGBoost model

This Student Performance dataset has an interesting range of values for the predictor column, `y_train`, which can be shown as follows:

```
y_train.value_counts()
```

The result is this:

```
11    82
10    75
13    58
12    53
14    42
```

15	36
9	29
16	27
8	26
17	24
18	14
0	10
7	7
19	1
6	1
5	1

As you can see, the values range from 5-19 with 0 included.

Since the target column is ordinal, meaning the values are numerically ordered, regression is preferable to classification even though the outputs are limited. After training a model via regression, the final results may be rounded to give the final predictions.

Here are the steps to score XGBRegressor with this dataset:

1. Start by setting up cross-validation using KFold:

    ```
    kfold = KFold(n_splits=5, shuffle=True, random_state=2)
    ```

2. Now define a cross-validation function that returns the **root mean squared error** using cross_val_score:

    ```
    def cross_val(model):
        scores = cross_val_score(model, X_train_transformed,
    y_train, scoring='neg_root_mean_squared_error', cv=kfold)
        rmse = (-scores.mean())
        return rmse
    ```

3. Establish a base score by calling cross_val with the XGBRegressor as input with missing=-999.0 so that XGBoost can find the best replacement:

    ```
    cross_val(XGBRegressor(missing=-999.0))
    ```

    The score is this:

    ```
    2.9702248207546296
    ```

This is a respectable starting score. A root mean squared error of 2.97 out of 19 possibilities indicates that the grades are within a couple of points of accuracy. This is almost 15%, which is accurate within one letter grade using the American A-B-C-D-F system. In industry, you may even include a confidence interval using statistics to deliver a prediction interval, a recommended strategy that is outside the scope of this book.

Now that you have a baseline score, let's fine-tune the hyperparameters to improve the model.

Fine-tuning the XGBoost hyperparameters

Let's start by checking n_estimators with early stopping. Recall that to use early stopping, we may check one test fold. Creating the test fold requires splitting X_train and y_train further:

1. Here is a second train_test_split that may be used to create a test set for validation purposes, making sure to keep the real test set hidden for later:

```
X_train_2, X_test_2, y_train_2, y_test_2 = train_test_
split(X_train_transformed, y_train, random_state=2)
```

2. Now define a function that uses early stopping to return the optimal number of estimators for the regressor (see *Chapter 6, XGBoost Hyperparameters*):

```
def n_estimators(model):
    eval_set = [(X_test_2, y_test_2)]
    eval_metric="rmse"
    model.fit(X_train_2, y_train_2, eval_metric=eval_
metric, eval_set=eval_set, early_stopping_rounds=100)
    y_pred = model.predict(X_test_2)
    rmse = MSE(y_test_2, y_pred)**0.5
    return rmse
```

3. Now run the n_estimators function, setting to 5000 as a maximum:

```
n_estimators(XGBRegressor(n_estimators=5000, missing=-
999.0))
```

Here are the last five rows of the output:

```
[128] validation_0-rmse:3.10450
[129] validation_0-rmse:3.10450
[130] validation_0-rmse:3.10450
```

```
[131] validation_0-rmse:3.10450
Stopping. Best iteration:
[31]  validation_0-rmse:3.09336
```

The score is as follows:

```
3.0933612343143153
```

Using our default model, 31 estimators currently gives the best estimate. That will be our starting point.

Next, here is a grid_search function, which we have used multiple times, that searches a grid of hyperparameters and displays the best parameters and best score:

```
def grid_search(params, reg=XGBRegressor(missing=-999.0)):
    grid_reg = GridSearchCV(reg, params, scoring='neg_mean_
squared_error', cv=kfold)
    grid_reg.fit(X_train_transformed, y_train)
    best_params = grid_reg.best_params_
    print("Best params:", best_params)
    best_score = np.sqrt(-grid_reg.best_score_)
    print("Best score:", best_score)
```

Here are a few recommended steps for fine-tuning the model:

1. Start with max_depth ranging from 1 to 8 while setting n_estimators to 31:

    ```
    grid_search(params={'max_depth':[1, 2, 3, 4, 6, 7, 8],
                        'n_estimators':[31]})
    ```

    The result is this:

    ```
    Best params: {'max_depth': 1, 'n_estimators': 31}
    Best score: 2.6634430373079425
    ```

2. Narrow max_depth from 1 to 3 while ranging min_child_weight from 1 to 5 and holding n_esimtators at 31:

    ```
    grid_search(params={'max_depth':[1, 2, 3],
                        'min_child_weight':[1,2,3,4,5],
                        'n_estimators':[31]})
    ```

The result is this:

```
Best params: {'max_depth': 1, 'min_child_weight': 1, 'n_
estimators': 31}
Best score: 2.6634430373079425
```

There is no improvement.

3.   You may guarantee some changes by forcing `min_child_weight` to take on a value of 2 or 3 while including a range of `subsample` from 0.5 to 0.9. Furthermore, increasing n_estimators may help by giving the model more time to learn:

```
grid_search(params={'max_depth':[2],
                    'min_child_weight':[2,3],
                    'subsample':[0.5, 0.6, 0.7, 0.8,
0.9],
                    'n_estimators':[31, 50]})
```

The result is as follows:

```
Best params: {'max_depth': 1, 'min_child_weight': 2, 'n_
estimators': 50, 'subsample': 0.9}
Best score: 2.665209161229433
```

The score is nearly the same, but slightly worse.

4.   Narrow `min_child_weight` and `subsample` while using a range of 0.5 to 0.9 for `colsample_bytree`:

```
grid_search(params={'max_depth':[1],
                    'min_child_weight':[1, 2, 3],
                    'subsample':[0.6, 0.7, 0.8],
                    'colsample_bytree':[0.5, 0.6, 0.7,
0.8, 0.9, 1],
                    'n_estimators':[50]})
```

The result is this:

```
Best params: {'colsample_bytree': 0.9, 'max_depth': 1,
'min_child_weight': 3, 'n_estimators': 50, 'subsample':
0.8}
Best score: 2.659649642579931
```

This is the best score so far.

5. Holding the best current values, try ranges from `0.6` to `1.0` with `colsample_bynode` and `colsample_bylevel`:

```
grid_search(params={'max_depth':[1],
                    'min_child_weight':[3],
                    'subsample':[.8],
                    'colsample_bytree':[0.9],
                    'colsample_bylevel':[0.6, 0.7, 0.8,
0.9, 1],
                    'colsample_bynode':[0.6, 0.7, 0.8,
0.9, 1],
                    'n_estimators':[50]})
```

The result is given here:

```
Best params: {'colsample_bylevel': 0.9, 'colsample_
bynode': 0.8, 'colsample_bytree': 0.9, 'max_depth': 1,
'min_child_weight': 3, 'n_estimators': 50, 'subsample':
0.8}
Best score: 2.64172735526102
```

The score has improved again.

Further experimentation with the base learner to `dart` and `gamma` resulted in no new gains.

Depending on the time and the scope of the project, it could be worth tuning hyperparameters further, and even trying them all together in `RandomizedSearch`. In industry, there is a good chance that you will have access to cloud computing, where inexpensive, preemptible **Virtual Machines** (**VMs**) will allow more hyperparameter searches to find even better results. Just note that scikit-learn currently does not offer a way to stop time-consuming searches to save the best parameters before the code completes.

Now that we have a robust model, we can move forward and test the model.

Testing model

Now that you have a potential final model, it's important to test it against the test set.

Recall that the test set was not transformed in our pipeline. Fortunately, at this point, it only takes one line of code to transform it:

```
X_test_transformed = data_pipeline.fit_transform(X_test)
```

Now we can initialize a model with the best-tuned hyperparameters selected in the previous section, fit it on the training set, and test it against the test set that was held back:

```
model = XGBRegressor(max_depth=2, min_child_weight=3,
subsample=0.9, colsample_bytree=0.8, gamma=2, missing=-999.0)
model.fit(X_train_transformed, y_train)
y_pred = model.predict(X_test_transformed)
rmse = MSE(y_pred, y_test)**0.5
rmse
```

The score is as follows:

```
2.7908972630881435
```

The score is a little higher, although this could be on account of the fold.

If not, our model has fit the validation set a little too closely, which can happen when fine-tuning hyperparameters and adjusting them closely to improve the validation set. The model generalizes fairly well, but it could generalize better.

For the next steps, when considering whether the score can be improved upon, the following options are available:

- Return to hyperparameter fine-tuning.
- Keep the model as is.
- Make a quick adjustment based on hyperparameter knowledge.

Quickly adjusting hyperparameters is viable since the model could be overfitting. For instance, increasing `min_child_weight` and lowering `subsample` should help the model to generalize better.

Let's make that final adjustment for a final model:

```
model = XGBRegressor(max_depth=1,
                     min_child_weight=5,
                     subsample=0.6,
                     colsample_bytree=0.9,
                     colsample_bylevel=0.9,
                     colsample_bynode=0.8,
                     n_estimators=50,
```

```
                        missing=-999.0)
model.fit(X_train_transformed, y_train)
y_pred = model.predict(X_test_transformed)
rmse = MSE(y_pred, y_test)**0.5
rmse
```

The result is as follows:

```
2.730601403138633
```

Note that the score has improved.

Also, you should absolutely not go back and forth trying to improve the hold-out test score. It is acceptable to make a few adjustments after receiving the test score, however; otherwise, you could never improve upon the first result.

Now all that remains is to complete the pipeline.

Building a machine learning pipeline

Completing the machine learning pipeline requires adding the machine learning model to the previous pipeline. You need a machine learning tuple after `NullValueImputer` and `SparseMatrix` as follows:

```
full_pipeline = Pipeline([('null_imputer',
NullValueImputer()),  ('sparse', SparseMatrix()),
('xgb', XGBRegressor(max_depth=1, min_child_weight=5,
subsample=0.6, colsample_bytree=0.9, colsample_bylevel=0.9,
colsample_bynode=0.8, missing=-999.0))])
```

This pipeline is now complete with a machine learning model, and it can be fit on any X, y combination, as follows:

```
full_pipeline.fit(X, y)
```

Now you can make predictions on any data whose target column is unknown:

```
new_data = X_test
full_pipeline.predict(new_data)
```

Here are the first few rows of the expected output:

```
array([13.55908  ,  8.314051 , 11.078157 , 14.114085 ,
12.2938385, 11.374797 , 13.9611025, 12.025812 , 10.80344  ,
13.479145 , 13.02319  ,  9.428679 , 12.57761  , 12.405045 ,
14.284043 ,  8.549758 , 10.158956 ,  9.972576 , 15.502667 ,
10.280028 , ...
```

To get realistic predictions, the data may be rounded as follows:

```
np.round(full_pipeline.predict(new_data))
```

The expected output is given here:

```
array([14.,   8.,  11.,  14.,  12.,  11.,  14.,  12.,  11.,  13.,  13.,
 9.,  13.,  12.,  14.,   9.,  10.,  10.,  16.,  10.,  13.,  13.,   7.,  12.,
 7.,   8.,  10.,  13.,  14.,  12.,  11.,  12.,  15.,   9.,  11.,  13.,  12.,
11.,   8.,
```

```
...
```

```
11.,  13.,  12.,  13.,   9.,  13.,  10.,  14.,  12.,  15.,  15.,  11.,
14.,  10.,  14.,   9.,   9.,  12.,  13.,   9.,  11.,  14.,  13.,  11.,
13.,  13.,  13.,  13.,  11.,  13.,  14.,  15.,  13.,   9.,  10.,
13.,   8.,   8.,  12.,  15.,  14.,  13.,  10.,  12.,  13.,   9.],
dtype=float32)
```

Finally, if new data comes through, it can be concatenated with the previous data and placed through the same pipeline for a stronger model, since the new model may be fit on more data as follows:

```
new_df = pd.read_csv('student-por.csv')
new_X = df.iloc[:, :-3]
new_y = df.iloc[:, -1]
new_model = full_pipeline.fit(new_X, new_y)
```

Now, this model may be used to make predictions on new data, as shown in the following code:

```
more_new_data = X_test[:25]
np.round(new_model.predict(more_new_data))
```

The expected output is as follows:

```
array([14.,   8., 11., 14., 12., 11., 14., 12., 11., 13., 13.,
       9., 13., 12., 14.,   9., 10., 10., 16., 10., 13., 13.,   7., 12.,
       7.],
          dtype=float32)
```

There is one small catch.

What if you want to make a prediction on only one row of data? If you run a single row through the pipeline, the resulting sparse matrix will not have the correct number of columns, since it will only one-hot encode categories that are present in the single row. This will result in a *mismatch* error in the data, since the machine learning model has been fit to a sparse matrix that requires more rows of data.

A simple solution is to concatenate the new row of data with enough rows of data to guarantee that the full sparse matrix is present with all possible categorical columns transformed. We have seen that this works with 25 rows from X_test since there were no errors. Using 20 or fewer rows from X_test will result in a mismatch error in this particular case.

So, if you want to make a prediction with a single row of data, concatenate the single row with the first 25 rows of X_test and make a prediction as follows:

```
single_row = X_test[:1]
single_row_plus = pd.concat([single_row, X_test[:25]])
print(np.round(new_model.predict(single_row_plus))[:1])
```

The result is this:

```
[14.]
```

You now know how machine learning models may be included in pipelines to transform and make predictions on new data.

Summary

Congratulations on making it to the end of the book! This has been an extraordinary journey that began with basic machine learning and pandas and ended with building your own customized transformers, pipelines, and functions to deploy robust, fine-tuned XGBoost models in industry scenarios with sparse matrices to make predictions on new data.

Along the way, you have learned the story of XGBoost, from the first decision trees through random forests and gradient boosting, before discovering the mathematical details and sophistication that has made XGBoost so special. You saw time and time again that XGBoost outperforms other machine learning algorithms, and you gained essential practice in tuning XGBoost's wide-ranging hyperparameters, including `n_estimators`, `max_depth`, `gamma`, `colsample_bylevel`, `missing`, and `scale_pos_weight`.

You learned how physicists and astronomers obtained knowledge about our universe in historically important case studies, and you learned about the extensive range of XGBoost through imbalanced datasets and the application of alternative base learners. You even learned tricks of the trade from Kaggle competitions through advanced feature engineering, non-correlated ensembles, and stacking. Finally, you learned advanced automation processes for industry.

At this point, your knowledge of XGBoost is at an advanced level. You can now use XGBoost efficiently, swiftly, and powerfully to tackle the machine learning problems that will come your way. Of course, XGBoost is not perfect. If you are dealing with unstructured data such as images or text, **neural networks** might serve you better. For most machine learning tasks, especially those with tabular data, XGBoost will usually give you an advantage.

If you are interested in pursuing further studies with XGBoost, my personal recommendation is to enter Kaggle competitions. The reason is that Kaggle competitions consist of seasoned machine learning practitioners and competing against them will make you better. Furthermore, Kaggle competitions provide a structured machine learning environment consisting of many practitioners working on the same problem, which results in shared notebooks and forum discussions that can further boost the educational process. It's also where XGBoost first developed its extraordinary reputation with the Higgs boson competition, as outlined in this book.

You may now go confidently forward into the world of big data with XGBoost to advance research, enter competitions, and build machine learning models ready for production.

Other Books You May Enjoy

If you enjoyed this book, you may be interested in these other books by Packt:

Hands-On Machine Learning with scikit-learn and Scientific Python Toolkits

Tarek Amr

ISBN: 978-1-83882-604-8

- Understand when to use supervised, unsupervised, or reinforcement learning algorithms

- Find out how to collect and prepare your data for machine learning tasks

- Tackle imbalanced data and optimize your algorithm for a bias or variance tradeoff

- Apply supervised and unsupervised algorithms to overcome various machine learning challenges

- Employ best practices for tuning your algorithm's hyper parameters

- Discover how to use neural networks for classification and regression

- Build, evaluate, and deploy your machine learning solutions to production

Mastering Machine Learning Algorithms- Second Edition

Giuseppe Bonaccorso

ISBN: 978-1-83882-029-9

- Understand the characteristics of a machine learning algorithm
- Implement algorithms from supervised, semi-supervised, unsupervised, and RL domains
- Learn how regression works in time-series analysis and risk prediction
- Create, model, and train complex probabilistic models
- Cluster high-dimensional data and evaluate model accuracy
- Discover how artificial neural networks work – train, optimize, and validate them
- Work with autoencoders, Hebbian networks, and GANs

Leave a review - let other readers know what you think

Please share your thoughts on this book with others by leaving a review on the site that you bought it from. If you purchased the book from Amazon, please leave us an honest review on this book's Amazon page. This is vital so that other potential readers can see and use your unbiased opinion to make purchasing decisions, we can understand what our customers think about our products, and our authors can see your feedback on the title that they have worked with Packt to create. It will only take a few minutes of your time, but is valuable to other potential customers, our authors, and Packt. Thank you!

Index

Made in United States
North Haven, CT
29 November 2023

44748786R00170